THE POLITICAL UNCOMMONS

In *The Political Uncommons*, Kathryn Milun presents a cultural history of the global commons: those domains, including the atmosphere, the oceans, the radio frequency spectrum, the earth's biodiversity, and its outer space, designated by international law as belonging to no single individual or nation state but rather to all humankind. From the *res communis* of Roman property law to early modern laws establishing the freedom of the seas, from the legal battles over the neutrality of the Internet to the heritage of the earth's genetic diversity, Milun connects ancient, modern, and postmodern legal traditions of global commons. Arguing that the logic of legal institutions governing global commons is connected to the logic of colonial doctrines that dispossessed Indigenous peoples of their land, she demonstrates that the failure of international law to adequately govern the earth's atmosphere and waters can be more deeply understood as a cultural logic that has successfully dispossessed humankind of basic subsistence rights. The promise of global commons, Milun shows, has always been related to subsistence rights and an earth that human communities have long imagined as 'common' existing alongside private and public domains. Utilizing specific case studies, *The Political Uncommons* opens a way to consider how global commons regimes might benefit from the cross-cultural logics found where Indigenous peoples have gained recognition of their common tenure systems in Western courts.

For

Albert Milun and Virginia Parrinello Milun

and

Randy Hanson

The Political Uncommons
The Cross-Cultural Logic of the Global Commons

KATHRYN MILUN
University of Minnesota Duluth, USA

ROUTLEDGE
Routledge
Taylor & Francis Group
LONDON AND NEW YORK

First published 2011 by Ashgate Publishing

Published 2016 by Routledge
2 Park Square, Milton Park, Abingdon, Oxon OX14 4RN
711 Third Avenue, New York, NY 10017, USA

Routledge is an imprint of the Taylor & Francis Group, an informa business

British Library Cataloguing in Publication Data
The political uncommons : the cross-cultural logic of the
global commons. -- (Law, justice and power series)
1. Global commons. 2. Environmental law, International.
I. Series II. Milun, Kathryn.
341.4-dc22

Library of Congress Cataloging-in-Publication Data

2010935098

ISBN 13: 978-0-7546-7139-8 (hbk)

Contents

List of Figures

Introduction

> A picture held us captive. And we could not get outside it, for it lay in our language and language seemed to repeat it to us inexorably. (Wittgenstein 1965: 115)

The commons is increasingly proposed as an economic and legal solution to global and regional problems. Commons are often thought of as collectively managed, shared resources. From the reduction of greenhouse gas emissions into our common atmosphere to the management of watersheds that straddle territorial boundaries, resources that extend beyond the jurisdictions of nation-states and outside the entrenched frameworks of the international order, the commons offers a new (and ancient) way of managing things we share. Certainly the Nobel Prize Committee understood this when they awarded the 2009 prize in economics to Elinor Ostrom for her lifelong work on the commons. Coming after the global economic collapse of 2008, the committee seemed to suggest that the intricate regulatory system of our global financial markets was not unlike the complex regulatory system of our climate: too fundamental to be left deregulated or mismanaged for the benefit of an elite few.[1]

As the global commons rises to adjudicate problems of a technologically and economically globalized earth, it is prudent to consider the history of its formation in international law. How has Western law managed common property at a global scale? What kind of social relations are implied in a commons? Will a new cosmopolitan class of citizens identify with the new global commons? Will the cosmopolitan class be a just vehicle for the concerns of non-Western peoples, for the voices of the global South? How have Indigenous commons persisted into the legal structures of modernity and what lessons do they hold for the global commons? Just as we have come to understand that the modern nation-state is supported not only by its legal and social institutions but by the news stories, novels, and artistic works that create the nation as an imaginary and exclusive community, so too the supports of the modern global commons go beyond the concepts of sovereignty and common property that we find in the legal documents. International law of the global commons is undergirded by a spatial imaginary whose outlines help explain why the global commons has so often failed to do what it says it does: manage things we all share for the benefit of all humankind. From the Roman concept of *res communis* to the early modern law of the seas,

1 The Tobin Tax, a tax on financial transactions, was proposed and supported by the Group of 77 and the European Union as a mechanism to fund the implementation of the 2009 Copenhagen agreement. The justification of a global tax on financial transactions that can be distributed to those in global need with regard to climate change is well on the way to understanding the financial system itself as a global commons.

the law of outer space, the radio frequency spectrum, and more recently the laws that govern the biodiversity of genetic material, the cultural history of the global commons foregrounds deeply rooted contradictions that can help explain the failures of international law to achieve its stated goal of managing what is shared by humankind for the common benefit of all.

In this book, I focus on a particular cultural aspect of the global commons: its spatial imaginary. More specifically, I focus on empty space and its role as an epistemic imaginary in the international law of the global commons. Cultural studies often provide an epistemological corrective to the forms of knowledge that underpin legal and social structures of the state (Sarat and Simon 2003). In this book, I argue that the metaphors and rhetoric of empty space carry into international law a very modern and powerful epistemological ground, evident in the colonial sovereignty that maintains the current configuration of modern nation-states, but obscured in more recent attempts to go beyond the international order of the state to create legal institutions of the global commons. Empty space is a key spatial imaginary of modernity. How does it persist in and respond to the challenges of post-colonial and post-modern forms of legal and social organization such as we see in attempts to govern domains of the earth as global commons? That is the question I explore in this book.

Indigenous Claims and the Global Commons

In December 2004 the front page of the *New York Times* reported that the Inuit, about 155,000 seal-hunting peoples scattered around the Arctic in both Canada and Alaska, will seek a ruling from the Inter-American Commission on Human Rights that the United States is threatening their existence by contributing substantially to global warming (Revkin 2004). Specifically, the charge points to the actions of the US Bush Administration which repudiated the Kyoto Protocol and refused to cut US carbon dioxide emissions, which make up 25 percent of the world's total and are a leading cause of the rising temperatures and sea levels whose drastic consequences are most dramatically seen by those communities living on the Arctic fringe.[2] The Inuit's legal move is unprecedented for the potential clout it has to shift the global warming issue from an environmental problem to an assault on

2 While the so-called developing world is more vulnerable to climate change (its people are more directly dependent on the natural resource base, more exposed to extreme weather events as we saw in the 2004 tsunami, and are less able economically and technologically to make needed adaptations), it is the industrial countries of the well-to-do North that contribute far more to the build up of greenhouse gases—the US is responsible for 30 percent—and who reap the greatest economic benefits in the process. The United States with its population over 250 million now emits the same amount of greenhouse gases as 2.6 billion people living in 151 developing nations (Speth 2004: 61). Most immediately, rising sea levels due to global warming are drastically changing the environments of the Arctic coast and tropical atolls. High mountain communities suffer in this category as well.

a people's basic human rights. While the Commission hearing the Inuit's claim has no enforcement powers, its declaration that the US has violated the Inuit's rights presented a new legal framework to pursue action against global climate change. Calling on a liability rule rather than a property rule, the Inuit claim sparked hopeful legal thinking. The *New York Times* suggested that the Inuit case "could create the foundation for an eventual lawsuit, either against the United States in an international court or against American companies in federal court." Citing legal experts, some from the very industries producing the noxious emissions, the *Times* reported, "if the Inuit effort succeeds, it could lead to an eventual stream of litigation, somewhat akin to lawsuits against tobacco companies." The application of the liability rule in the US brought forth litigation and popular campaigns addressing the culture of smoking which lead to the most successful national change in citizens' behavior in recent history: cigarette smoking is no longer allowed to contaminate the air in public places. The legal analogy comparing the successful protection of US public air space from tobacco smoking with the desired protection of the global atmosphere from fossil fuel burning was a hopeful one. It reminded citizens of how law can work to create effective social change.

In 2004, the moment seemed propitious for the Inuit's petition since industrial countries, including the United States, had concluded in recent reports and studies that global warming linked to heat-trapping smokestack and tailpipe emissions is contributing to large-scale environmental changes in the Arctic. Just one month previous to their claim, an assessment of Arctic climate change by 300 scientists for the eight countries with Arctic territory, including the United States, concluded that "human influences" are now the dominant factor in the alarming rate at which the Arctic is warming, a rate that is projected to continue by as much as 18 degrees Fahrenheit by 2100.[3] As the warming melts northern ice it causes a dramatic increase in freshwater released into the North Atlantic. According to scientists at the Woods Hole Oceanographic Institute, it is the largest and most dramatic oceanic change ever measured in the era of modern instruments (Gagosian 2003). The impact on Arctic ecosystems, including sea ice, permafrost, forests, and tundra is enormous.[4]

How can we explain the spark of hope raised in 2004 around the Inuit claim?[5] How do we account for the striking possibility that Indigenous peoples, nonstatist

In the not so distant future this will increasingly include coastal areas of the North such as the Netherlands and Florida.

3 See the online report "Impacts of a Warming Arctic: Arctic Climate Impact Assessment (Overview)" (Arctic Climate Impact Assessment 2004).

4 The mechanism is complex, but scientists basically explain that dumping freshwater into the ocean risks disrupting the Gulf Stream by blocking its release of heat which would in turn disrupt the ocean currents that pull warm waters of the stream northward. Rivers were dumping seven percent more freshwater into the Arctic Ocean in 2002 than in the 1930s with global warming cited as the most likely cause. Bruce Peterson et al., "Increasing River Discharge to the Arctic Ocean," *Science*, December 2002: 2171–2173.

5 As of this writing, the Inter-American Commission on Human Rights had declined to rule on the Inuit complaint. "The agency told the Inuit Circumpolar Conference, which

social actors who, since the European colonization of the globe, have always been excluded from positions of power, may have some cultural and legal leverage missing from the nation-states meeting in Copenhagen in 2009 or Kyoto in 1992 to use legal instruments at national and international levels to fight global warming? Two answers come immediately to mind. First, nation-states may have lost certain powers to effect change at a global level. The political economy of the global market system has changed in the last decades and global elites, corporate entities and other nonstate social actors have new powers to use states for their own interests. Nation-state structures themselves have become more flexible in the new global economy, sometimes going against their own interests to seek greater gain in the global economy.

The second answer lies in the way international law has defined the atmosphere as a domain of the global commons. Perhaps international law itself has set the earth's nonterritorial environments up for ruin. Global commons are vast domains described in international law as regions belonging to no one individual or nation but ostensibly protected by law for just use by all the earth's citizens. From this legal perspective, commons are natural spaces made accessible for general use, exploitation or dispossession by various technological innovations in the modern era: the high seas opened to colonial trade and later the ocean's fisheries and deep seabed minerals opened to industrial exploitation; the earth's atmosphere open to air travel and the orbital pathways of outer space to satellite launches; the radio frequency spectrum inhabitable to cell phone and computer networks; and finally, the biodiversity of the earth viewed as DNA codes containing genetic blueprints of all forms of life.[6] International law describes all these global commons domains as theoretically lying outside the territorial sovereignty of states.

represents 150,000 people in northern Alaska, Canada, Russia and Greenland, that there was insufficient evidence of harm. Inuit leaders said they would seek a hearing to present more evidence" (Revkin 2006).

6 Legal scholars define the global commons as four jurisdictions where sovereignty is shared globally: the oceans, the atmosphere, outer space and telecommunications, and Antarctica (Vogler 1995, Buck 1998). In this book I include biodiversity as an emergent global commons domain. I will not, however, address the status of Antarctica as global commons for the following reasons. Unlike the legal regimes that govern the high seas, outer space and telecommunications, the atmosphere, and biodiversity, Antarctica is governed by a treaty headed by a consortium of scientists from the twelve nations who conduct research on the subcontinent. The Antarctic Treaty was signed in 1959 by Argentina, Australia, Belgium, Chile, France, Great Britain, Japan, New Zealand, Norway, South Africa, the Soviet Union, and the United States. Since recent discoveries suggest the presence of oil, gas, and mineral supplies on Antarctica's outer continental shelf, relations between the signatories have become strained. Many developing nations have argued that the Antarctic Treaty System should be converted into a United Nations regime. Because of its special governing structure involving scientists restricted to only twelve countries, Antarctica's status is like no other global commons domain. I plan to address Antarctica separately in a future article.

In practice, however, the outside status of the global commons has often been a legal fiction. New technologies have always led to further internalization and privatization of the global commons. The high seas, for example, have increasingly been brought into the territorial jurisdiction of coastal states: the original zone of territorial waters reflected the distance of canon fire but by the last Law of the Seas Convention economic development zones allow states to extend from their shores a claim to 200 and 350 mile economic development zones that enclose the fish, energy, and mineral sources in these areas.[7] Further privatization of the global commons occurs in other domains as well: the gene pool that comprises the global commons of biodiversity is privatized by intellectual property rights; the radio frequency spectrum used for wireless access to the internet and cell phones is moving toward a system of proprietary rather than user rights; and outer space, a domain which the 1967 Outer Space Treaty declared a non-militarized zone, has not ceased being developed by states for military purposes since the former Soviet Union sent Sputnik into orbit in 1957 and flight patterns of Cold War nuclear missiles territorialized the Cold War skies much as satellite systems carrying weapon defense technologies promise to territorialize the geostationary orbits under continuing state initiatives popularly known as Star Wars.

Even when the global commons do remain outside the territorial governance of states and individuals, international law has not succeeded in protecting them from devastating exploitation.[8] The oceans and atmosphere have become garbage dumps of the industrial age and the phenomenon of global warming, only recently validated by scientific regimes, has still to find an effective legal instrument to recognize the seriousness of its threat.[9] Legally described as nonstate space, outside

7 Ninety percent of the world's fisheries are now enclosed in these coastal economic development zones. According to Boris Worm et al., in *Science*, the current mismanagement of ocean fisheries has lead to enormous biodiversity loss on ocean ecosystems. Fish stocks have collapsed in nearly one-third of all ocean fisheries. All commercially valuable world fish stocks could completely collapse by 2048 (2006). (Fisheries are collapsed when yields fall to less than 10 percent of the recorded maximum catch during the period 1950 to 2003.)

8 For recent discussion of the failure of international law to protect the global commons from pollution, resource depletion and privatization, James Speth offers a historical review and critical analysis of post 1970s international law of the following global commons domains: ozone layer depletion; climate change; desertification; deforestation; biodiversity loss; freshwater resources; marine environment deteriorization; toxic waste trade; and acid rain (2004: 75–116). See also Young 1997, Hunter 2000.

9 See the report of the National Academy of Sciences which states: "Recent scientific evidence shows that major and widespread climate changes have occurred with startling speed … (G)reen house warming and other human alternations of the earth system may increase the possibility of large, abrupt and unwelcome regional or global climatic events." National Research Council (2002). Scientists at the International Geosphere-Biosphere Program have warned: "The evidence is now overwhelming that (rising temperatures) are a consequence of human activities … (W)e are now pushing the planet beyond anything experienced naturally for many thousands of years. The records of the past show that

territorial sovereignty, global commons are not protected as domains that belong to everyone, *res communis*. Instead international law treats them as domains that belong to no-one, *res nullius*. "The 'state of nature' for the global commons is *res nullius*," laments international relations scholar John Vogler (1995: 17). Given their commons structure in international law, the global commons appear to be corrupted beyond our ability to correct. Why then should Indigenous peoples be so well poised to intervene in the corruption of the global commons?

A Second Grotian Moment

Some international legal scholars suggest that the recent leverage of marginal social actors in the world political system is a sign that the system itself is undergoing fundamental change. Richard Falk, the eminent scholar of international law, once remarked that Hugo Grotius' seventeenth-century work on the law of nations marked a similar moment of profound societal change on a global scale. "A Grotian moment," Falk calls it, "a time in which a fundamental change in circumstances (creates) the need for a different world structure and a different international law" (Falk 1983: 272, Roling 1990: 297–98, Buck 1998). Falk was referring to the passing of feudal society, the rise of the nation-state, and the development of a law among nations for which Grotius had written the foundational documents describing the form of statist sovereignty that would eventually become international law. Is the Inuit claim evidence of a second Grotian moment?

In her book *The Global Commons* legal scholar Susan Buck asks whether the changes we are coming to call globalization signal a second Grotian moment. Her conclusion is ambivalent: Grotius' international law among nations, codified and strengthened over the centuries, still appears to operate for powerful multinational corporations and for the world's developed nation-states. The first Grotian moment is still with us. Indeed, several recent factors give Buck pause: "government policy makers are increasingly forced toward a globalized view of the world environment, triggered by recognition of impending disasters (such as) the depletion of the ozone, global warming, acid deposition and the destruction of the rain forests" (1998: 173). The instant telecommunication systems that make global assessments of environmental conditions immediate, and the role which developing countries like

---

climate shifts can appear abruptly and be global in extent, while archeological and other data emphasize that such shifts have had devastating consequences for human societies" (Alverson, Bradley, Pedersen et al., 2001: 27). The most likely mechanism for abrupt climate change is the disruption of ocean currents such as the Gulf Stream. Computer models suggest that a shutdown of the Gulf Stream would lead to winters twice as cold as the worst winters on record in the Eastern United States (Gagosian 2003: 8). Scientists have outlined the effects of abrupt climate change: extensive biodiversity loss; extreme weather events such as extraordinary droughts, floods, heat waves, and hurricanes; sudden regional cooling; sea level rise; coral bleaching; public health risks, and major new social stresses within and between countries (Speth 2004: 61).

China are playing as holders of valuable natural resources and potential industrial polluters on a heretofore inconceivable scale are all new factors to consider.[10] The global commons, those domains that international law has always placed outside the sovereignty of nation-states, cannot be managed by the so-called developed nations without the consent of the developing ones. This calls for changes in the law of nations, Buck argues; the creation of a different kind of world government, a second Grotian moment.

Buck's assessment is significant but incomplete. Governance of the global commons does require the consent of developing nations, and international law has not yet been an effective instrument for those countries to make themselves heard.[11] But the Inuit are not a developing nation. The reason that native peoples like the Inuit have a unique voice in international law of the global commons is because they have always had a unique position in the international legal order. As the global commons increasingly became a global sink for the pollution of the industrial world in the last 50 years, Indigenous peoples were becoming more adept at strategically using their unique status within post-World War II structures of intensified nation-building. The spatial and life practices of Indigenous peoples have always challenged the statist legal system that was built during the centuries-long first Grotian moment.

The Inuit, for example, challenge Western categories of legal thinking in international law in at least two ways, both intricately connected to new forms of spatial organization including those of the global commons. First, the Inuit are not organized as a nation-state. Their legal identity for purposes of the 2004 petition against the US is comprised of villages and communities that span the coastline of the Arctic sea regardless of where it crosses the territorial boundaries of Canada and the United States. Secondly, when the Inuit provide videotaped statements for the petition from elders and hunters describing the harmful effects of global warming to their way of life, they do not use legal categories from Western law but rather categories that come from their own traditions and common sense experience (Watt-Cloutier 2004). In this way, descriptive categories of space not embedded in the territorial spatial imaginary of Euro-American states make their way into a Western court and demand recognition.[12] Once recognized in the

10 As predicted, in 2009 China surpassed the US in CO_2 emissions (Wong and Bradsher 2009).

11 Note the frustration of the Group of 77 (developing countries) who were effectively dismissed from negotiating the final agreement at the Copenhagen summit when the US, China, Brazil, India, and South Africa forged a last minute, three page document which "did not meet even the modest expectations that leaders set for this meeting, notably by failing to set a 2010 goal for reaching a binding international treat to seal the provisions of the accord" (Broder 2009: A1).

12 See the discussion by Robert A. Williams, Jr. on how traditional storytelling practices of Indigenous peoples in Western venues of international law have succeeded in introducing native people's complaints in frameworks that demand new legal categories in order to find remedy (1990). See also Torres and Milun's discussion of how US legal

form of a legitimate legal claim, these new spatial descriptions, with their various metaphors, narratives and worldviews, can provide not only the leverage with which to force Western legal categories into negotiations, but also new spatial imaginaries for the tools of international law. For these reasons the Inuit's claims may become an important and effective way to introduce change to the ineffective, dominant forms of spatial thinking on the global commons.

The emergence of a second Grotian moment, then, can be observed when we consider challenges to neo-liberal globalization from the perspective of the global commons, the complex spatial imaginary it deploys, and the common history it shares with the colonization of Indigenous peoples. The recent, contentious inclusion of Indigenous peoples at national and international levels does indeed suggest a second Grotian moment. It also suggests that Western spatial imaginaries are, broadly speaking, changing under pressure from the non-territorial and mixed territorial spaces that are emerging in the era of globalization.

Res Nullius and Empty Space versus the Ecological Perspective: The Outlines of a Political Uncommons

The global commons are often described and treated in international law under the doctrine of *res nullius*, things or space which cannot be governed and therefore belong to no-one. As such, domains of the global commons exist in a category that overlaps with the legal category *terra nullius*, land belonging to nobody, a colonial doctrine of sovereignty used by European states to dispossess Indigenous peoples of their land in the eighteenth and nineteenth centuries. Historical references to both *terra nullius* and *res nullius* domains show that global commons and Indigenous peoples are caught in an epistemic imaginary where metaphors of vacant, empty space support a legal rhetoric that legitimates dispossession. Like the "political unconscious" described by literary critic Fredric Jameson to show how political ideologies operate subliminally in the storytelling devices of a culture, empty space operates as a "political uncommons" in the legal descriptions of the global commons in international law (Jameson 1981). Within the persuasive authority of legal discourse deeply embedded in the cultural traditions of the West, empty space furthers an agenda of dispossession despite a rhetoric of shared sovereignty. In this regard, the international law of the global commons shows that globalized space can work as the kind of primitive accumulation strategy Marx described for the early phase of capitalism: dispossession *tout court*.[13] Working alongside the greed

---

traditions, in particular the structures of precedent and rules of evidence, do not provide an adequate arena to hear stories from American Indian plaintiffs that bear witness to historical and present acts of injustice (1990).

13 Political geographer David Harvey has argued that the term globalization often disguises what are in fact simply modes of primitive capitalist accumulation. (Talk given at the Globalization Conference at University of California, Santa Barbara in 2003.)

and power of overdeveloped northern states, international law employs empty space as a particular spatial imaginary that lends rhetorical force to legitimate the privatization and exploitation of the global commons.

Cultural geographers tell us how key metaphors are often used to organize spatial thinking into regions.[14] *Res* and *terra nullius*, first steps in the legal organization and dispossession of spaces that do not fit the territorial spatiality of European nation-states, carry the rhetorical force to create regions. In *The Political Uncommons* I argue that empty space is a key regional metaphor for the vastly different, unbounded domains of the global commons. In international law, *res* and *terra nullius* show how empty space functions as a powerful spatial imaginary behind doctrines that overtly describe domains of public space belonging to all the earth's citizens even as they covertly enable these domains to be treated as if they belonged to no-one. If globalization foretells the possibility of a second Grotian moment, a world government that radically departs from the earth's modern history of dispossession and colonial territoriality, *The Political Uncommons* argues that it does so only when international law no longer makes empty space the regional metaphor for the creation of the nonstate space of the global commons. And, if global commons can be disentangled from the web of *res nullius* legalities, then, I argue, Indigenous peoples too, given their common history of nonstatist standing in international law, may likewise gain a new voice in world politics as they are recognized in a legal idiom that has moved beyond the cultural logic of empty space.

The Inuit's current leverage in world politics relies on a spatial form of being-in-the-world whose authority was at once eliminated by the territorial nation-state and allowed to remain as a residual moment in international law. Finding the right term to describe their special politico-spatial identity is difficult. Up until now I have been referring to their special spatial status in an abstract Western way by calling it nonstate space. This is deceptive. To say that Indigenous peoples are nonstate social actors is to overlook their cultural difference. It erroneously places Indigenous peoples in the same legal category as that other nonstate social actor of increasingly powerful nonterritorial global status in the past quarter century: the multinational corporation. Certainly in US Federal law Native American tribes have been encouraged to deal with their nonstate status by incorporating themselves. The modern corporation, however, is a rather recent legal invention. Giving a profit-oriented enterprise the legal rights of a human being is a development that does not surprise us only because we have become accustomed to its face (Buck 1998: 176). Multinational corporations do overshadow national governments in many international spheres. Indeed, as many observers of contemporary neo-liberal global capitalism note, never before in world history have corporate

14 See, for example, Popper and Popper's work on the Buffalo Commons Project in the Great Plains of the US Deborah E. Popper and Frank J. Popper, "The Buffalo Commons as Regional Metaphor and Geographic Method," *The Geographical Review* 89, no. 4 (October 1999): 491–510.

interests unconnected with the interests of a nation-state so regularly determined international structures and policies. The most obvious difference between multinational corporations and Indigenous peoples as nonstate social actors in international law is their economic power. If both groups have leverage (albeit drastically unequal) within nation-state frameworks of sovereignty, multinational corporations have this leverage because, contra many critics of neo-liberal global capitalism, they have not broken out of the old legal mode and continue to operate within the context and benefits of the international law among nations. The 2008 bailout of insolvent multinational insurance agencies and banks by national governments is a case in point. Multinational corporations are enabled by the first Grotian moment whose laws are defined through the spatial categories of the nation-state and colonialism.[15]

Indigenous peoples' leverage, on the other hand, comes from the legal difference they maintain despite the colonial and statist framework of international law. They may be nonstate social actors but that is not what is so important about their contribution to the transformation of the global commons.[16] The Inuit have leverage in international law because they make a human rights claim that cannot be understood apart from their land. They bring a specific spatial dimension to the law. The multinational corporation, on the other hand, claims rights in the nonstate space of the global marketplace. Both involve their own kind of spatial thinking expressed in the metaphors and images they use to make their claims. While corporate claims are not "landed" and thus tend to invoke images and metaphors of unlimited, abstract, empty space, Indigenous peoples' claims are landed and tend to carry very different, ecologically minded spatial metaphors. Indigenous claims are landed, but still in nonstate space. This complex difference is the contribution Indigenous peoples make to our spatial thinking about the global commons. Unlike the nonstate space of multinational corporations and neo-liberal capitalism, Indigenous nonstate spatial thinking is above all unthinkable without the land. Indigenous nonstate space occupies habitats of long-standing cultural value in the land. When critiquing and composing regional metaphors for the global commons, the Inuit and the other two cases of Indigenous land claims I examine later in this book reveal the importance of cultural understandings that persist in nonstatist lands. Landed understanding of nonstate space brings metaphors of limited space into international arenas. The metaphors of empty, unlimited space, on the other hand, metaphors so useful to the abstractions of numbers and money, come to international law from an entirely different, imperialistic historical project.

---

15 I explore this more fully when I discuss the success of multinational corporations in thwarting the Common Heritage of Mankind principle in international law in Chapter 4.

16 Some progressive social analysts see the legal leverage of Indigenous peoples as stemming from their special ability to incorporate themselves and enter the economic arena from the powerful, legally protected status of the corporation. See *What Can Tribes Do? Strategies and Institutions in American Indian Economic Development*, ed. Stephan P. Cornell and Joseph Kalt (Los Angeles: American Indian Studies Center, UCLA, 1992).

If Indigenous peoples have contributed the sense of limited, nonstate space in the global commons, it is because they begin from an ecological perspective. From an ecological perspective there is first of all no "outside" to the earth's living systems. There is no ecological way to think of "waste products" and "side-effects" in natural systems because there is no "waste" or "side" in nature, just complex, interactive systems. The global commons, then, from an ecological, Indigenous perspective is not "outside." From the statist perspectives of modern economics and international law, on the other hand, the global commons retains an outside status: the commons are legally outside territorial states and the pollution and other side effects of industrial life (called "externalities" in economic terms) are side-products the costs of which are scarcely if at all factored into our dominant system of capitalist production.

The ecological perspective the Inuit bring to international law includes cultural relations to the land that preceded the colonial mentality of *vacuum Domicilium*, a legal doctrine used by Europeans as they settled the West to justify dispossession of native peoples. Seventeenth-century English political philosopher John Locke, for example, built his theory of natural rights to private property based on arguing that the Americas were undifferentiated expanses, a kind of empty space which Europeans were justified in occupying and eventually possessing as their agricultural labor added a surplus value missing in the cultures of the Indigenous inhabitants. In his well known chapter on property in the 1690 classic, *Two Treatises of Government*, Locke presciently offered a metaphor for what may well characterize the fate of the global commons today: "In the beginning all the world was America" (Locke 1988: II.49.1). The European projection of an undifferentiated, homogenous quality onto the diverse, heterogeneous (and unknown) terrain of the New World is the preamble for the justification of the European natural rights theory of property which dispossessed Native Americans of their land.

Metaphors of empty space pervade colonial thinking and create a cultural logic that applies beyond domains of land. Locke's other famous metaphor, the *tabula rasa* (empty slate), was used to explain why the dominium of European-style thinking should be extended to nonEuropean minds. "Let us suppose," wrote Locke, "the mind to be, as we say, white paper, void of all characters, without any Ideas: how comes it to be furnished?"[17] The *tabula rasa* argument (originally in Aristotle) makes Euclidean space—everywhere the same, static, uniformly subject to the same laws, and abstract in the sense of being empty—the universal foundation of Reason. Thus empty, homogeneous space in Locke is an originary abstract space that can serve as a foundation for the seizure of that space by the state or by individuals.

17 See the entry "*table rase*" (French for *tabula rasa*) in André Lalande, *Vocabulaire technique et Critque de la Philosophie* (Paris: Presses Universitaire de France, 1983: 1099). The editor notes that the expression *table rase* probably came into French philosophical discourse thanks to Leibniz who ridiculed Locke's theory of a foundational empty space.

In addition to the perspectives of *res* and *terra nullius*, the other main way in which international law describes the complex space that lies outside the territory of the law of nations is through the law of the high seas. The early legal description of the high seas comes from Dutch scholar and humanist Hugo Grotius. Modern legal scholars generally focus on the bulk of Grotius' writings that famously describe interstate space: the rules and rights for exchange among emergent nation-states.[18] Indeed, Grotius' early modern description of laws for interstate space has earned Grotius the reputation of "the father of international law" or, as Richard Falk notes, our first "Grotian moment." In *The Political Uncommons* I argue that a second Grotian moment compels us to instead examine the body of law that grew up around the "outside" space of states, the space of the global commons. This means turning our focus to one of Grotius' lesser known works, *Mare Liberum* written in 1609 (1916). *The Free Seas* (or *The Freedom of the Seas*) is a treatise on the laws that apply on the high seas. Rediscovered and translated into English in the late nineteenth century, *Mare Liberum* argues that the seas must be legally protected as nonterritorial space. No one European colonial nation should govern the seas, Grotius wrote; rather they should be open for the free usufruct right of all. As the first description of a global commons in modern international law, Grotius legal and spatial thinking about the high seas is an important document. Since the last century, I argue, its arguments have entered every subsequent legal description of a global commons regime from outer space to biodiversity.

The relation between empty space and maritime space in Grotius and later legal thinking is complex.[19] Unlike Locke's vision of natural domains as empty, extensive, homogeneous space, Grotius' description of the high seas gives a paradoxical account of natural domains as space which is both homogeneous and heterogeneous, at once possessible, unpossessible and possessive. Amenable to, but more complex than, the metaphorics of empty space, the law of the seas has provided extended maritime metaphors of open, nonterritorial, nonstate space to legal thinking on the global commons. Along with Locke, Grotius and his legal description of the oceans, I argue, provides the other key regional metaphor for all the diverse forms of the global commons today. Like the empty space metaphors Locke uses to describe domains over which proprietary rights can be asserted, metaphors of maritime space dominate the description of modern commons domains over which only usufruct rights can be asserted. Both sets of

18 Grotius' most influential work in international law is *De Jure Belli ac Pacis* (1625) translated into English in 1682 as *The Rights of War and Peace*, by Jean Barbeyrac, ed. Richard Tuck, 3 vols (Indianapolis: Liberty Fund, 2005). The work is more than a discourse on the rules of war and the rights of citizens during wartime. It became a source of the modern idea of natural rights, the doctrine that all human beings equally are by nature free to dispose their persons and their possessions as they think fit. Natural rights, in this view, are the foundation of law and government and are not granted by the state.

19 I provide a close reading of *Mare Liberum* in Chapter 3, focusing on the complex kinds of space Grotius envisioned in the first global commons: *res nullius, res communis, res publicae*.

metaphors describe nonstate, nonterritorial space, but they project different spatial imaginaries into legal thinking about the global commons. Importantly, neither of these metaphorical approaches to the space of the global commons is ecological. Neither of them supplies the metaphors and spatial imaginaries that we see in the Inuit approach to global space.

The metaphor of empty, unlimited, homogeneous space has followed Western legal traditions as the first step in describing and conceptualizing all new global spaces opened up by Western technological know-how—whether it be navigational technologies on the seventeenth-century open seas, rocket technologies in twentieth-century outer space, or bioengineering inventions in the genetic domains of the twenty-first century. More recently, the powerful reach of multinational corporations, along with the banking institutions and trade agreements they inspire, have provided models of globalized space that appear to benefit from the law of nations framework devised by Grotius and Locke. To rethink and change the course of dispossession that accompanies international law's first steps at describing unbounded "natural" space, we must consider how differently ecological spatial thinking works. A colonial spatial imaginary created the law of the seas and the international law of colonial nations. That spatial imaginary supports the dispossessive agenda in the global commons.[20] The Inuit appear best able to challenge dispossessive laws in the global commons because as nonstate social actors working from an ecological perspective, they have a strategic advantage over citizens of nation-states.

The Cultural Logic of Empty Space

Empty space in modernity, broadly speaking, is a cultural logic. In its most general sense, a dominant cultural logic is a kind of hegemonic norm. In terms of international law, the cultural logic of empty space refers to an "epistemic imaginary," an image repertoire of figural cultural assumptions that undergird the supposedly neutral conceptual system behind a legal argument. The laws governing the global commons offer not only a reason-based understanding of common space. They also use figural schemas and metaphors to render the unimaginable depths and reaches of the global space they seek to regulate. These images are rarely overt operators in legal discourse. They generally lie hidden in disparate ways throughout the law's field of reference. What I find in all areas where the global commons is under construction is an image of empty space that is linked to earlier spatial imaginaries supporting colonial sovereignty and the law of the high seas. *The Political Uncommons* seeks to make explicit these connections and show their material impact.

---

20 For an example of the capacity of the international law of the seas to create empty space in the ocean commons, see Peter H. Sand, "Diego Garcia: British-American Legal Black Hole in the Indian Ocean?" *Journal of Environmental Law*, January 2009: 1–25.

International law is embedded in a broader cultural system where the metaphorical power of empty space is also at work. There is no doubt that empty space has played a key role in how common space has been imagined, created, lived in, and critiqued in Western modernity. Sociologists, for example, speak of the "emptying" of time and space that took place when the universal global map and world-standard time were instituted: "Empty space only comes into existence on an institutional level once the world has been thoroughly explored and universal degrees of latitude and longitude established," notes sociologist Anthony Giddens, critical of the disembedded social relations that come when this indefinite extension of time and space becomes systematically integrated into the day-to-day activities of everyone (Giddens 1994: 3). Those who use the metaphor of empty space to describe this ever further reach of abstraction into the everyday experience of modern life usually equate empty space with homogeneous space.[21]

More recently, however, we find empty space used in a more positive sense as a poststructuralist trope associated with democracy in a postmodern era. Political theorist Claude Lefort, for example, considers that with the radical change in society that accompanied the late eighteenth-century French Revolution and its unprecedented transformation of democracy—what Alexis de Tocqueville had called "the democratic invention," when power was suddenly said to emanate from inside the social (from the people) rather than from an external source (the king)—suddenly the place from which power derived its new legitimacy could not be represented as an organic totality. This new, unrepresentable social site of legitimacy Lefort refers to as "the image of an empty place." "In my view," Lefort writes in *The Political Forms of Modern Society: Bureaucracy, Democracy, Totalitarianism*, "the important point is that democracy is instituted and sustained by the *dissolution of the markers of certainty*. It inaugurates a history in which people experience a fundamental indeterminacy as to the basis of power, law and knowledge, and as to the basis of relations between *self* and *other*" (Lefort 1986: 279). In this "antifoundationalist" formulation, empty space is no longer homogeneous and abstract. It is a virtual space whose unbounded complexity promises diversity and possibility. Advocates for the Internet's open access and neutrality thus often make claims that the experience of virtual global space produces a new kind of democratic citizen (a "netizen"), a global commoner.[22]

21 In a similar fashion, the Italian philosopher Giorgio Agamben notes the function of empty space in modernity as the communication gap that separates a subject formed through experience from a subject formed through knowledge. Abstract categories of modern knowledge—of both the natural and the social sciences—have authority in modernity while the categories of knowing gained through experience—emotional knowing, intuition, dreams, but also the storytelling modes of a culture (the novel, music, poetry)—are undervalued and underfunded. Agamben schematizes the two realms as unable to communicate over the gulf of empty space that will not function as a common denominator. See *Infancy and History: On the Destruction of Experience (Radical Thinkers)* (London: Verso, 2007).

22 See for example the conclusion to David Bollier's history of the struggle to build the Internet as a global commons in *Viral Spiral: How the Commoners Created Their Own*

These two examples illustrate how empty space has become a way to describe both the curse of our time (disembedded social relations) and the saving potential of our time (social democracy).

Why is the cultural category of empty space doing this paradoxical work at this historical moment? Anthropologists who study the cultural dimensions of the enormous transformations we moderns are experiencing as space is extended, accelerated and shrunk by communication, travel and market technologies are quite aware that when metaphors of spatial emptiness are used they often refer to something that is as yet unrecognizable in the society, something that is unrepresentationally trying to make itself known. For some this is a sign of a paradigm shift, a first or second Grotian moment. For others the changes brought by the accelerated form of globalized modernization are "sometimes carelessly reduced and summarized in expressions like 'homogenization of culture' or 'world culture'," says French anthropologist Marc Augé who invites us to give it close ethnographic scrutiny (1995: 39–40). In *The Political Uncommons* I take up the challenge to study spatial dimensions of modernity with the eye of a cultural anthropologist.

Space has traditionally been an important concept in anthropology. Spatial and temporal grammars were key areas of study for ethnographers out to find the generative forms behind the world-making ways of pre-industrial cultures (Whorf 1956). As a cultural concept in post-industrial cultures, space is in the process of being redefined and redeployed by urban geographers, literary theorists, sociologists, historians and anthropologists, all of whom have now made space a vibrant and transdisciplinary category for social analysis.[23] The metaphoric operations of empty space in the global commons in international law provide a sort of field site for an anthropological approach to empty space as a cultural operator in modernity. In this way a study of the international law of the global commons can contribute to more general philosophical thinking about common space in modernity.

Outline of the Book

The Political Uncommons is an interdisciplinary work that uses research methods and theories from critical geography, cultural anthropology, international relations, law and the humanities. The aim of the book is at once descriptive (a description of the conceptual and material work of empty space in domains of shared sovereignty

---

Digital Republic (New York: The New Press, 2008). Bollier contends that the Internet advances democracy by making individuals into "history making citizens."

23 See, to begin with, Michael Crang and N.J. Thrift, *Thinking Space (Critical Geographies)*, ed. Michael Crang and N.J. Thrift (London: Routledge, 2000). See also my first book, Kathryn Milun, *Pathologies of Modern Space: Empty Space, Urban Anxiety and the Recovery of the Public Self* (New York: Routledge, 2007).

in modernity), analytic (an interpretive analytics of what it means to inhabit common domains of the earth as they are increasingly defined through the work of empty space in international law), and finally interventionist (a suggestion of how to go beyond these colonial spatial categories by understanding and supporting the legal leverage which Indigenous peoples bring to Western law's failure to protect common space). Along with the Inuit, I seek to enter the debate on environmental issues from a perspective that makes prominent the Euro-American colonization of the earth in the modern era. The environment in this book is being thought through the history of globally common space in international law.

Chapter 1 offers a case study of biodiversity as an emergent domain of the global commons. Biodiversity is an emergent name for nature when it is imagined spatially and protected legally as a global commons. Many diverse and contradictory intentionalities are at stake when environmentalists, biotech corporations, genetics, advertising agencies, ecologists and international lawyers depict nature as a global commons of biodiversity. Following the cultural logic of empty space in the modern transformation of nature to biodiversity, I employ an interdisciplinary approach showing how empty space will be explored in the rest of the book as a complex, covert cultural operator in international law. At the end of this chapter I use the material on biodiversity to raise questions about Giorgio Agamben's political theory of the state of exception, offering the ecological and Indigenous challenges to global commons regimes as evidence that empty space may be dominant but is being challenged in complex ways.

Chapters 2, 3, 4, and 5 turn to the global commons of the high seas, outer space and the radio frequency spectrum (on which the Internet and other modes of telecommunication function)—and the way in which international law initially brings these commons into its jurisdiction under the doctrine of *res nullius* (space that belongs to nobody). *Res nullius*, I argue, is the doctrine through which the cultural logic of empty space works in international law. Once a space is declared legally "empty" of the social relations of belonging, these spaces can achieve the status of *res communis* (things which belong to everyone) if states can agree on the proper conventions. Without such conventions, these commons remain *res nullius* and legally open access to a seemingly limitless exploitation, privatization, and a variety of unregulated practices. Much of the global commons today endures in this latter state. Here it tends to be framed in a rhetoric of *res communis*, space that belongs to everybody, even as in practice it is treated as *res nullius*, space that belongs to nobody. Understanding the paradoxical and dynamic relation between *res nullius* and *res communis*, I argue, allows us to better understand the rhetorical strategies that keep the global commons malingering in its present dispossessive state.

Thus, Chapter 2 looks at the doctrine of *res nullius* as a semantic field in international law. It examines the role of *res nullius* in the description of the contemporary global commons and studies the inseparable relations between *res nullius* and *terra nullius*, the colonial doctrine of sovereignty used both to legitimize late nineteenth-century actions that dispossessed Native peoples of their land and (as *territorium nullius*) to describe regions of the high seas in early twentieth century textbooks of international law. This complex picture of the legal description of the global commons, I argue, allows us to better grasp the paradoxical logics operating in the international law of global commons today. Chapter 3 takes three historical moments in the life of *res nullius* as a legal concept and follows its move from Roman law to the law of the Internet. The most important discovery of this chapter is the role of *res nullius* in Grotius' treatise on the law of the seas. I demonstrate how conceptual and imagistic legal thinking about the high seas, their visual qualities and ungovernable nature, came to dominate political thinking on Western commons regimes to this day. In Chapters 4 and 5 I explore how maritime law became the basis of the law of outer space. By looking at the first several years of papers presented by jurists at the International Conference on the Law of Outer Space (1957–1960) I note the conceptual and political struggles that in the end resulted in maritime law's vertical extension into outer space. *Res nullius*, it turns out, was a crucial operator in rendering the utterly diverse spatial realm of "outer space" representable in the descriptive legal categories used for the high seas. In these chapters I consider how debates over the just distribution of commons resources in such diverse spatial domains were nonetheless framed by the same *res nullius* type logic: whether referring to deep seabed mineral extraction and mining on the moon or fishing rights and licensing of the geostationary orbits, the winning arguments written into the international law of the global commons use the concept of *res nullius* fashioned in the law of the seas. What difference, I ask, do these different spatial tropes make in the practice of distributive justice? I also compare specific cases of environmental protection and liability that invoked the law of the seas (dumping nuclear waste and creating legal "black holes" in the high seas), the law of outer space (contamination by the crash of a Soviet nuclear satellite in Canada) and the law of territorial land (Chernobyl). Interesting differences in liability can arguably be related to different kinds of spatial thinking that persist in these legal domains despite the imposition of the conceptual maritime framework of *res nullius*.

Examining the effects of *res nullius* empty space and residual spatial imaginaries on the global commons leads us to ask what the governance of the earth's shared spaces might be like if not informed by the cultural logic of empty space carried in international law's *res nullius/terra nullius* framework. In Chapters 6 and 7 I take up this question by looking at two cases where the legitimacy of *terra nullius* has been revoked in recent years and considering what these cases can tell us about how to create a more just law for the global commons. When *terra nullius* is revoked law faces the immediate problem of how to help decolonize the earth by recognizing spatial schemas previously nullified by colonial legal categories. Recognition of Indigenous peoples' rights is inseparable from this process. *Terra nullius* was revoked by the International Court of Justice in the Western Sahara (1976) where a state of war ensued for decades; it was revoked by the High Court of Australia (1991) where Native Title was enacted and Indigenous peoples have been empowered to negotiate with white ranchers, multinational corporations and federal agents. In both cases, the revocation of *terra nullius* has allowed empty space to give way to paradoxical encounters and solutions as the newly legitimated, precolonial, non-Western, nomadic notions of belonging to the land are suddenly used by Indigenous peoples to argue and negotiate claims in courts whose legal logic is still defined by Western notions of territorial property. These cases allow us to consider how common space in modernity might look otherwise if not governed by a legal imaginary grounded in a colonial spatial sensibility. They invite us to better understand the issues of self-determination faced by Indigenous peoples who seek to assert non-Western forms of sovereignty on an earth that has been so thoroughly saturated by the colonial logics of empty space.

In the conclusion I suggest what the cultural analysis of spatial thinking in the global commons can contribute more broadly speaking to both a philosophical and a practical discussion of common space in an increasingly globalized, homogenized modernity. In the conceptual map of modern, secular knowledge drawn during the European Enlightenment, the German philosopher Kant, a geographer himself, proposed that a universal idea of common space was fundamental to the project of making Reason and not Religion the basis of peaceful co-existence among the different peoples of the world. Kant's map of modern knowledge shows the epistemological assumptions that underlie the organization of many Euro-American social institutions, from international law to the modern university. The Eurocentric idea of common space proposed by Kant, as well as its attendant notion of common sense, has been widely attacked by social thinkers in many fields—from geography to urban planning to political theory—who argue that it did for modern knowledge what we have described empty space doing in international law. I point to another legal tradition of commons in the West, one persisting in Indigenous rights and in the Forest Charter of the Magna Carta, and note recent interpretations of its value as a global tool for an alternative kind of commons protection and creation in international law.

Chapter 1
An Emergent Global Commons: Biodiversity—A Case Study of How Culture becomes Law and Nature becomes Empty Space

> So what is biodiversity? My belief is that the variety of life on the planet is like an extra-ordinary complex, unfinished, and incomplete *manuscript* with a hugely varied alphabet, an ever-expanding lexicon, and a poorly understood *grammar*. Nonetheless, some scholars (for example, Charles Darwin) have been able to translate enough of the *text* to apprehend that it speaks of profound matters concerning our origins and our destiny. Ripping the *manuscript* to pieces because we want to use the *paper* makes little sense, especially if the *manuscript* says that 'to survive you shall not destroy what you don't understand.' Our mission as ecologists must be *to interpret the meaning* of biodiversity. The urgent need for this mission, and our current ecological ignorance, must be forcefully communicated to the public. (Ecologist D.M.S.J. Bowman cited in Nabhan 1997: 20, my emphasis)

> From the moment when biotechnologists insert a single gene from, say, a bacterium into the genetic code of a crop plant to produce a 'transgenic' variety, they have staked their claim on the plant and all of its descendants. Farmers are contractually barred from saving any seed they produce from such a variety, and plant breeders can't use its pollen—unless they pay the corporation that owns it. It is as if *an author* compiled *a thick novel* entirely from *the writings of other authors*, added one *original word*, *copyrighted the book*, and then claimed ownership of each *sentence* individually. (Cox 2002)

The term "biodiversity" is a recent addition to the public vocabulary. Generally speaking, biodiversity is a new word to refer to the abundant variety of life on earth. It is a current popular science word for nature that has arisen out of academic and activist discourse and made its way into common culture and law precisely at the moment when the variety of life on our planet is being lost at an unprecedented scale in human history.[1] Indeed, the growing consensus of biologists is that we

---

1 The term "biodiversity" (short for biological diversity) was advanced in the 1980s by a concerned community of scientists, nongovernmental organizations (NGOs) and others to take the place of the 1970s term "endangered species" in public and political

are entering a sixth mass extinction of life on earth: the five previous caused by asteroids, volcanism, and other natural phenomena, but this emergent sixth mass extinction a result of human transformations of the earth (Wilson 2002). The word "biodiversity" thus has a big job to do in the common culture and in the domain of law: it must designate nature as a field of differences (variety); it must indicate that we are at risk of losing this diversity if we do not find better ways to govern it; and it must speak to a spatial sensibility about life on a planetary scale. A planetary scale! What kind of spatial sensibility is this?

Where do we begin to get a sense of such a vast commons jurisdiction? Since the senses alone cannot provide a common experience of space on such a massive scale, spatial metaphors are called in to help. Metaphors are part of our spatial imaginary and law relies on such metaphorical thinking to circumscribe what it aims to protect. In the first two epithets above, biodiversity is an expression that relies on a particular metaphorical framework to describe nature as a commons domain: biodiversity is likened to a "manuscript" or a "book" that has "words," "sentences," "grammar," to be "interpreted" and "authors" whose "original writings" can be protected by law through "copyright." Written language is the dominant metaphor used to describe this newer sense of nature that is at once made apparent by recent biotechnologies and under threat by human populations. This chapter looks at the metaphor of writing/language that Western culture implicitly attaches to the term biodiversity in order to communicate the sense of massive political space of this newest area of the global commons. I argue that, within the metaphor of written language, empty space is the implicit trope that carries the dominant spatial imaginary behind biodiversity. Empty space, then, is a rhetorical strategy. It uses metaphors of writing and analogies from Western law governing the high seas to advance arguments about global commons, making these arguments appear logical and necessary when in fact they involve historical and cultural preconceptions, colonial power relations, and economic reductionism.

A further argument of this chapter involves biodiversity as a new jurisdiction of international law. Biodiversity is an emergent domain of the global commons. Only recently has it taken its place in international law next to other regions of the global commons—Antarctica, the oceans, the atmosphere, outer space, and telecommunications networks. Legal descriptions of biodiversity refer to it as "the gene pool," a genetic commons that is quickly being enclosed by corporations staking patent claims to domains of genetic code. The spatial imaginary attached to biodiversity thus encompasses the shift from a broad cultural domain of nature to a region of shared sovereignty described by international patent law. Contemporary legal discussions of nature as biodiversity reveal the persistence of a cultural logic of empty space based in eighteenth-century notions of nature and property rights.

At the end of this chapter, the complex picture of biodiversity as a spatial imaginary is considered alongside recent arguments by political theorist Giorgio

---

consciousness. To emphasis that species die because of habitat destruction, new emphasis was placed on the diversity of ecosystems of which species are functioning parts.

Agamben concerning the spatial logic of modern sovereignty. The global commons, I argue, offers a challenge to Agamben's controversial position. This chapter, then, opens our investigation of the cultural logic of empty space in the global commons. It shows why a deeper examination of this logic is called for in the jurisprudence of international law. And finally, it indicates how the in-depth analysis of the doctrine of *res nullius* we take up in subsequent chapters can contribute to recent debates in the political theory of globalization.

Spatial Metaphors for Nature in Medieval, Classical and Post-Modern Eras

Consider for a moment the metaphor that ecologist D.M. Bowman uses to describe biodiversity in the first epithet above. Biodiversity, writes Bowman, is an "unfinished, incomplete manuscript" which has an "ever-expanding lexicon." Nature here is imagined as a text, a text with an unclear message but one clear injunction about how to govern it: "to survive you shall not destroy what you don't understand." A modern western reader would have no trouble with the analogy of biodiversity as a manuscript. After all, since the European Middle Ages writing has been one of the most commonly used metaphors to refer to nature in the Western tradition. In the European Middle Ages, "The Great Book of Nature," was written by the hand of God. As the philosopher Michel Foucault noted:

> (During this epoch, t)here is no difference between the visible marks that God has stamped upon the surface of the earth, so that we may know its inner secrets, and the legible words that the Scriptures, or the sagas of Antiquity, have set down in the books preserved for us by tradition. The relation to these texts is of the same nature as the relation to things. (1973: 49)

The resemblance between the (sacred) text and the (text of the) world is complete. Since the European medieval worldview assumed that all things existed in God, the universe possessed a profound unity. Spatially that unity could be depicted in the way objects were placed next to each other within the frame of a picture.

Even where it appears to a modern, secular viewer as mere empty space, the background space of the medieval picture is actually full of the epistemologically assumed relations between God and the natural world that are expressed in the metaphor of an incorporeal (therefore flat) God who has written the Book of Nature. Thus, says art historian Pierre Francastel:

> the age was satisfied with a representation of juxtaposed spaces, no distance between things, everything, man and objects, being attributes of God. Simply out of respect, divine objects and persons are not situated within any *naturalistic order*, no matter how minimal. The opposition is between the incorporeal—and therefore flat—essence, and its attributes. (Francastel 1967: 36, my emphasis)

Figure 1.1 Hieronymus Bosch, the Haywain c. 1485–90 (triptych)
Source: Prado, Madrid.

Now compare the medieval spatial imaginary with the sense of space implied in Bowman's contemporary metaphor of biodiversity as an "incomplete manuscript." The profound unity of the medieval world is not signaled in Bowman's metaphor which implies that Nature's diversity is both incomplete and in the process of happening (the lexicon is still growing, is still being written).

Bowman's contemporary metaphor of the incomplete and dynamic "manuscript" of biodiversity is much closer to the classical eighteenth-century worldview where nature no longer resembled the word of the Scriptures but suddenly existed in a new scientific relation to writing: God no longer wrote the truth of nature but turned the task over to the taxonomical efforts of the emergent scientist who could represent the God-given world in tabular form.

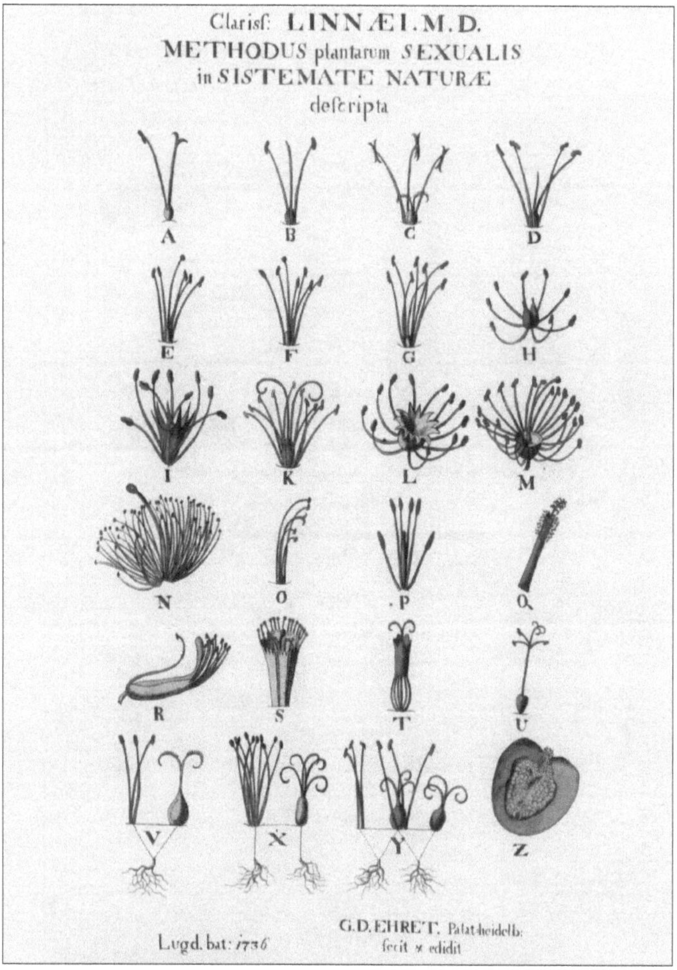

Figure 1.2 Georg Dionysius Ehret's illustration of Linnaeus's sexual system of plant classification, 1736

Source: Linnaeus, Special Collections, Library, University of Otago, New Zealand.

To better grasp how, today, the metaphor of a written nature carries both an epistemological and a political logic that would dispossess rather than sustain biodiversity, consider a full-page advertisement published in 1998 in the *New York Times* entitled “Biodiversity.”

Figure 1.3 Monsanto advertisement on biodiversity
Source: *New York Times*, June 2, 1998, D3. © 1998 Monsanto Company (Historical advertisement used with permission).

The advertisement is sponsored by Monsanto, a company which has the dubious distinction of being the first multi-national corporation to obtain a US patent on a form of plant life (Barlett and Steele 2008). Since its world-wide foray into genetically-engineered seeds and food products, Monsanto has updated the legend associated with its logo and no longer promotes itself as a player in agricultural, chemical, and pharmaceutical industries but rather as "A Life Sciences Company." Alongside its economic and technological power, Monsanto has the means to influence through advertisements like these the cultural perception of nature as a relationship between science and life.

Many things could be said about the description of nature offered in the promotional advertisement Monsanto placed in the *New York Times* to publicize their sponsorship of the Hall of Biodiversity at the American Museum of Natural History. The images of animals appear to stand for the earth's biodiversity. They are featured as eighteenth-century-styled scientific drawings of discrete species. This is the vision of nature, the advertisement suggests, Monsanto is protecting. Why would Monsanto be interested in protecting nature as a classically styled scientific series of discrete organisms? Perhaps Monsanto simply hopes to gain cultural capital from being associated (albeit stylistically) with a classical tradition of scientific work, intellectual labor from an era where science was not commercially driven. Certainly there is another advantage to Monsanto in placing nature in this eighteenth-century representational order. The eighteenth-century stylistic borrowing allows Monsanto to connect with a deeper cultural logic by placing its depicted life forms against a backdrop of empty space. In the advertisement, empty space is the background of taxonomical classifications whose stylistic conventions do not require depiction of an organism's habitat or relational life. Decontextualization is a key rhetorical function of empty space when used as a (back)ground for modern life. It connotes the authority of science with its visual codes of the neutrality of homogeneous space. Thus the Monsanto advertisement appears, on the one hand, to support the notion of nature's biodiversity as disconnected entities in empty space.

On the other hand, the printed message in the Monsanto advertisement contradicts the image's sense of disconnectedness. Contrary to what we see in the image, in the printed text Monsanto repeats that biodiversity is about interconnectedness and interdependence. The Monsanto text reads:

> All of life is interconnected. So without a supporting cast of millions of species, human survival is far from guaranteed. This variety and interdependence of species is what's called biodiversity. And it matters to Monsanto in particular. Because our business depends on making discoveries in the world of genetic information. Information that is lost forever when a species becomes extinct. Information that offers solutions in agriculture, nutrition, and medicine never before thought possible. For a population that's growing. On a planet that's not. (Monsanto 1998)

The choice of discrete images appears to contradict the advertisement's printed message that biodiversity, which is "interconnected" and "interdependent," should be viewed as something so intricately bound together that it cannot be separated without harming human life. The advertisement's text implies that biodiversity is a nonexcludable part of human life. In terms of property law, to exclude humans from this life source would be a basic violation of their common property right. Biodiversity, Monsanto says, belongs to everyone. In international law this is called *res communis*, things belonging to everyone. In short, it is a commons.

Reading more closely, however, the nature of the Monsanto commons become clear: "Our business," Monsanto states, "depends on making discoveries in the world of genetic information." Monsanto's practical use of nature as recombinant DNA—genetic material which it mines, engineers, patents, and sells in various forms—bespeaks an entirely Lockean, natural rights claim to ownership. This view of biodiversity is what international law describes with the doctrine of *res nullius*, things that belong to nobody and are therefore available for privatization. It appears then that these images in empty space are actually helping us as a culture make the transitions from life to species to genetic information. And it is the latter that Monsanto protects by claiming patents. If biodiversity is our global culture's collective attempt to legally describe the diversity of life as *res communis*, something belonging to everyone, it remains entirely suspicious that Monsanto places this life in abstract, empty, eighteenth-century-styled space. Such empty space is in fact the depiction of life in a *res nullius* domain. Indeed the Monsanto advertisement provides an example of how empty space acts as an epistemic imaginary, a spatial metaphor that prepares the way for a logical argument about the way things really ought to be understood. Empty space is the figural cultural logic that helps Monsanto covertly argue that nature's diversity belongs to no-one and ought therefore to be excludable, legally open to private property claims.

The Monsanto advertisement reveals the cultural as well as juristic tendency to create *res nullius* while ostensibly professing *res communis*. Environmental strategists have recently recognized the political and spatial complexity of protecting biodiversity as a global commons. Protecting biodiversity as discrete endangered species may lead to a weakened political agenda since the real cultural problem lies in getting the public to imagine complex habitats rather than individual species. Kent Redford of the Nature Conservancy explains it this way:

> (The) use of just species as a measure of biodiversity resulted in conservation efforts focusing on relatively few ecosystems while other highly threatened ones were ignored. Species do not exist in a vacuum, and any (valid) definition of biodiversity must include the ecological complexes in which organisms naturally occur and the ways in which they interact with one another and their surroundings. (Cited in Nabhan 1997: 20)

Culturally speaking, empty space is a "recognizable" figure, a normative spatial representation that naturalizes a tacit Lockean argument relating nature to rights in property and, by extension, the surplus value that can be created by selling that property. Simple in itself, empty space is extremely difficult to "see." Many conservationists were late to realize that they needed a counter-representational spatial figure to represent nature as complexity.[2] Legal activists similarly struggle to find doctrines that effectively describe the complexity of nature without succumbing to the rhetorical force of our culture's keystone figure of empty space.

The Monsanto advertisement provides a visually sustained argument about the contemporary global commons that uses a prior cultural logic involving eighteenth-century notions of nature and, if empty space does its work well, of rights in property relations that were intimated in that earlier era. A brief historical detour will further allow us to examine how, in the early classical period, empty space was used to support a reconceptualization of nature consonant with a nascent theory of rights and a colonial worldview.

Empty Space as a Metaphor for Nature: Locke, *Tabula Rasa*, Surplus Value and the Dispossession of Native America

In *Changes in the Land: Indians, Colonists and the Ecology of New England*, ethnohistorian William Cronon describes how early seventeenth-century American legal thinking viewed land through the lens of an epistemic imaginary of empty space (Cronon 1983). Colonial theorist John Winthrop, Cronon explains, resolved conflicting sovereignty issues relating to the land practices of Native Americans by arguing that there were two ways of owning land in colonial New England, one natural and one civil. A natural right to the soil had existed, Winthrop claimed, "when men held the earth in common every man sowing and feeding where he pleased." When individuals began to raise crops, keep cattle, and improve the land by enclosing it, Winthrop said, their actions gave them a superior, civil right of ownership. "As for the Natives in New England," he wrote, "they inclose noe Land, neither have any setled habytation, nor any tame Cattle to improve the Land by, and soe have noe other but a Natural Right to those Countries." By this argument, only those fields planted by Indian women could be claimed by Native Americans as property. "(T)he rest of the country," wrote Winthrop, "lay open to any that could and would improve it." The legal doctrine of *vacuum*

2 For an example of a counter-image to represent nature as complexity, see the fascinating account of the Buffalo Commons, a regional metaphor proposed by geographers (Popper and Popper) to transform the monocultural devastation of the US Great Plains. Finding the appropriate metaphorical figure in this case played an important role in being able to gain public support to construct an ecologically minded solution to decades of biological and civil decline in the region. Similar regional metaphors are needed to legally protect biodiversity as a *res communis* commons. Deborah E. Popper and Frank J. Popper, "The Buffalo Commons as Regional Metaphor and Geographic Method," *The Geographical Review* 89, no. 4 (October 1999): 491–510.

Domicilium described land waiting to be inhabited by a more productive people. "In a vacant soyle," wrote the minister John Cotton, "hee that taketh possession of it, and bestoweth culture and husbandry upon it, his Right it is" (Winthrop in Cronon 1983: 56–57).

There is a good deal of work being done by empty space in Winthrop's argument. Cronon rightly notes that it was not so much the emptiness of Indian-inhabited lands that made colonial theorists see New England's native peoples as inhabitants of *vacuum Domicilium.* It was the fact that these non-Europeans worked the land only for subsistence. Because they did not produce surplus value (capital) from their land, the Indians could lose the right of ownership in the eyes of the early colonial theorists. Thus empty space is linked to the production of a form of property that creates surplus value.

The same links among empty space, Indigenous lands, and surplus value are probably most famously made in the early seventeenth-century by English political theorist John Locke. The foundational image of undifferentiated expanses that Locke uses in his well known chapter on property in the *Two Treatises of Government* is of pre-European America. "In the beginning," Locke wrote in 1660, "all the world was America" (II.49.1). This projection of an undifferentiated, homogenous quality onto the diverse, heterogeneous (and unknown) terrain of the New World was the preamble for the justification of the European "natural rights" theory of property which dispossessed Native Americans of their land. It functioned logically in the same way as another writing metaphor, the *tabula rasa* (empty slate), did in Locke's arguments to extend the dominium of Reason to non-European minds. "Let us suppose, then," wrote Locke in *An Essay on Human Understanding*, "the mind to be, as we say, white paper, void of all characters, without any Ideas: how comes it to be furnished?" (2.1.2). The *tabula rasa* argument (originally in Aristotle but ridiculed by Locke's contemporary Leibnitz) makes Euclidean space—everywhere the same, static, uniformly subject to the same laws, and abstract in the sense of being empty—the universal foundation of Reason. Thus empty, homogeneous space in Locke is an originary abstract space that can serve as a rhetorical foundation for the seizure of that space by the State or by individuals.[3]

The connection between the image of Native North America as a homogeneous expanse and Locke's theory of surplus value is worth further reflection to grasp the

3 Leibniz most probably made the expression *tabula rasa* known to French philosophical discourse by his ridicule of Locke's empty space argument: "(Les partisans de Locke) supposent qu'au commencemnet l'âme est une table rase, vide de tous caractères et sans aucune idée … Cette tabula rasa, dont on parle tant, n'est à mon avis qu'une fiction que la nature ne souffre point." (Locke's supporters) suppose that in the beginning the mind is a blank slate, empty of all characters and ideas … (Lalande 1983: 1099). In our own era, it is the French philosopher Gilles Deleuze who will make Leibniz's philosophical system a starting point for describing a foundational space that is not grounded in emptiness, a point we will return to in our final chapter. See Gilles Deleuze, *The Fold: Leibniz and the Baroque*, trans. Tom Conley (Minneapolis: University of Minnesota Press, 1992).

links between a spatial imaginary and an economic order whose legacy is still very much our own. William Cronon explains it this way:

> Locke sought to explain how people came to possess unequal rights to a natural abundance he supposed had originally been held in common; to accomplish this task, he explicitly contrasted the societies of Europe with those of the American Indians. 'In the beginning,' he said, 'all the world was America.' In that original state, possession was directly related to the labor one spent in hunting and gathering: one could own whatever one could use before it spoiled. What enabled people to accumulate wealth beyond the limits of natural spoilage was something Locke called 'money.' Bullionist that he was, he thought of money as gold and silver which could be stored as a resource of permanent value without fear of spoiling. But the way he actually used the word 'money' was an odd hybrid between a simple medium of exchange that measured the value of commodities, and *capital*, the surplus whose accumulation was the motor of economic growth. It was capital—the ability to store wealth in the expectation that one could increase its quantity—that set European societies apart from precolonial Indian ones. (1983: 78)

By contrast, Cronon notes, "what the Indians owned—or more precisely, what their villages gave them claim to—was not the land but the things that were on the land during the various seasons of the year" (65). The Indian conception of property as something closer to a set of limited usufruct rights was evident in the names Indians attached to the New England landscape. The names signified not so much possession as use: Pokanoket, in Plymouth County, Massachusetts, meant "at or near the cleared lands"; Anitaash Pond, near New London, Connecticut, meant, literally, "rotten corn," referring to a swampy location where corn could be buried until it blackened to create a favorite Indian delicacy (65). While the Indians used ecological labels to describe how the land could be used, the English typically created place names which either recalled localities in the old country or they gave a place the name of its owner. From the perspective of the cultural logic of empty space, what most interests us here is how a notion of empty space persistently accompanies the dispossession and decontextualization of Indian lands and precedes the recontextualization of those lands in an English worldview, one tied to the creation of surplus value.

The doctrine of *vacuum Domicilium*, then, is part of a more general cultural logic associated with a modern spatial imaginary whose primary characteristic is empty space. Locke's writing shows how the legitimation arguments of modern English sovereignty in the Americas begin with the rhetorical creation of empty, or socially emptied, space. When natural rights theorists like Locke argue for a natural right to property, nature in their schema is like *res nullius*, something belonging to no-one and thus open to privatization.

Empty Space as a Rhetorical Strategy in Contemporary International Law of Biodiversity

To this day, empty space remains a rhetorical strategy in how law describes and governs the variety of biological life. Interest in the control over life forms dates back to ancient times and has been a strategic economic issue since at least colonial times. In his discussion of the cultural history of the law surrounding biodiversity, anthropologist Michael Flitner notes several changes in the way Western law frames nature. For thousands of years, seeds were traditionally saved by farmers and used in planting the next year's crops. Attempts to restrict the export or the use of certain organisms or seeds increased in the eighteenth and nineteenth centuries, but in most if not all cases it still turned out to be impossible in the long run to physically prevent the removal of these organisms from the territories of those seeking to own them. Thus, most of these highly utilized species—corn, tomatoes, peppers, peanuts, sunflowers, and such—spread all over the globe until the beginnings of the twentieth century when a slow but steady change in the focus of interest began to take shape. The new science of genetics helped to systematize crossbreeding in Northern countries, and henceforth it was "the variability within species, varietal diversity" that became more and more interesting. "What geneticists saw and needed was not the organism as an entity anymore, but rather as an accumulation of properties each of which could be treated separately as a building-block for novel varieties" (1998: 149–50).

As a thought experiment, consider how we might picture or provide a metaphor for the evolving concept of the variety of the natural world. How might an advertiser or political activist, for example, portray nature as organisms abstracted into a set of properties that could be further separated and then recombined? What sort of spatial imaginary accompanies this radically new way of thinking about nature that is at first characterized by abstraction and separation of entities but then at the point of recombination is characterized as a virtual cornucopia of potential for unlimited emergences of new genetically modified entities? These new, virtual entities might be predictable and controllable, or they may be unpredictable with uncontrollable consequences that end up, like so many other side effects of industrial production, as "externalities" with no institutional liability attached to their potentially damaging effects. How could this virtual, dynamic sort of space be represented as an object of human governance? Recall that Monsanto solved the problem of representing biodiversity in its promotional advertisement by a nostalgic use of eighteenth-century scientific drawings. Empty space functioned as a rhetorical strategy in covertly furthering Monsanto's ownership claims over nature even as Monsanto showcased, in the text of the advertisement, nature as an interconnected commons. But even if they had wanted to, could Monsanto have found a spatial image to represent biodiversity as a limitless potential of nature, as recombinant DNA, and as a universal jurisdiction where all citizens, including future generations, share rights to the potential wealth of nature?

Four Legal Tools to Frame Nature

In contemporary international law the global commons status of biodiversity is defined by four seminal documents which would govern all transnational corporations invested in what is known as "biodiversity prospecting." In these documents the spatial imaginary of emptiness described thus far both persists and is challenged. The four new legal tools add to previous thinking about global commons in modern international law. Past laws characterize the diversity of the natural world as "genetic resources." They assume that the loss of genetic resources is an unavoidable by-product of agricultural modernization. The new laws, on the other hand, while they often use the vocabulary of genetic resources, establish a link between conservation and the use of species or ecosystems. Thus they recognize that biological life as a repository of genetic information is more than a "resource" for human use and exploitation. They recognize a social relationship, conservation, as an inherent quality to be protected in species variety.[4]

The following brief examination of these four legal documents looks at the implied spatial imaginaries and the social relationships that the laws protect in the form of a global commons of biodiversity.

The Convention on Biological Diversity (CBD) is one of the key agreements adopted at the Earth Summit in Rio de Janeiro in 1992, is a contradictory proposal: it creates the legal framework to make the variety of life on earth at once a commons and private property. The CBD has been signed by 187 countries including the United States, which then never went on to ratify it.[5] Article One of the CBD provides for three things: the conservation of biological diversity, the sustainable use of its components, and the fair and equitable sharing of the

---

4 The German philosopher Martin Heidegger warned back in the 1950s that the world-making ways of technology in post World War II Western culture included a new description of nature as resource. "Resourcing" the world, is what Heidegger called it. Critical cultural theorists have since emphasized the social relations that such resourcing obfuscates. See Martin Heidegger, *The Question Concerning Technology and Other Essays*.

5 A major weakness of the treaty mechanism in international law: after the painstaking work of conventions and protocol, governments may simply go against years of negotiations and decide not to ratify. The United States in particular, and especially since 2001 under the Bush Administration, has a history of not participating in international treaties, from the Convention on the Rights of the Child (the US is apparently the sole nonsignatory nation) to the Convention on the Elimination of All Forms of Discrimination Against Women (where the US is not one of the 173 signing nations). The US joins Libya in being among the very few states that have not ratified the Convention on Biological Diversity. Neither has the US ratified the Law of the Sea Treaty (a point we will return to in later chapters). Since 2001 the US has opposed the treaty to establish an International Criminal Court; it has abandoned the climate treaty's Kyoto Protocol; it has declared it will pull out of the 1972 anti-Ballistic Missile Treaty; threatened to withdraw from international conferences on racism and illegal trafficking in small arms, the list goes on and on (Speth 2004: 110–111).

benefits arising out of the utilization of "genetic resources" (United Nations 2009). In this document, access to and benefit sharing of commons resources is brought into a legally binding arrangement at the global level for the first time in Western history. Exactly how benefits are to be shared is to be worked out on individual bases but the treaty generally supports the use of intellectual property rights, even if only tentatively, when it comes to "living material." It protects genetic resources by making nation-states the controlling agents of the common pool of genetic material on their territories and by encouraging corporations to make bilateral contracts (generally not open to the public) with the states where they collect their resources. Thus the CBD articulates a paradoxical commons logic, not unlike the Monsanto advertisement, where access and benefit sharing are required to be communal while at the same time individualist property rights (in the form of patents) are also available (Flitner 1998: 149–56).

The Agreement on Trade-Related Aspects of Intellectual Property Rights (TRIPS) is the second legal instrument to circumvent biodiversity as a global commons (World Trade Organization 2009). It proposes a Lockean commons in terms of the work of empty space. TRIPS obliges all World Trade Organization states to provide some form of patent or patent-like protection around plant varieties.[6] Thus this second legal tool treats biotechnology as an instrument for authorship—like a pen, typewriter, or computer—and nature as a screen of immense virtual potential on which science could draw, as it were, enclosures around various life forms. TRIPS' rhetorical convention of authorship allows multinational companies to, for example, take a traditional medicinal plant cultivated over generations by Indigenous peoples, introduce slight genetic modifications, and claim proprietary rights for a commercial brand of herbal remedy, excluding local peoples from continuing traditional practices at a commercial scale. Thus TRIPS disavows social relationships that exist in low-tech labor on genetic material and protects industrial scale and high-tech labor.

The rhetorical argument for authorship and patent protection in the global commons of biodiversity reveals the inherent colonial relations protected in TRIPS. A case in point is the neem tree in India. The tree contains an extract that has been effectively used for thousands of years by Indian farmers as a pesticide. When the US company W.R. Grace began extracting this substance in the late twentieth century, the TRIPS agreement legitimized the patent Grace placed on the extraction process and on the related compounds. Grace even moved its production sites to India and tried to put the local Indian producers out of business. Indian activists

6 Because Article 27.3.b of TRIPS allows member states to "provide for the protection of plant varieties either by patents or *by an effective sui generis system* or by any combination thereof," it introduced the "sui generis" concept that has allowed some countries to reject the compulsory introduction of plant patents. See Philippe Cullet, "Plant variety protection," *International Environmental Law Research Centre*, 2003, http://www.ielrc.org/content/f0304.htm (accessed December 1, 2009).

opposed to TRIPS' protection of Grace's property rights in neem have argued that Grace's processes and chemical compounds are simply scaled up versions of what local farmers have been making for ages (Vandana and Radha 1996).

Just as the rhetoric of empty space in patent law is linked to the protection of colonial power relations where the Indigenous labor goes unrecognized, the spatial rhetoric describing genetic material as genetic resources is linked to a *terra vacantis* view of nature where the productive forces of the environment in human life go unrecognized. Thus among environmentalists there is also strong legal resistance to the patenting of genetic material allowed under TRIPS. Monsanto's exclusive ownership of genetically modified alfalfa seeds was protected under TRIPS. But in 2007, a US Federal judge in San Francisco ruled that the US Department of Agriculture had violated environmental impact laws by deregulating Monsanto's genetically-modified seeds without showing the environmental impact of genetically engineered crops outside the laboratory (Barlett and Steele 2008). TRIPS protects Grace and Monsanto's proprietary interest in genetic material by emptying these biodiverse life forms of their complex social, cultural, and ecological relations. Introducing cultural history and environmental impact to the legal arena, biotechnology no longer acts as a mere writing tool whose creative products exist against the backdrop of nature as a blank slate. Legal challenges to biodiversity enclosure under TRIPS use cultural variety and ecological complexity to establish a counter-narrative that undermines the dominant legal rhetoric grounding life forms in empty space.

The International Treaty on Plant Genetic Resources for Food and Agriculture popularly known as the International Seed Treaty, is the third legal tool to govern biodiversity (United Nations Food and Agriculture Organization 2009). The Seed Treaty creates an international framework for seed in line with the national framework provided by the Convention on Biological Diversity. While the CBD brings plant genetic material under the jurisdiction and sovereignty of national governments, it does not provide a universal jurisdiction for agricultural genetic material. The Seed Treaty views mainstay crops like rice, wheat, maize, and potato as international phenomena crossing countries and continents. The Treaty recognizes humans' historical impact on biological life. Experts estimate that there were once 10,000 types of food crops. Today, only 150 crops feed the greater part of the world's population. Twelve of these crops provide 80 percent of humans' dietary energy. The Seed Treaty thus identifies for conservation and protection 64 major food crops deemed essential to the food security of the globe. As multinational seed-breeding companies flood the market with small numbers of highly selected and often genetically modified seeds, genetic variety is being lost.[7] Over millennia, farmers across the globe have bred and saved seeds, preserving seed varieties that

7 One effect of such reductions in the diversity of plant sources available for food is that, as climate change creates a need for more hearty varieties, the genetic pool of seeds resistant to cold winters and hot summers will dwindle.

grow in remote tropical islands and frigid plains. They have been passing this information along from generation to generation. The Treaty thus aims to establish a seed-bank that would act as a global gene pool to preserve and protect genetic variety in these 64 food crops. All nation-signatories to the Treaty would have access to others' seed banks on the condition that, if a commercial product results from this seed sharing, the owners will pay 1.1 percent of the product sales into the Treaty's benefit-sharing fund. The Seed Treaty thus aims to encourage seed saving and sharing by farmers and by corporations. Advocates who agree to the ambiguous property status of this global commons see the Seed Treaty as a model for the sharing of other genetic materials deemed essential for the well-being of humankind, such as influenza viruses for vaccine production.

With regard to the global commons, the Seed Treaty is important because it counterbalances the privatization of patent law by placing agricultural biodiversity in a distinct class of genetic property belonging to all humankind. It does this by invoking the Common Heritage of Mankind Principle. The idea of a universal jurisdiction was first articulated in debates concerning the International Law of the Seas. It arose along with the postcolonial demands of the 1970s which sought to make Northern, industrialized countries share with their poorer Southern neighbors the monetary benefits of commercial mining in ocean seabeds of the global commons. The Common Heritage Principle was later employed in the Moon Treaty to cover extraterrestrial mining.[8] Use of the Common Heritage Principle in the Seed Treaty makes agricultural biodiversity analogous to the inorganic matter under the seabed and on the moon, placing both potential seed and mineral wealth within a universal jurisdiction. The Seed Treaty's benefit-sharing fund would be used to pay poor farmers who conserve seed varieties on their own and continue passing them on to future generations.[9]

In addition to establishing agricultural genetic material as a global commons, the invocation of the Common Heritage Principle from the Law of the Seas allows the Seed Treaty to recognize, for the first time in international law, farmers' rights as collective, residual rights as opposed to individual property rights. Farmers form

8 For a full discussion of the complexity and potential of the Common Heritage Principle, see Kemal Baslar, *The Concept of the Common Heritage of Mankind in International Law* (The Hague: Kluwer Law International, 1998).

9 To date 121 countries have signed the Treaty. Notably, the US is not among them. Even proponents of the Treaty note that the provisions concerning access and benefit sharing, which constitute the most important part of the Treaty in practice, are largely lacking in specificity. In 2006 the second meeting of the Treaty's Governing Board could not meet because signatory nations had not paid for the administrative costs. More importantly, farmers' groups accused key governments of not enforcing the reciprocity agreement that requires industries that patent new breeds of seed (even those produced by farmers) to share 1.1 percent of profits from sales with farmers. In 2009 the provisions for profit sharing with farmers are still merely voluntary. Negotiating documents can be found on the United Nations web site of the Commission on Genetic Resources for Food and Agriculture at http://www.fao.org/ag/cgrfa/default.htm.

a legacy class of stewards of the global genetic commons. Their rights are framed like the rights of Indigenous peoples in the US: they are residual rights connected to ancestral traditions residing with the group even as the dominant structure of sovereignty and property in which the group lives is changing in ways that are contradictory or incompatible with their traditional forms of using and holding tenure. Thus, just as Native Americans secured residual rights in hunting, fishing, land use, and self governance even though the United States government and its individual citizens had (by force) become the territorial occupiers and possessors of the Indigenous peoples' land and waterways, so too do farmers protected under the Seed Treaty maintain original (albeit highly compromised) rights to save, use, exchange, and sell farm-saved seeds, even though plant breeding through biotechnology has transformed the political economy of agriculture through patents and intellectual property rights.

Despite its outline of a global commons through the Common Heritage Principle and its designation of farmers as a transnational, global class of common property owners, the Seed Treaty is no match for the corporate agricultural landscape that is dramatically changing farmers' age-old practices. In the United States, a country which has not signed up to the Seed Treaty, Monsanto has successfully brought suits within the framework of the Convention on Biological Diversity against farmers in Indiana and North Dakota for "stealing" its transgenic variety of corn. From the moment biotechnicians insert a single gene from, say, a bacterium into the genetic code of a crop plant to produce a "transgenic" variety, that plant and all of its descendents can be claimed as the property of the laboratory, even though research increasingly shows that transgenic pollen and seed, like all pollen and seed, can easily escape the fields in which they were originally planted. Farmers who use Monsanto's seeds are contractually barred from saving any seed they produce from such a variety, and plant breeders are not allowed to use its pollen—unless they pay the corporation that "owns" it. So, when Monsanto's wandering herbicide-resistance genes turn up in a farmers' non-transgenic fields, current international law allows Monsanto to successfully charge that the farmer pilfered the seed. Under current US law, when transgenic seed and pollen travel, their property rights travel with them (Cox 2002).

Even if the US had signed the Seed Treaty, it would not protect farmers against such claims of theft, even if the seeds in question originated in the group of 64 crops protected under the Treaty. Thus, even though the Seed Treaty creates a global commons jurisdiction of agricultural genetic material and a collective agency with property rights to this commons, the Treaty does not appear to protect either farmers or the common pool resource of food crops from private property claims by corporations like Monsanto which mine the genetic potential of these common pool resources. Based on the Common Heritage Principle, the Seed Treaty protects the past heritage but not the future potential of what it deems the most important agricultural seeds. The Treaty recognizes the biodiverse, historical legacy of these seeds as an intrinsic value and places that value in a common property regime, while at the same time recognizing the future potential of the seeds as a commercial value which it gives away to the highest bidder who need only voluntarily assent to share in a small fraction of the profits. In short, under the Seed Treaty, the seeds' heritage belongs to all humankind, but its potential belongs to nobody. Belonging to nobody, they belong to anybody, that is to say, anybody who can invest in the biotechnology needed to create large-scale commercial value from genetic manipulation. Thus the Seed Treaty describes a global commons domain imbued with the contradiction we have noted previously: a *res communes* that is indistinct from a *res nullius.*

The Genetic Commons Initiative is the fourth legal tool to protect the biodiversity of the earth (World Social Forum 2002). This grassroots initiative attempts to solve the contradiction noted in the Seed Treaty by declaring that the gene pool of the entire earth should be protected as a global commons. "Our initiative improves upon other international agreements dealing with this issue in one very fundamental aspect," says Vandana Shiva, Director of the Research Foundation for Science, Technology, and Ecology in India, one of the Treaty's founding NGOs. "Unlike other initiatives, we oppose the extension of intellectual property rights to any living thing as well as the components of the living things." The initiative would outlaw all multinational corporations, like Monsanto, who are currently protected by TRIPS and the CBD from exploiting critical genetic materials for private gain (UKabc 2002).

The Genetic Commons Initiative rejects the Common Heritage Principle and the legal precedence of voluntary benefit-sharing attached to this. The Initiative follows in a long-standing critique of the Common Heritage Principle, noting the ineffective form of authority the principle has historically delivered and thus viewing the principle as a vehicle to perpetuate the unequal distribution of wealth between the global North and South.[10] Instead of a heritage, the Treaty Initiative refers to the genetic commons, virtual and actual, in terms of a "legacy": "We proclaim these truths to be universal and indivisible ... that the global gene pool, in all of its biological forms and manifestations, is a shared legacy and, therefore, a collective responsibility."[11] The word *heritage*, in English refers to the property

10 The criticism refers to the development of the Common Heritage Principle in the 1970s and 1980s into a UN Authority with power to manage the mineral resources on the ocean sea-bed. The Authority was stacked with people representing the interests of the industrialized nations and did not succeed in distributing the wealth of the sea-bed to all countries of the United Nations, particularly those of the South. For a deeper discussion of the Common Heritage Principle, see Chapter 3.

11 The English text of the Treaty appears to studiously avoid the term "heritage" (as in the Commons Heritage Principle). However the Treaty's English terms "gene pool" and "genetic commons" are generally translated in the romance language versions of the Treaty as "*Patrimoine*" (*patrimoine génétique de la Terre, Patrimonio Genético Común, patrimonio genetico della Terra*) which correspond to the romance language translation of the Common Heritage Principle: *patrimoine commun de l'humanité*. In the civil law tradition, there is no exact translation of the English term or concept of "heritage": the

that is bequeathed to an *heir* after the death of the original (often biologically related) owner. The term *legacy*, on the other hand, comes from the ecclesiastic world and originally refers to the domain ruled over by the *legate*, a person who had received orders or responsibilities from the Pope, himself the representative of the Divine on earth. Thus, etymologically, the term "legacy" referred to in the English version of the Genetic Commons Initiative has roots in a realm of things that are passed down from a sacred domain, *res sacrae*, things belonging to the gods.[12] While there is no reference to a sacred domain in the legal text itself, the Initiative studiously avoids all reference to the domain of property (including the idea of common property). Thus it defines all living things as part of a universal, biodiverse genetic commons and protects the entire commons from privatization/ enclosure:

> Therefore, the nations of the world declare the Earth's gene pool, in all of its biological forms and manifestations, to be a global commons, to be protected and nurtured by all peoples and further declare that genes and the products they code for, in their natural, purified or synthesized form as well as chromosomes, cells, tissue, organs and organisms, including cloned, transgenic and chimeric organisms, will not be allowed to be claimed as commercially negotiable genetic information or intellectual property by governments, commercial enterprises, other institutions or individuals. (World Social Forum 2002)

It takes its mandate from "our increasing knowledge of biology," making knowledge itself an authoritative and common domain that brings "obligations" as opposed to "information" to all earthlings.

---

concept of *patrimoine* "is not equivalent with the concept of "heritage" (. I)n the French legal tradition the difference between the English estate of a deceased person and the patrimony is that the patrimony attaches to a living person and the estate does not." See Jane Ball, "The Boundaries of Property Rights in English Law: Report to the XVIIth International Congress of Comparative Law," *Electronic Journal of Comparative Law*, December 2006: 12. Of equal interest is the translation issue regarding the legal concept of "trust." A "trust" in law is specific to the English common law tradition and thus the term "trust" in the Genetic Commons Treaty ("The Parties to the treaty ... further agree to administer the gene pool as a *trust*") remains untranslated in all three romance languages. For the English text of the Treaty and its translations in these three romance languages, see The Foundation on Economic Trends, *Treaty to Share the Genetic Commons*, 2003–2009, http://www.foet.org/past/GeneticCommons.html (accessed January 1, 2010).

12 While there is no reference to a sacred domain, Jeremy Rifkin, an important force in the Treaty's development, notes, "Perhaps more than anything else, the Treaty Initiative is a positive affirmation of the *sacred integrity* of the earth's genetic inheritance and of our shared rights and duties to defend this integrity and to ensure that it is used for the benefit of all humanity and does not become the exclusive commercial monopoly of anyone. See Jeremy Rifkin, "Biotech Century Treaty to Share Genetic Commons," *Jeremy Rifkin Office: The Foundation on Economic Trends*, 2003–2009, http://www.foet.org/past/GeneticCommons.html (accessed January 1, 2010).

Significantly, the Treaty Initiative to Share the Genetic Commons is the only one of the four legal documents discussed above that allows Indigenous peoples to be signatories on a par with nation-states. In the Genetic Commons Initiative both kinds of political entities, states and Indigenous peoples, become "stewards" of the global commons of biodiversity and the political doctrine of a "trust" is invoked:

> The Parties to the treaty—to include signatory nation states and Indigenous Peoples—further agree to administer the gene pool as a trust. The signatories acknowledge the sovereign right and responsibility of every nation and homeland to oversee the biological resources within their borders and determine how they are managed and shared. However, because the gene pool, in all of its biological forms and manifestations, is a global commons, it cannot be sold by any institution or individual as genetic information. Nor can any institution or individual, in turn, lay claim to the genetic information as intellectual property.

Similar to our recognition in the Introduction to this volume concerning the Inuit case and the special role of Indigenous peoples in legally leveraging a global commons domain for the atmosphere, the Treaty Initiative to Share the Genetic Commons also recognizes that Indigenous peoples have a fundamental role to play in the construction of a global commons domain of biodiversity. As previously noted, there is a key contradictory spatial logic shared by Indigenous peoples and the global commons. Legally, global commons exist within international sovereignty frameworks that protect bounded, statist territoriality, privatization, and commercial exploitation. Spatially, global commons are both inside and outside of the nation-state. In modern political regimes, Indigenous peoples have long lived with this spatial contradiction. They have become expert in asserting residual rights in sovereignty frameworks dominated by the nation-state model. Furthermore, in the United States, Native Americans have used the trust doctrine—a doctrine of Federal Indian law that makes the US government responsible to protect tribes from disadvantageous non-Indian commercial exploitation—to challenge unscrupulous land grabs and other forms of mistreatment. In this fourth legal tool, then, the farthest reaching attempt to create a global commons of biodiversity gives Indigenous peoples a special legal role: by invoking the trust doctrine, the category of *res sacrae*, and the spatial complexity of a type of sovereignty that is both inside and outside national boundaries, the Genetic Commons Initiative aims to successfully construct a *res communis* global regime where national governments have previously constructed globalized *res nullius* commons.

All four legal attempts to describe the global commons of biodiversity, then, are caught in the same struggle, namely that between global *res nullius* domains where individuals, corporations, and national governments hold rights to enclose common property to their unique advantage, and global *res communis* domains where collective entities like farmers, Indigenous peoples, humankind, and future generations hold rights to participate on a par with nation-states to collectively hold common property. The spatial rhetoric supporting an inside and outside to sovereignty issues concerning the global commons undergirds this struggle.

The Cultural Logic of Empty Space in Biodiversity Law

The cultural logic of empty space persists in a biodiversity commons that can be enclosed by legal arrangements promoting patent law and other forms of intellectual property rights. In this endeavor, it is enabled in metaphors coming from the discourse of writing. Theoretically speaking, writing has been linked in several key moments of Western modernity to a particular way of relating to nature and human nature via empty space. This relationship persists in the general trend in Northern, overdeveloped countries to translate information—genetic material, but also archived photographs and newspapers, etc.—into code which can now be further manipulated into electronic data such that even the four building blocks of DNA can be reduced to, as some cultural theorists have called them, the two digits of our age: X and O. Practically speaking, code allows patent or rights owners to charge fees to those seeking to recombine material or access information. Many have argued that claims to creative authorship made by multinational corporations on the part of their research laboratories stretch the limits of the legal imagination. Such claims use a language of entitlement that comes from the early nineteenth-century romantic tradition of the writer or author as an individual creative genius facing a blank page. But this category of creative propriety appears wholly unsuited to our own historical period where the sources and forms of wealth are tied less and less to industrial production and increasingly to information—genetic, electronic, and proprietary.[13]

In addition to the metaphorics of writing, there is another rhetorical domain that dominates Western legal thinking about global commons. When we consider why laws governing the earth's biodiversity so easily lead to a *res nullius*

13 According to legal scholar James Boyle, the increase in intellectual property rights in domains like genetic engineering "is a bad thing for both reasons of efficiency and justice; it leads us to have too many intellectual property rights, to confer them on the wrong people, and dramatically to undervalue the interests of both the sources of and the audiences for the information we commodify ... (T)he unconscious use of the author paradigm has wide-ranging negative effects, with costs in areas ranging from biodiversity and the production of new drugs to the shape of the international economy and the structure of the computer industry" (xi). Because this legal arrangement does a bad job of protecting the sources of wealth, it is detrimental to a commons framework. "Even a conventional economic analysis," Boyle notes, "supports the idea that it is in the interest of those who are exploiting a "commons" to make sure that the commons continues to exist. The author vision blinds us to the importance of the commons—to the importance of the raw material from which information products are constructed" (xiv). James Boyle, *Shamans, Software, and Spleens: Law and the Construction of the Information Society* (Cambridge, MA: Harvard University Press, 1996).

commons when aiming to construct a *res communis* commons, we are lead to consider why the law of the seas provides the dominant analogy for understanding global commons in international law. The Seed Treaty borrows the principle of a "common heritage" for the domain of genetic material from the United Nations' convention on the Law of the Seas. In that maritime legal document the notion of "common heritage" was created to refer to how the economic benefits from minerals mined in the international waters of the oceans' deep sea beds were to be equitably distributed. Several years later the Common Heritage Principle is used in the Moon Treaty to define that celestial orb as a commons for purposes of equitable benefit sharing from future mineral extraction. In all three domains where the CHP was used—the plant genetic, the oceanic, and the extraterrestrial—the notion of space as *res communis* eventually gives way as signatories from industrialized countries reframe the global domain as a form of commercial value. The agency of technologically developed Northern nation-states dominates the commercial frame and these nonstate, *de jure res communis* domains become *de facto res nullius*, their common wealth privatized and extracted.

Why does international law sustain such an overlap in its definition of globally common property whose wealth is harnessed by human systems? On the one hand, global commons are imagined as in a more or less "blank slate" condition where there are no relevant institutions because they "belong to no-one" (*res nullius*) and, on the other hand, global commons are seen as property with institutionalized restrictions on user rights because they belong to everyone (*res communis*). Why this oscillation between *res nullius* and *res communis*? As legal anthropologists and historians can tell us, traditional commons tenure systems in small scale societies are not *res nullius* type open access (Ostrom 1990). Modern nation-states make particular use of the *res nullius* doctrine because it captures the scope of the global as an economic, surplus value. Beyond power and greed, there is also a more pervasive cultural explanation for why the global commons' economic value so readily dominates its various ecosystem and use values. The seemingly unimaginable expanse of the global in modernity lends itself to being represented by economic value because, beyond the logic of precedent, the law of the seas provides a kind of numerical value of zero in its dominant concepts and metaphors. It provides a kind of common denominator for how we think of global commons in domains as diverse as outer space and biodiversity. Moreover, the oscillation between *res communis* and *res nullius* which is continually undermining the creation of the global commons is related to an enduring Western form of juridical logic, one which is tied to the law of the seas. Throughout the history of the global commons, the high seas stand for the place outside of national boundaries, devoid of social institutions, the ungovernable par excellence. The tautologically unsuccessful attempts to create a law of the ungovernable seas has come to dominate the legal framework that undermines the creation of a successful global commons.

In the coming chapters I look at how the law of the seas has provided the conceptual framework for all relations of sovereignty with respect to the modern global commons. Empty space is operative as a cultural logic in the extensive metaphoric work which makes the law of the seas the foundation for the legal imagination as it moves into places as diverse as outer space, the Internet, and biodiversity. In this regard it is interesting to note that, except for the Treaty Initiative on the Genetic Commons, the spatial imaginary at work in international juridical descriptions of modern global commons appears to be in various ways anchored in the high seas. But what if we are indeed at a historic turning point in our global history of legal thinking about commons, a second Grotian moment? Many legal thinkers point to the Internet with its open source software, self-organizing user systems and creative commons licenses as the new paradigm for our global commons imaginary (Benkler 2006, Lessig 2002, Bollier 2008). One could also point to seeds, as framed by the World Social Forum in its Genetic Commons Initiative. Both domains might be more useful than the oceans as the basis of Western thinking about globally shared domains.

Empty space, then, is a rhetorical strategy that uses metaphors of writing and analogies from Western law governing the high seas to enable arguments about global commons to appear logical and necessary when in fact these arguments involve historical and cultural preconceptions, colonial power relations, and economic reductionism.

Empty Space as a Cultural Operator in Political Theory

While empty space is at the heart of modern thinking about global commons, it also has a long history in political theory in the foundational discussions of Western, statist sovereignty. The cultural logic of empty space is related to recent arguments in political theory about the spatial logic of a globally-extended model of Western sovereignty. The *res nullius* seas and their extension by analogy through international law to all areas of the global commons raise issues of a spatial logic that is in some ways similar to the notion of zones of exception described by the Italian political theorist, Giorgio Agamben. In *Homo Sacer: Sovereign Power and Bare Life* (1998) and *The State of Exception* (2005) Agamben suggests that globalization be considered in light of a political logic of exclusion and exception that is increasingly becoming the logic by which all the world's citizens are defined, organized and regulated.[14] Following the work of German political philosopher

14 Agamben goes further and argues that the biological life of citizens is also regulated by this logic of exception, a logic which he claims as an extension of Foucault's notion of biopower and biopolitics. In this book I am more interested in the political logic of exception and less interested in its value as an updated articulation of Foucault's thesis on biopolitics. For a criticism of Agamben's use of the concept of biopower in this regard, see Paul Rabinow and Nikolas Rose, "Biopower Today," *Biosocieties* 1, no. 2 (2006): 195–217.

Carl Schmitt, Agamben notes that the way that Western law has created territorial jurisdictions and has extended its juridical thinking across the earth:

> always implies a zone that is excluded from law and that takes the shape of a 'free and juridically empty space' in which the sovereign power no longer knows the limits fixed by the *nomos* as the territorial order. Schmitt himself assimilates this zone 'beyond the line' to the state of exception, which 'bases itself in an obviously analogous fashion on the idea of delimited, free and empty space' understood as a 'temporary and spatial sphere in which every law is suspended …'. (Agamben 1998: 37)

Western sovereignty, Agamben argues, is a political order with this particular logical form: just as in symbolic logic we say that the exception is created by the rule, so in Western sovereignty the zones of exclusion are created by the sovereign power of the state. Moreover, Agamben claims, Western sovereignty is not just a political order made up of an abstract order of rules and regulations, their location in one arena and their absence in another. It is a biopolitical order, an order that claims to tell the truth about the bodies and life forms it locates in its sovereign domains and zones of exception. Thus Agamben cites the case of Germany under National Socialism: the people (in this case, the German Volk) are those homogeneous bodies (the biopolitical bodies or master "race") that are free to live in the state; those who belong in the zones of exclusion (the concentration camps)—which, of course, are also very much a part of the state since they were created and maintained by it—are simply those biopolitical bodies who are the other of the homogeneous master race: the Jews, the Gypsies and so forth. Race here is a biopolitical category. It is a notion about biological life that has become indistinct from the political rules of citizenship. Race is therefore a notion about nature that is at once created by the state but at the same time created to stand for something existing entirely outside the state. In this way, Agamben argues that the Western individual's body and life forms are supported and regulated by means of a spatial logic that is quite ancient in Western culture: it is a logic which conceals a point of intersection between the juridico-institutional and the biopolitical models of power.

The ancient character of the spatial and biopolitical logic that describes nature in this model, Agamben shows, goes back to some of the earliest treatises of political theory in the Western tradition. For Agamben, the zone that exists in the "state of exception," exists in what Hobbes famously called "the state of nature," a "juridically empty space" that could erupt anywhere, at any time, whenever the state dissolved. "In the classical epoch of the *ius publicum Europaeum*, the zone corresponded to the New World, which was identified with the state of nature in which everything is possible (Locke: 'In the beginning, all the world was America')" (36). For Agamben, both the Hobbesian state of nature and the state of exception that characterized the zones of the concentration camp belong to the same political logic:

> They are two sides of a single topological process in which what was presupposed as external (the state of nature) now reappears, as in a Mobius strip or a Leyden jar, in the inside (as the state of exception), and the sovereign power is this very impossibility of distinguishing between outside and inside, nature and exception, *physis* and *nomos*. The state of exception is thus not so much a spatiotemporal suspension as a complex topological figure in which not only the exception and the rule but also the state of nature and law, outside and inside, pass through one another. (37)

For Agamben, Western sovereignty is now going through a time when the two distinct zones described by Locke and Hobbes ("the New World" vs. Europe; and "the State of Nature" vs. the state of law) have not only become more clearly manifest as inner and outer spaces (the Nazi concentration camp that exists inside the German state as its own state of exception) but have gone one step further, turning into a spatial logic where the two zones are no longer distinguishable from each other. A zone of indistinction. In the current restructuring of Western sovereignty under forces of globalization, Agamben claims we are experiencing a new, more expansive aspect of this topological zone of indistinction. Thus, after the First World War when:

> the entire system of the reciprocal limitations and rules of the *ius publicum Europaeum* (was) brought to ruin ... what has happened and what is still happening before our eyes is that the 'juridically empty' space of the state of exception (in which law is in force in the figure—that is etymologically, in the *fiction*—of its own dissolution, and in which everything that the sovereign deemed de facto necessary could happen) has transgressed its spatiotemporal boundaries and is now, overflowing outside them, is starting to coincide with the normal order in which everything again becomes possible. (38)

Within the thesis of *Homo Sacer* written in the early 1990s, as market capitalism became globalized on an unprecedented scale, the chaotic and violent events that Agamben witnessed—in particular the collapse of the former Soviet Union and the war in ex-Yugoslavia—are seen not as regressive forms of political organization (reversions to a state of nature, as it were) but as "premonitory events ..." that "announc(e) the new *nomos* of the earth, which (if its grounding principle is not called into question) will soon extend itself over the entire planet" (38). More recently in *The State of Exception* (2005), Agamben updates his argument that the global extension of post-Enlightenment Western sovereignty carries the logic of the state of exception along with it by including the case of the "pre-emptive" war and then military occupation of Iraq lead by the United States in 2003. Under the banner of bringing freedom and democracy, but in fact exempt from United Nations' sanction and outside of international law, the US has made itself exempt from the Geneva Convention on the treatment of prisoners of war in its prison camps at Abu Ghraib, Guantanamo Bay, and various places in Eastern Europe.

Globalization, according to Agamben, expands the zone of indistinction and with it a sense of possibility where potentially anything can happen. What kind of potentiality is this? For Agamben, it is the kind of freedom that exists only because it is imagined as the freedom that would exist if the sovereign law were not operative. Potentiality here is nothing other than the antithetical, excluded Hobbesian state of nature that is internalized as the state of exception (the camp) and now normativized as the way things are in a state of absolute freedom. This is in fact a particular notion of freedom (and potentiality) that gets its sense (and its power) from the *fiction* that freedom, as Agamben says, is a "delimited, free and empty space," a "temporary and spatial sphere in which every law is suspended" (1996: 38).

The "freedom" and consequent implosion of the deregulated markets of globalized financial capital in 2008 appear to support Agamben's thesis. The deregulated financial domain that became a dominant global norm was in fact a particular way of packaging the potential security risks of loan repayment or liquidity. All markets depend to some extent on units, measurements, and other regulated standards. Deregulated, this market became a zone of exception.

There is a deep connection between the spatial imaginary Agamben locates in Western political theories of sovereignty and the cultural logic we have been discussing so far, the cultural logic of empty space. The notion of freedom associated with the topological figure of the zone of exception is also present in international law in the fiction of the high seas as a free, open access, *res nullius* commons. However, by expanding the scope of Agamben's thinking to include how juridically empty space of *res nullius* is challenged by ecosystems managed as *res communis* and by the persistent wedge of Indigenous forms of land tenure in international law, *The Political Uncommons* points to the strengths and weaknesses of Agamben's powerful argument concerning modern sovereignty and the fate of the biological life caught in its dominium. A counter-hegemonic understanding of the political world in late modernity must certainly deal with the juridico-institutional power of the cultural logic of empty space as Agamben argues in his work on the zone of exception. From the perspective of the global commons, however, our attention remains how *res nullius* global commons are challenged by commoners and Indigenous peoples who use international law to create habitats without the logic of the exception, in spite of the cultural logic of empty space.

Conclusion: Habitats of Empty Space

The topological figure set forth in Agamben's political theory recalls many elements of the cultural logic of empty space noted throughout this chapter. The cultural and legal representation of nature in the early modern English period included Winthrop's and Locke's discussion of land as *vacuum Domicilium* and *tabula rasa*, decontextualized common ground for the extension of private property. Early scientific depictions of nature also provided a background of abstract, empty space for a focus on a taxonomy of discrete species. In the late twentieth century, abstract, empty space persisted in the representation of biodiversity at the popular visual level in Monsanto's advertisement sponsoring the 1998 Hall of Biodiversity at the American Museum of Natural History. Into the twenty-first century, the regime of intellectual property rights over genetic material in the international seed treaties continues the European romantic paradigm of individual authorship, a labor process that springs *ex nihilio* and thus supports the Lockean theory that labor gives an individual natural right to property.

At the cusp of the new millennium, however, we saw that the sovereignty expanding description of nature underlying the practice of genetic engineering shows empty space to be not so much static and abstract as dynamic and virtual. As a virtual space of potentiality, empty space in genetically modified nature appears to be a sphere whose definition approaches that given by Agamben: a topological figure of a zone of exception giving way to a zone of indistinction. In this regard, the cultural logic of the spatial imaginary underpinning Western theories and practices of sovereignty over nature shows a dynamic potentiality to empty space. The oceans, that first great global commons, provide the perfect figure for this topological dynamic potentiality: the oceans are a space both outside the territorial sovereignty of states and yet marked by those states as their own nonstate space where anything—from pirates, to nuclear testing, to radioactive garbage dumping—can happen with impunity. The failures of the Common Heritage Principle, rising as it does out of the Law of the Seas, to protect the biodiversity of the earth from enclosure by sovereign corporations, is further proof of the epistemic power of empty space in modernity. Empty space, then, is a persistent feature in both the early and late modern examples of sovereignty discourse, but the make-up of that emptiness changes over time from static abstraction to dynamic motion and potentiality. It is the task of the coming chapters to track and explicate these hegemonic forms of emptiness as rhetorical, legal strategies that support neocolonialist expropriation in domains of the global commons.

A further task of *The Political Uncommons* is to take up the challenge of describing historically persistent counter hegemonic spatial imaginaries that have strategic potential in our legal framework to build more equitable, sustainable global commons. In this light, I recall the words of ethnobiologist Gary Nabhan who notes that "while biologists have been writing epitaphs for species, linguists have been doing the same for the Indigenous languages left on the planet ... more than a quarter of all languages still spoken on earth already have fewer than one thousand speakers and will soon be moribund." Not manuscript or writing but language itself, he suggests, is a better metaphor for the current fate of biodiversity. "Soon," Nabhan notes:

> whatever we can read about biodiversity will be written in less than 5 percent of the languages that have existed since Gutenberg's print revolution. Other culture's ways of speaking and singing about the richness of plants and animals

> around them will have been lost, even if the local biota itself is not lost by that time. (1997: 21)

In modernity, the death of the world's diverse languages and Indigenous peoples is indeed a fitting analogy for what has become of nature as an inadequately protected domain of biodiversity in international law. There are many reasons to connect the death and health of our ecosystems with the fate of Indigenous peoples.

Moreover, recall what happened to the Western understanding of language in modern linguistics … In the early twentieth century, the Swiss linguist Ferdinand de Saussure put forth a theory of language as a sign system that was to become influential not only in modern linguistics but in philosophy as well. In order for Saussure's theory of language as linguistic signs to work coherently, he had to assume that language represented a sphere of human endeavor that was fundamentally different, indeed fundamentally split off from the natural world: he had to assume a nature/culture split. That is to say, Saussure had to assume that all languages referred to diverse, culturally defined worlds that had one characteristic in common: they all existed against a spatial background that was devoid of culture, devoid of social relations. Language was a world-making device that existed, Saussure argued, against a background of homogeneous, culturally empty space. This empty background was nature. It was nature as a form of life that was devoid of all symbolic meaning.[15] It was nature as empty space. Like the empty space in which early taxonomists placed entities of the natural world, like the empty space in which the Monsanto advertisement placed its biodiverse species, modern linguistics too placed language in nature as empty space. Thus for the modern scientist and the modern linguist, nature became a kind of zero sign, a sign that refers to nothing but itself (and, in this case, to itself as nothing).

I single out Saussure's theory to show how pervasive the cultural logic of empty space is to modern thinking. If language is to be a key metaphor for thinking about biodiversity, as we have seen at the beginning of this chapter, then Nabhan's comments remind us that language should not be considered even metaphorically as existing outside of a habitat, outside of the worlds it struggles to make sense of. Our appreciation of the problem of the referent in Saussurian linguistics challenges us not to imagine language, or biological life (Monsanto), or democracy (Lefort), in a "naturalized" or "socialized" habitat of empty space.

Before taking up this challenge, however, I turn my attention to producing a deeper understanding of the cultural logic of empty space by following its operations in the international law of the global commons. In the following

15 The argument is of course more complex. For those who are interested in seeing how Saussure's theory of the sign was deconstructed to reveal nature as an empty referent, as mere empty space, see Jacques Derrida, *Of Grammatology*, trans. Gayatri Chakravorty Spivak (Baltimore and London: Johns Hopkins University Press, 1976). See also Uri Eisenzwieg, "An Imaginary Territory: The Problematic of Space in Zionist Discourse," *Dialectical Anthropology* 5 (1981): 261–285.

chapters I analyze how *res nullius* has functioned as the zero sign of international law and note the complex spatial thinking that connects all domains of the global commons to the early law of the seas.

PART I
Res Nullius/Terra Nullius and the Epistemic Imaginary of International Law

International law is like a radar system. It creates a gridded screen where certain peoples and cultures appear and others disappear. They disappear because they fall under the radar: they have no standing in the jurisdictional radar system and therefore cannot be seen on the grid. Along with Indigenous peoples, many nonstate entities have fallen under the legitimizing radar of international law in the modern period. Commons are one of them. When Indigenous peoples and commons vaguely appear as indistinct spots on the screen, it is only because they have persisted in the modern legal order in some residual way: a treaty that was never abrogated by the state; a common law tradition like "estovers," (the amount of free wood a commoner can gather in the forests) whose premodern lifeworld (a pre-fossil fuel economy) no longer exists. Global and regional commons lack robust institutions that would make them recognizable in international law. In this introduction to chapters 2, 3, and 4, I outline the cultural perspective I take to describe the spatial, epistemic imaginary that underlies these colonial, "uncommoning" legal doctrines.

International relations literature defines contemporary *res nullius* domains as "areas or resources that do not or cannot by their very nature fall under sovereign jurisdiction" (Vogler 1995: 2). In other words they are "ungovernable" in terms of the sovereign jurisdiction of states. By default, then, many regions of the global commons are treated as ungovernable, *res nullius* domains. *Res nullius* also overlaps with the legal doctrine of *terra nullius*, a foundational concept of colonial sovereignty: if land belonged to no-one, it could be considered open for colonial acquisition.[1] The legal logic behind both doctrines is that because these lands or spaces "belong to no-one," they are therefore either open to legitimate

---

1 *Terra nullius* as a legal definition for land on its way to colonial status is part of a network of rules agreed upon among European powers during the period of their imperial expansion. Basically, there were three ways to legitimately acquire new territory: either (1) through conquest, (2) by cession (which generally meant "voluntary" (sic) handing of territory by one government to another by treaty or sale) or (3) by settlement, where "settlement" often meant the "discovery" and occupation of uninhabited lands, lands referred to as *terra nullius*.

appropriation or acts of sovereignty or, if ungovernable as such, open to usufruct rights by sovereign entities as well as by other political and commercial actors. This juridical logic informs the algorithm that creates the gridded radar screen of international law. Historical practices reinforce this logic. Legal descriptions of global commons domains have often been initiated not by claims that they belong to everyone, but rather by first claiming that they "belong to no-one." As such, these domains are often first defined not in terms of any positive relation or any inherent human or ecosystem qualities of the space itself but rather in terms of a lack of qualities, of a relation to no-one. The initial legal description of these commons therefore signals an absence on the radar screen. The historical tendency to label domains of the earth falling outside the territorial boundaries of European states as *terra* and *res nullius*, a tendency to place them outside before bringing them inside the jurisdiction of the law of nations, means that the doctrines of *terra* and *res nullius* act as zero signs, as a zero degree for the establishment of international law.

The idea of zero signs comes from semiotics (the study of sign systems) where zero signs are signs that refer only to themselves.[2] The number "zero," for example, which entered Western mathematics when the Arabic numerals displaced the Roman system of counting, does not point to something else, as do the integers "one," "two," "three," and so forth. It refers only to itself, that is, to itself as "nothing." While the reference to nothing may be its most obvious feature, the zero sign also acts a covert organizing device. To say that *res nullius* and *terra nullius* are zero signs of international law means that while they refer to domains devoid of state sovereignty, they also are key organizing devices for the larger picture of sovereign order in which they reside.

To better understand this epistemological argument about the cultural imaginary of empty space in international law, consider another analogy. Instead of thinking about the legal order as a radar screen, imagine it works like a one point perspective grid.

Just as with the radar grid, imagine that Alberti's grid is produced by entering the coordinates of the foundational sovereignty concepts of international law. In the Renaissance machine of one-point perspective, the grid is an artist's tool to create a representation of the world. With regard to international law, *res* and *terra nullius* would be the invisible spot in the one-point linear perspective picture, the

2 The linguist Roman Jakobson described the zero sign as a significant absence where the absence of any explicit signifier functions by itself as a signifier. Silence, for example, can in fact convey information, a "pregnant pause," as we might say. Literary critic Roland Barthes described the functions of the zero sign in logic, in the structuralist ethnographies of Lévi-Strauss (the notion of mana) and in rhetoric, where, carried on to the connotative plane, the absence of rhetorical signifiers constituties in its turn a "stylistic signifier." Roland Barthes, *Writing Degree Zero*, trans. Annette Lavers and Collin Smith (New York: Hill and Wang 1968: 77). In linguistics, the zero sign appears as the unmarked term in the imperative mode: an implied, albeit silent, listener.

zero point that refers back to the perspective of the painter standing outside the frame but following the imperatives of colonialist, statist principles. The invisible inside point and the ostensible outside point are the devices that organize all the objects of the world drawn inside the frame following the spatial grid. All objects in the frame of the picture are now lined up in a grid-like homogeneous space. This is the epistemic structure in which the global commons is caught today.

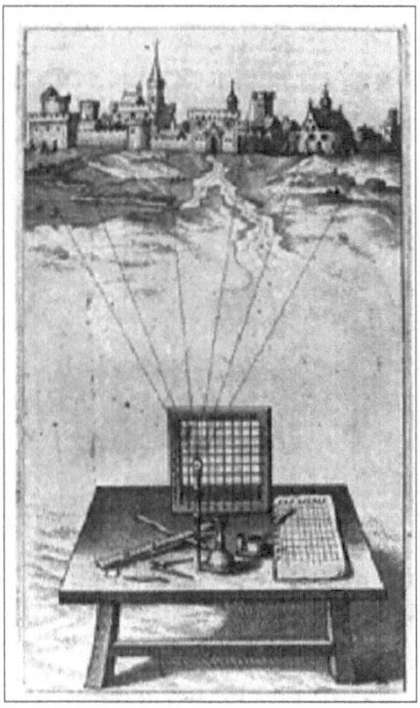

Figure PI.1 Alberti's one point perspective grid
Source: Russell Naughton (2003) "Drawing Aids to Perspective," http://www.acmi.net.au/AIC/DRAWING_MACHINES.html.

Consider how the one-point linear perspective painting establishes the painter's subjective point of view as an objective point of view. Any other individual onlooker will also see the world organized as the painter did. As all other viewers imperceptibly take on the painter's point of view, they learn to objectify themselves, to erase their particular subjectivity and take on the subject position of the painter. Again, in the legal analogy, that subject position is created by the foundational concepts of international law. A point outside the frame, then, is both the organizing device for the relational grid of homogeneous space produced inside the frame, and the position from which any other viewer is obliged to view the world thus represented/organized.

In the Western world, we are habituated to viewing the world in this way. We have built machines—cameras—that do this even better than a painter can. And we have come to view this way of seeing as "realism," as the way things naturally are. So, too, for most people who use the tools of international law to create, protect, or pillage our world. While I have used the one-point perspective system as an analogy to describe the workings of specific doctrines of international law, this system is actually a much more foundational platform of our culture. In the Western and global world order, it uses us more than we use it. It is part of our epistemological framework, the way we moderns see and make sense of the world. The German philosopher Immanuel Kant described epistemology as a (cultural) net that you throw out into the ocean (world). You are mistaken if you think that the fish you catch represent the contents of the sea. The contents of your net represent a partial view of the life of the ocean; but they represent a good view of the size of the holes in your net. Depending on your net, you might catch salmon and whitefish, but not krill or shrimp. The fisherman's net is like the grid in our one-point perspectival drawing machine. It is a cultural means of (partially) capturing the world around you. And it is a clever and powerful way because it reduces the world to one viewpoint and tricks people into thinking that this is, on the one hand, a subjective viewpoint (instead of a cultural machine). On the other hand, it tricks people into thinking that they are viewing the world from an objective viewpoint because they will share the same view with every onlooker who stands in the viewer's prescribed position. Such is the homogenizing power of the visual machines of our culture. And such is the rhetorical power of the epistemic imaginary behind international law.

Of course there are other perspectival strategies that work differently than the one-point perspective common in Western, European art. In Chinese traditions, for example, several points of view may be arranged inside the frame creating an effect of heterogeneous space with a moving perspective where we as viewers are in that world, not outside of it. In the seventeenth-century print by Wan Hui, the Emperor is seen moving through various scenes throughout his southern empire—high up on a bridge, at street level with commoners, and so forth. There are many perspective points in the picture representing a viewer standing on a mountain, then on a rooftop, then on a street.

In Western traditions, to reiterate, we have come to use a predominantly one-point linear perspective to represent the world around us. One-point perspective images have become naturalized and the process of how we came to see the world in this way is no longer evident. Indeed we tend to call such perspectival arrangements "realistic" even though they are static and highly formalized depictions of the world employing Western visual techniques just as Wan Hui's print uses formalized non-Western visual techniques.[3]

3 The analogy has been used most famously by Michel Foucault, *The Order of Things: An Archeology of the Human Sciences* (New York: Vintage, 1973). But see in particular the collaborative study of one point perspective by artist David Hockney and physicist Charles Falco set forth in David Hockney, *Secret Knowledge: Rediscovering the Lost Techniques of the Old Masters* (New York: Viking Studio, 2001).

In the landscape of international law, global commons are "depicted" in (or caught in the net of) the juridical coordinates of *res* and *terra nullius*. These doctrines, which create legal black holes on the face of the earth, are like the vanishing point in the linear perspective painting. They are a "naturalized" space that refers both to nothing but itself (the global commons of the atmosphere and the oceans, for example, are simply "nature" in its free, unbounded form, outside the spatial grid of territorial states, apparently empty of any social relations: they are *res nullius*) and also to a hidden outside perspective (the global commons are also domains of the earth seen from the perspective of colonial sovereignty: they are *terra nullius*). Moreover, just as we can actually know a great deal about the outside position of a one-point perspective painting—the geometric optics allow us to calculate, for example, the height and approximate distance of the painter from the canvas—so can we analyze the hidden colonial juridical dimensions of a global commons whose "natural," nonstate status was in fact imagined (created) from the perspective of a colonial legal order.

The global commons may appear off the grid or under the radar, so to speak, of statist territorial thinking. In fact they occupy a far more complicated spatial position. To the extent that international law maintains the commons as "outside" effective forms of governance, as free open-market domains, it succeeds in fitting these commons domains in a homogeneous spatial grid. But, to the extent that international law succeeds in creating a commons governance regime over these utterly heterogeneous forms of space—the seas, outer space, radio frequency waves, the earth's atmosphere—it brings a different organizing principle into Western juridical categories. For the most part, such dissonance can be treated as a distortion to the system and thus be expunged. The Common Heritage Principle we saw in Chapter 1 is a good example. The commons principle that would protect and equitably predistribute the wealth industrialized countries made from patenting and selling genetic materials was, in several of the legal tools, simply expunged. In the UN Convention on Biodiversity and the WTO Agreement on Trades and Tariffs the Common Heritage Principle was absent. When it was included, as in the Seed Treaty, it was a nonbinding, voluntary mechanism that was for the most part ignored by nation-states which did not follow through by taxing seed companies in their jurisdictions and sending the monies collected to an international trust fund for farmers. In the Genetic Commons Initiative the Commons Heritage Principle was considered such a useless and corrupt principle it was not even mentioned. Indeed we know very little about how a commons principle can make its way into international law. We can examine the process by which principles and concepts of such utter difference are kept out of international law—just as we can examine the process by which the painter of a one-point perspective representation organized their grid. But to understand how such heterogeneous principles and concepts would work within the system of international law, to learn how such difference would communicate with the homogenous whole, is another story.

The fact is that the spatial heterogeneity of the global atmosphere, the oceans, outer space, and the Internet do persist and demand new kinds of recognition in international law. So do the land tenure systems of non-European, Indigenous peoples, whose non-nation-state perspectives also propose a different geometry of human relations to the earth. These perspectives of Indigenous land tenure and global commons are only recently gaining legal recognition in Western conceptual systems of international law. Concepts like "the self-determination of peoples" and "aboriginal or native title" are examples of the later. Recognizing that global commons share a juridical logic of exclusion and then inclusion with the ancestral lands of Indigenous peoples puts us in a better position to investigate and understand how both domains are intertwined as they emerge from the shadow perspective of *res/terra nullius* and demand new legal expression in international law.

To return to our analogy then, just as the vanishing point of linear perspective showed us the hidden perspective or "subject" position of the painter (and therefore the possibility of there being other perspectives from other painters, other subject positions), so too can a deeper understanding of *res nullius* reveal hidden limitations of the colonial-based sovereignty of *terra nullius*. Instead of referring to a "lack" (a relation to no-one), the zero sign of *res/terra nullius* will expose the grid of complicitous relations international law organizes under the sign of *res nullius*. It will also point to the potential for law's representing other non-*res nullius* perspectives.

Figure PI.2 Scene in a Tea House by Okumura Masanobu (1745)
Source: Robert Vergez, *Early ukiyo-e master: Okumura Masanobu*. Tokyo and New York: Harper & Row, 1983.

The history of emptied space in international law gives us a particular vantage point from which to view legal attempts to govern the global commons and legal terms of dissention from Indigenous tenure systems, some of which are gaining legitimacy in Western legal contexts. Viewing the global commons and Indigenous land tenure rights from this combined perspective in international law is like looking at the mixed perspective painting by eighteenth-century Japanese artist Okumura Masanobu.

The painting shows the influence of colonialist Dutch culture as it entered Japan in the eighteenth century. Note that inside the building the Japanese printmaker borrows the Western system of one point linear perspective. Outside, through the windows of the building, however, nature maintains the roaming perspectival view common to the Japanese tradition of landscape painting in this period. Different perspectival systems next to each other create heterogeneous space. Reading the cultural history of the global commons in international law is like viewing this image. Scenes from the often violent, homogenous perspective of Western international law treat global commons and Indigenous land tenure systems as next to nothing: they are the outside of the privileged Western legal perspective. At the same time what is depicted as "outside" has other organizing perspectives, other stories to tell. Through the history of the doctrines of *res* and *terra nullius*, commons and Indigenous perspectives are presented in homogenizing Western categories. And yet, there are glimpses of global commons and Indigenous peoples speaking and producing change in the Western tradition of international law, even as they maintain their difference.

In the chapters that make up Part I, I investigate the role played by the doctrines of *terra* and *res nullius* in governing the global commons. I focus on three points: first, the paradox that *terra* and *res nullius*—spaces that belong to no-one—are integrally related to the way international law describes the global commons (*res communis*)—as spaces belonging to everyone (Chapter 2); second, the historical changes in the concept of *res nullius* as it moves from the experience of seventeenth-century European powers navigating the high seas to attempts to govern outer space and privatize the radio frequency spectrum and the Internet (Chapter 3); and finally, liability for environmental disasters in three *res nullius* territories covered by three different jurisdictions—the Law of the Seas, The Law of Outer Space and Customary (land-based) International law. Liability law worked in some jurisdictions and not in others. I show how the spatial complexity of the open seas and outer space allow their respective legal regimes to go beyond the inside/outside logic enabled by the metaphor of homogeneous, empty space so effective in maintaining territorial sovereignty on land.

Chapter 2

Terra Nullius, *Res Nullius* and *Res Communis*: A Conceptual Confusion of Terms

> It may, therefore, now be regarded as a universally accepted rule of International Law that the open sea is free for the common use of all nations ... It is not so much *res nullius* as *res communis omnium*. (Hershey 1912: 217)

> The 'state of nature' for the global commons is *res nullius*. (Vogler 1995: 17)

Introduction

Despite the distinction contemporary texts of international relations make between the legal doctrines of *terra nullius* and *res nullius*, there is a persistent confusion of these terms at nearly every level of their usage. To add to this confusion, international law often collapses the doctrine of *res nullius*, things that belong to no-one into *res communis*, things that belong to everyone, things that have the legal status of "commons." The result is that the current legal conceptualization of commons is compromised by an imperialist spatial imaginary that persists in the doctrines of *terra* and *res nullius*. Since the post-World War II era of decolonization and the various revocations of *terra nullius*, it seems clear to legal scholars and lay people alike that *terra nullius* represents a now officially outdated colonial doctrine of sovereignty. With the revocation of *terra nullius* international law recognizes that Indigenous lands never did belong to nobody. What is not yet clear, however, is that *res nullius* carries on the spatial arguments of *terra nullius* into our attempts to legally define and care for the environments that we hold in common. At the bottom of this confusion lies the cultural logic of empty space. This chapter scrutinizes the confusion between *terra nullius* and *res nullius* in contemporary international relations, in the semantic features of the legal terms, and in the historical texts that legitimate colonial sovereignty.

Res Nullius, *Terra Nullius* and the Global Commons

In *The Global Commons: A Regime Analysis*, international relations scholar John Vogler struggles to clarify the doctrines that inform contemporary legal descriptions of the global commons and to articulate the distinctions between *res nullius*, *terra nullius* and *res communis*.

> The original characteristic of a commons is 'open access.' It is available for use by anybody and its goods are 'non-excludable' and free for the taking. A commonly used legal description is *res nullius*—literally the property of no-one. This does not imply that, like undiscovered land (*terra nullius*) during the great age of maritime exploration, the right to exclusive use of such resources could be seized. In international law this is avoided under the doctrine of 'common property' (*res communis*). For over 100 years this has been applied to the fish and mammals of the high seas, where 'no single user can have exclusive rights to them, nor the right to prevent others from joining in their exploitation'. (Birnie and Boyle 1992 cited in Vogler 1997: 4)

The scholarly literature claims that *res nullius* global commons are unlike lands seized under the imperialist doctrine of *terra nullius* because they become "common property" (*res communis*) rather than private or State property. Setting aside the distinction between *res nullius* and *terra nullius* for the moment, note how *res nullius* has been collapsed into *res communis* in this description. What makes the global commons both *res communis* and *res nullius*? Unlike *terra nullius* the global commons does not allow for exclusive use by any (sovereign) party. "Nonexcludable open access" is the policy term used to describe *res nullius* domains. Thus a legal term which is virtually synonymous with the concept of a "free marketplace" in capitalist economics has a categorical overlap with a term which defines the modern global commons. In other words, *res communis* and *res nullius* are terms which oscillate in international law. This is a curious conflation. If unlimited use is what defines common property in international law there would be no way to institute limits in this space. Indeed, after his description of open access commons that are given limits under the doctrine of *res communis*, Vogler himself goes on to describe how several ocean fisheries and the whale population have been brought to near extinction under the legal rubric of "common property." Becoming common property (*res communis*) then, has not stopped the areas from being "free for the taking" (*res nullius*). It is as if *res communis* and *res nullius*, belonging to no-one and belonging to everyone, produce the same effect: both lead to nearly unlimited exploitation in international law. Why should *res nullius*, a category of things that are ungoverned or ungovernable, overlap with *res communis*, the legal category of things that are governed in common? In order to answer this question we must go back to the relation between *res nullius* and *terra nullius*. Contrary to Vogler and the standard description of these terms in international relations, we need to ask whether the two terms really are separate, or whether in fact *res nullius* carries over to the shared space of the global commons the colonial spatial imaginary of empty, homogeneous space. In other words, is the imaginal space that once served colonial powers in legitimizing the seizure of that space now serving commercial exploitation by legitimizing the expropriation or dispossession of commons space from its citizenry?

Historical and Semantic Considerations of *Terra Nullius* and *Res Nullius*

First, do *terra nullius* and *res nullius* really refer to different kinds of space? A look at some typical examples of these terms in late nineteenth- and early twentieth-century international law show a general confusion between the terms as well as outright disagreements about what the terms meant. Even the two dominant languages of international law, French and English, have different translations of the Latin term *terra nullius*. In English *terra nullius* is translated as "land belonging to no-one" (Lindley 1926, Falk 1970). In French it is translated as "territoire sans maître," literally "territory without a master" (Fiore 1885, Fauchille 1925).

As a mode of imperialist expansion in the late nineteenth century, *terra nullius* or *territorium nullius* is associated with treating the lands of various nonEuropean peoples as empty of legitimate sovereignty and therefore open for acquisition or protectorate by a European crown or nation-state. It was the General Acts of the Conference of Berlin (1886)—signed by all major European states and the United States of America—which established the doctrine of *territorium nullius* for use in Africa, and codified the procedure by which a state could take legal possession or assume a protectorate on the east and west coasts of Africa by using this doctrine. The declaration of the Berlin Conference was further solidified by a study commissioned by the European-based Institute of International Law in 1888 to bring theoretical clarification to the process by which European states occupied their African territories.[1] The debates surrounding the legitimacy of the doctrines of *territorium* and *res nullius* figure in that study, reported by Institute fellow Ferdinand von Martitz and published in the Institutes' journal, *LAnnulaire de l'institut de droit international.* The following excerpts show the theoretical indistinction between the doctrines of *territorium nullius* and *res nullius* as employed in these debates.[2]

> Est considérée comme *territorium nullius* toute région qui ne se trouve pas effectivement sous la souveraineté ou sous le protectorat d'un des Etats qui forment la communauté du droit des gens, peu importe que cette région soit, ou non, habitée. (Martitz 1887–1888)

---

1 The Institute of International Law won the Nobel Peace Prize in 1904. Its journal, *Annulaire de l'institut de droit international*, published the institute's studies and is the source of several of the following exerpts. The Institute's report on the Berlin Conference was divided with regard to the issue of what constituted a land as *res nullius, territorium nullius,* or *terra nullius.* Their final report took a rather cynical and "practical" approach to the outcome of the Berlin Conférence by stating that the conference was meant to not define which kind of African peoples could be colonzied but rather to avoid territorial fights among European powers as had occured in the last century in North America.

2 My analysis is meant to address nothing more than how the use of the terms *res nullius* and *territorium nullius* figure in the logic of arguments discussing the legitimacy of European sovereignty in Africa.

> We consider *territorium nullius* to comprise any region which is not effectively under the sovereignty or the protectorate of one of the States that make up the community of the law of nations, regardless of whether that region is inhabited or not. (All translations from the French are mine)

Elaborating on the status of inhabitants of lands considered *territorium nullius*, inhabitants labeled "*sauvages*" and "*demi-barbares*" (savages and semi-barbarians), the report takes a ambiguous stand, demonstrating that from the viewpoint of colonial law, Indigenous identity is related to the same spatial ambiguity between outside and inside that the political theorist Giorgio Agamben noted with regard to the "zone of indistinction" in Chapter 1. Thus Martitz continues,

> On ne pourra même dire strictement que ceux-ci sont en dehors de la communauté du droit des gens. Mais ils n'en sont pas members. (Ibid.)

> One cannot strictly say that they are outside the community of the law of nations. But they are not members of that group.

Indigenous peoples are not outside the law of nations, but neither are they inside ("members"). Continuing with this spatially contradictory metaphor, the author notes that for legitimate possession of a territory inhabited by Indigenous peoples, the articles of the Berlin Conference require the tribal chief to hand over his authority to the representative of the occupying state. To explain how such Indigenous authority is in fact not a form of recognizable (and now ceded) sovereign authority (which might make the Indigenous peoples recognized members of the law of nations), the jurist offers the analogy of the relation between *territorium nullius* and *res nullius* as if to say, there are two kinds of sovereignty just as there are two kinds of nobody:

> Le droit international ne connâit pas 'des droits des tribus indépendents.' Les arrangements qui aujourd'hui se passent réglièrement avec des chefs des tribus sauvages seront indispensables pour se fixer dans un territoire occupé; *territorium nullius, c'est autre chose que res nullius*. Mais le titre de possession international n'est pas *dérivatif;* il reste *originaire.* (Ibid.)

> International law does not recognize 'the rights of independent tribes.' The arrangements that take place regularly today with the chiefs of savage tribes are indispensable for establishing oneself in an occupied territory; *territorium nullius is not the same as res nullius.* Title of possession in international law is not derivative, it remains originary. (My emphasis)

So, *territorium nullius* is territory belonging to an Indigenous nobody—a nobody who is still somebody because they are not completely "outside" the law of nations (even though they are not members); while *res nullius* is land that belongs to a real nobody who inhabits a true outside to the law of nations. Since true *res nullius* nobodies cannot hand over authority because they are nonexistent, the jurist seems to say, one should not assume that an Indigenous nobody who resides in an ambiguous zone of the law of nations has actual title to hand over. Title, in international law, does not derive from anything, including nobodies. Title is originary. It originates in certain laws agreed upon by certain nations. But aren't Indigenous peoples within the law of nations? Yes, they are within, but they are not members … and so on and so forth.

Beyond the zone of contradiction in the above quotes, the jurists' assertion that *territorium nullius* is not the same as *res nullius* is itself contradicted by contemporary historical documents. One report, from an 1886 article debating whether Germany could occupy an African territory which was close to a territory occupied by Great Britian, uses the term "territoire sans maître" (*terra nullius*) interchangeably with "territoire *res nullius*":

> La note du 10 juin 1884 affirme le droit de l'allemagne à l'occupation d'un territoire *res nullius* et d'y proteger ses nationaux, lors même qu'elle n'aurait pas l'intention d'y créer un établissement politique, mais un simple établissement colonial délégué à une compagnie ayant un caractère officiel, ainsi que l'Angleterre l'avait fait à Bornéo, et il combat l'étrange théorie de vouloir écarter le protectorat d'une tierce puissance étrangère sur un territoire *sans maître* au profit d'une puissance *coloniale voisine*. (Jooris 1886: 241)

> The note of June 10, 1884 affirms Germany's right to the occupation of a *territory res nullius* and its right to protect its nationals on that territory, even if it did not intend to create a political establishment there but rather a simple colonial one delegated to a company having an official character, just as England had done in Borneo, and (furthermore) it takes issue with the strange theory that would dismiss the protectorate of a third foreign power on a territory *sans maître* (*terra nullius*) to the advantage of a neighboring colonial power. (My emphasis)

The passage is typical of the confusion and seemingly interchangeable usage between *terra nullius* ("territoire sans maître") and "territoire *res nullius*." In this case imperialist Germany asserts its right to form a protectorate in Africa on a territory belonging to no-one (*res nullius*) and to demand that Great Britain not try to separate this protectorate from one of Germany's European allies who also resides in Africa on territory belonging to no-one (*terra nullius*).

Not only is there confusion between the terms, but the terms themselves are often accompanied by synonyms like "absent" and "vacant." Such adjectives reveal that *terra nullius*/*res nullius* are political terms whose colonial spatial imaginary is constructed around empty space. Note the following definition of *terra nullius* from a French manual of international law published in 1925:

> Lorsqu'on parle d'un territoire *vacant* et *sans maître* cela ne veut pas dire que le territoire doive être absolument sans habitants. Pour qu'un territoire soit *res nullius*, il suffit qu'il y ait sur lui *absence* d'autorité. (Fauchille 1925: 697)
>
> When we speak of a *vacant* or masterless territory (*terra nullius*) we are not saying that the territory must be absolutely uninhabited. For a territory to be *res nullius*, it is sufficient for there to be an *absence* of authority. (My translation and emphasis)

Once again *territorium nullius* ("territoire sans maître") elides with *res nullius*. It also provides an exemplary instance of how an imaginal space of emptiness is formed in a place that is admittedly inhabited. Emptiness, associated with the political form under which those inhabitants are organized, becomes virtually synonymous with the habitats of nonstatist peoples. During the second wave of European colonization the doctrine of *terra nullius/res nullius* was commonly used by European powers to justify colonial acquisitions (Salomon 1889, Griache 1945, Kiss 1966).[3]

In an American text of international law from 1926 the connection between vacant lands and lands which are inhabited but "absent of authority" is once again clear, but in this text "the high seas" is added to the list of *territorium nullius* making it, again, indistinguishable from *res nullius*. Thus the text lists:

> Areas which are *territoria nullius* and open to acquisition by Occupation may consist of:
>
> 1. Uninhabited lands
> 2. *Lands inhabited by individuals who are not permanently united for political action*
> 3. Lands which have been abandoned by their former occupants
> 4. Lands which have been forfeited because they have not been occupied effectively
> 5. *Seas* that are almost or entirely surrounded by land which fulfills one of the above conditions
> 6. *The belt of the ocean* bordering on land which fulfills one of the above conditions …
> 7. *Portions of the open sea* adjoining the territorial belt—by accretions to the neighboring land.

3 See Alexandre-Charles Kiss, *Répetoire de la pratique française en matière de droit international public* CNRS, Paris, 1966, v.II, no. 247, p. 138 (Italy) and no. 253, p. 144 (France).

These listed areas are open to acquisition and a reign of full sovereignty. However, to the list is added the postscript: "The open sea, though *territorium nullius*, is not now susceptible of sovereignty, save in certain cases where prescriptive rights are claimed to sedentary fisheries on the sea-bed" (Lindley 1926: 80). This list then brings the habitats of Indigenous peoples into a spatial imaginary that includes the seas.

Despite the exhortation noted at the beginning of this chapter by international relations scholar Vogler not to confuse the global commons with doctrines of colonial sovereignty, despite his insistence that the open seas were not *terra nullius* but rather *res nullius* which were governed as *res communis*, it is clear that *terra nullius* and *res nullius* are often indistinguishable. Their complicity reveals the colonial doctrine of *terra nullius* as the shadow cast over both *res nullius* and *res communis*.

State Space, Nonstate Space and a New Category which is Neither

If *terra/res nullius* refers to empty (yet often times inhabited) space, what is the semantic frame of the space that is not empty, the space against which this inhabited emptiness is measured? It is quite clear from late nineteenth-century legal writings that the "not empty" space is made up of forms of political organization and action associated with the European state. Thus the President of the European Institute of International Law, Alphonse Rivier, summed up portions of the Institute's debate on the 1885 Berlin Conference on the interpretation of *terra nullius* and the European occupation of Africa with the following remarks:

> Un Etat, c'est un corps politique organisé; une tribu nomade ne sera pas un Etat. Des qu'il y a apparence d'organisation, c'est-a-dire l'existence d'un Etat, il n'y a plus lieu d'occupation pure et simple, (*res nullius*) mais a protectorat: c'est qu'a admis l'Allemagne dans l'Afrique méridionale.[4]

---

4 Rivier goes on to remark: "La tendence a reconnaître des Etats et a traîter comme tels des corps politiques rudimentaires ou insignifiants est, du reste, si forte qu'au Congo les Etats européens voilent leurs occupations sous l'apparence de traités avec les petits chefs indigènes: rien n'est moins sérieux que ces traités ou un chef sans importance, un petit tyran local, vend des droits de souveraineté douteux contre quelques pièces de cotonnade ou quelques bouteilles de rhum." (The tendency to recognize States and to treat as such rudimentary or insignificant political bodies is, moreover, so strong that in the Congo European States cover their occupations with the appearance of a treaty with some Indigenous chief. Nothing could be less serious than these so-called treaties where an insignificant chief, a petty local tyrant, sells doubtful sovereignty rights for a few pieces of cotton cloth or a few bottles of rum.) Remarks reported in Ferdinand Von Martitz, "Examen de la théorie de la conférence de Berlin de 1885, sur l'occupation des territoires," *Annulaire de l'institut de droit international* (P. Weissenbruch) 2 (1928): 711.

> A State is an organized political body; a nomadic tribe is not a State. As soon as organization appears, in other words, the existence of a State, there is no longer a question of occupation pure and simple, (*res nullius*) but of a protectorate: this is what Germany admitted in southern Africa.

Laws legitimizing colonial actions of late nineteenth-century European states find their clearest example of inhabited *terra nullius*, inhabited emptiness, in lands traversed by nomads. The nomadic tribe is indeed the antithesis of the state and therefore subject in the international law of this period to legitimate colonization. Note, however, that even when Africa did produce recognizably *de facto* states, these states did not have enough authority to resist capture by the European state: instead of becoming colonies they could become protectorates. Although there appears to be a good deal of ambiguity surrounding the doctrine of *terra nullius* concerning what kind of political organization constituted a nonstate and therefore a legitimate target of colonial acquisition at the turn of the last century, as soon as European states began colonizing what they considered "weak states"—the Ottomon Empire, Morocco, Tunisia, and Zanzabar, it was clear that *terra nullius* as "territoire sans maître" referred simply to non-European lands.

As European powers debated the emptiness and nonstate status of what became their African colonies, the United States invented a new category for a form of sovereignty that was somewhere in between: the "domestic dependent nation." Nineteenth-century European debates on legitimate sovereignty are an extension of earlier medieval debates on the continental presence of heretics and non-Christians. The European sixteenth century carried this ecclesiastical context into the so-called New World, claiming that lands of pagans and infidels could belong to the Christian nation that "discovered" them. The Papal Bull of 1493 established a line of demarcation between Spanish and Portuguese possessions in the New World, staking out a clear distinction between legitimate (European) states and nonstate domains that could be legitimately possessed. The clarity of this distinction was nevertheless challenged by many early modern jurists (Lindley 1925: 12–13, Seed 1992). Hugo Grotius, the early modern Dutch jurist, for example, offered a notion of limited or divided sovereignty in international law that added further ambiguity to the distinction of state and nonstate space. The high seas, Grotius argued, were domains of such shared sovereignty. Grotius' argument introduced the concept of usufruct rights as a form of limited sovereignty that could exist alongside the full sovereignty of the state (Dickason 1988). While Grotius's ideas about limited sovereignty on the high seas would not take hold in international law until the nineteenth century, it is important to consider how his maritime arguments would eventually link legal thinking about nonstate space to legal conceptions of limited sovereignty for Indigenous peoples in settler states like the US.

In the nineteenth century Grotius' idea of limited sovereignty was used in the landmark US case of the *Cherokee Nation v. Georgia* (1831) when US Supreme

Court Justice John Marshall used Grotius' concept of usufruct rights to argue that the Cherokee were a "domestic dependent nation." This novel term for limited sovereignty would become fundamental to the status of Indian tribes in the United States. In this case Marshall argued that:

> (T)he condition of the Indians in relation to the United States is perhaps unlike that of any other two people in existence. In the general, nations not owing a common allegiance are foreign to each other. The term *foreign nation* is, with strict propriety, applicable by either to the other. But the relations of Indians to the United States is marked by peculiar and cardinal distinctions which exist nowhere else.
>
> … Though the Indians are acknowledged to have an unquestionable, and, heretofore, unquestioned *right to the lands* they occupy, until that right shall be extinguished by a voluntary cession to our government; yet it may well be doubted whether those tribes which reside within the acknowledged boundaries of the United States can, with strict accuracy, be denominated foreign nations. They may, more correctly, perhaps, be denominated *domestic dependent nations*. (Cited in Getches and Wilkinson 1986: 47)

Justice Thompson's dissention in the *Cherokee* case cited the 1758 work of Swiss jurist Emer de Vattel, *The Law of Nations*, to argue that the Cherokee did indeed meet the requirements of sovereignty, understood as a limited concept in international law:

> It is sufficient if it be really sovereign and independent: that is, it must govern itself by its own authority and laws. We ought, therefore, to reckon in the number of sovereigns those states that have bound themselves to another more powerful, although by an unequal alliance. The condition of these unequal alliances may be infinitely varied; but whatever they are, provided that the inferior ally *reserves* to itself the sovereignty or the right to govern its own body, it ought to be considered *an independent state*. (Ibid. 50, my emphasis)

The idea that Indigenous peoples held reserved rights, never relinquished basic usufruct rights in the land, persists in the Indian reservation system in the United States. US law does not recognize aboriginal title, but some have argued that its justification exists in international law going back to Vattel's *Law of Nations* (Gagne 1983).

Reserved rights of Indigenous peoples thus form a new kind of territoriality in Western legal systems. Legal precedent for this kind of spatial thinking goes back to ideas of limited, usufruct rights articulated in international law of the high seas, areas we now refer to as global commons.

Summarizing the Confusion of *Res Nullius, Terra Nullius* and *Res Communis*: State and Non-State Space

As a means of summarizing the argument thus far, consider how the two dominant languages of international law translate the term *terra nullius.* The English translation, "land belonging to no-one" carries the sense that the space in question has a passive potential for belonging, for becoming property. The French translation "territoire sans maître" (territory without a master) suggests that the space has no masterful authority over itself and no authority in relation to other authorities. The Latin term *nullius* adds a further dimension: the dative form of *nullus—ne* "not" and *ullus* "any' from *unus* "one"—literally means a relation to the "not one." Continuing this semantic language game, *res/terra nullius* carries the meaning of space or land of the "not one."[5] In terms of the spatial imaginary supporting these legal concepts, both semantically and historically, the "one" in relation to which *res* and *terra nullius* are lacking is a master as a unitary form. The "one" is the European state. The "not one," then, the *res nullius*, is the nonstate. And nonstate space is also the global commons, the global commons as a form of nonstate, empty space.

All these meanings go into the cultural logic behind the legal concepts of *res* and *terra nullius*. Taken together they help explain the rhetorical force behind the categorical overlap and consequent oscillation between *res nullius* and *res communis*. Both *res nullius* and *res communis* share one feature: both refer to tenure not held by any one "masterful" subject. Logically speaking, even though the categories of *res nullius* and *res communis* are not alike—*res communis* presupposes a common or collective form of subjectivity or mastery while *res nullius* presupposes an individualist subject (be that a state or a person) as potential future possessor or master—their shared aspect is that neither of them are presently governed by a unitary form of subjectivity, the state. They share the space of the "not one," nonstate space. Both *res communis* and *res nullius* are nonstate space.

---

5 In poststructuralist political theory, the space of "the not one" is defined as the space of the multitude, a subjectivity or sovereignty characterized by its multiple identities and its lack of a foundational myth or common denominator. For a discussion of the how such nonstate space expands Western conceptual thinking with regard to sovereignty in a globalized era, see Michael Hardt and Antonio Negri, *Multitude: War and Democracy in the Age of Empire* (New York: Penguin Press, 2004). Hardt and Negri follow philosophers Gilles Deleuze and Feliz Guattari's formulation of the dangers and potentials in smooth-nonstate (as opposed to striated, state) space (see Gilles Deleuze and Félix Guattari, *A Thousand Plateaus: Capitalism and Schizophrenia*, trans. Brian Massumi (Minneapolis: University of Minnesota Press, 1987)). More recently Hardt and Negri have sought to conceptualize the commons aspect of this nonstate space in Michael Hardt and Antonio Negri, *Commonwealth* (Cambridge, MA: Belknap Press of Harvard University Press, 2009).

Figure 2.1 Thought picture of *res nullius* and *res communis* as nonstate and interstate space

When the statist thinking of international law does imagine *res communis*, it does so by abstracting it to a form which can be inhabited collectively by states: interstate space. Historically, interstate space has been framed in international law as nonexcludable, open access commons—the high seas and outerspace being exemplary domains. The spatial imaginary behind laws that articulate economic and political behavior of nations in these spaces is highly abstract. Indeed, these conceptions of shared but abstract space work especially well with the ideology of an invisible hand of a "free market" that can effectively regulate commons use. Grotius and other legislators called this abstraction "natural law." Marx and other political thinkers critiqued the naturalization of abstraction as a regulative social value.[6]

Both *res communis* and *res nullius* are legal fictions that allow states to extend themselves into the space of commons by making that space both interstate and nonstate space. Interstate space brings an abstract, homogeneous quality to the commons when it describes commons domains as infinite, boundless space and legislates unlimited forms of use. In this respect states keep the commons (un)governable, by which I mean they maintain the commons outside legal frameworks which would effectively restrict the agency of states. They govern it in a form that allows them to keep it ungovernable and therefore free for a dangerously unrestrained use.

International law shows that unrestrained use of global commons by states, (interstate space) can lead to interstate war as well as to a demand for self-limiting regulations on use. Indeed in interstate space, states may collectively decide to limit their sovereignty (although their history suggests that they will do otherwise). The other outcome of governing the commons as homogeneous open access interstate space is that as it oscillates towards *res nullius* it becomes nonstate space. This means that nonsovereign entities have as much right as sovereign ones to use nonstate commons. Nonstate space can be inhabited effectively by various social actors: multinational mining companies, for example (as we shall see in the case of the ocean seabed and the Moon), as well as nongovernmental organizations like Greenpeace (as we shall see in the case of whale protection).

In sum, at the level of a spatial imaginary, the rhetoric of global commons oscillates in international law between *res communis* and *res nullius*. This involves abstracting the commons so that they might function as homogeneous space.

Terra/Res Nullius and *Res Communis*: "Who Owns the Oceans? No-One and Everyone"

With this historical and semantic background the connection between nomadic lands and the more recent referent of *terra/res nullius*, the global commons, becomes clearer. As categorical objects of *terra nullius*, both domains are characterized by their relation to the state via the mediation of empty space. It is evident that the modern state has a (now repudiated) history of legitimizing the colonization of what it called "backward territories" and the exploitation of what

6 In particular see Henri Lefebvre's masterwork on abstract space, *The Production of Space*, trans. Donald Nicholson-Smith (Oxford: Basil Blackwell Ltd., 1991).

it terms "natural resources" assisted by the rhetorical notion of empty space. What has been less clear is how the state maintains its colonialist relation of dominance over Indigenous lands and the environment today by means of the category of shared or common space (*res communis*).

Res communis is thought in international law through the mediation of empty space. *Res communis* overlaps with the concept of *res nullius* which itself is linked to *terra/res nullius* which stands for a type of space that can either be seized because it isn't "governed" or not seized because it cannot be "governed." *Terra/res nullius* as a category of things which are ungoverned or ungovernable, also often overlaps with the legal category of *res communis*, things which are held in common—held in common by either state forms (interstate space) or by nonstate forms like nomadic groups. At the level of its conceptual tools, then, international law of the global commons supports the oscillation between *res communis* and *res nullius*. This conceptual confusion means that the commons are more easily subjected to forms of governance that reflect the policies of *terra nullius*: unilateral, hierarchical centralized assertions of sovereignty. The ambivalence surrounding *res nullius* and *res communis*, or rather this usurpation of common property by *res nullius* legalities, leaves the conceptual sphere of international law with a powerful lack of imagination and even intolerance for forms of governance which reflect *res communis*. Thus tenure systems that are regulated but noncentralized, multilateral, even nomadic face enormous obstacles to being thought as legitimate in international law.

Reduced to statist terms, such *res communis* or "commons" are areas like US national parks, areas which are "owned" by a state that expelled the area's Indigenous, heterogeneous forms of sovereignty in order to render the terrain governable as homogeneous space. Expanded to a global scale, *res communis* bear the symptom of the complex contradiction of the indistinction between *res communis* and *res nullius*. "Who owns the sea at present?" asks the environmental editor of the *Daily Telegraph*, Britain's largest selling newspaper. "The short answer" he responds, "is everyone and no-one" (Clover 2005). In any discussion of today's global commons, the norm appears as this contradictory idea that no-one and everyone own global commons. Empty space and its juridical corollary *res nullius* are part of the spatial repertoire of the political uncommons. They form the epistemic imaginary behind legal and popular thinking that shapes global commons today.

Taken together then, colonized nomadic lands and the global commons reveal a similarity at the level of the spatial imaginary of international law: the shared feature of a degree zero, empty space. The rhetorical function of the figure of empty space in international law is to permit the oscillation between *res communis* and *res nullius*. The further investigation of *res nullius* in the following chapter reveals how this spatial imaginary took shape in the conceptual system of modern international law.

Chapter 3
Res Nullius—The Tragedy of the (Modern Global) Commons: From Grotius and the High Seas to the Internet

Introduction

Taking three "moments" in the life of *res nullius* as a concept of international law, Chapter Three examines the evolving epistemic imaginary that informs this legal doctrine as it finds its way into historical arguments defining the modern and postmodern global commons. First, I look at *res nullius* as a doctrine of Roman law reinterpreted in the eighteenth century by German philosopher Immanuel Kant in a key enlightenment argument for a secular, universal basis for modern justice. Second, I analyze the doctrine of *res nullius* in a sixteenth-century text often hailed as one of the founding documents of modern international law, Hugo Grotius' *Mare Liberum* (The Freedom of the Seas). *Res nullius* is part of a complex spatial logic that makes the oceans the basis of modern thinking on global commons.[1] Third, I examine the presence of *res nullius* in legal arguments describing the governance of the radio frequency spectrum and the Internet, leading examples of postmodern global commons struggling against enclosure today.

The following chapter does not claim to be a history of the doctrine of *res nullius* in the global commons. Rather, it is a cultural study of the rhetorical force of an evolving spatial imaginary that persists around the doctrine of *res nullius* in the modern commons. Therefore, instead of taking a chronological approach to the topic, this chapter is construed as a "history of the present" as the philosopher Michel Foucault intended the term: a genealogy of a present problem, the failure of international law to create an effective global commons jurisdiction. The history is eclectic and partial. It focuses on the appearance of the *res nullius* doctrine

---

1 See, for example, how Grotius and the law of the seas have been used as the basis for thinking about ownership of human, plant, and seed DNA (Jasper A. Bovenberg, "Mining the Common Heritage of our DNA: Lessons Learned from Grotius and Pardo," *Duke Law and Technology Review*, 3, 8, 2006: 1–19); about the intellectual property (Carol M. Rose, "Romans, Roads, and Romantic Creators Traditions of Public Property in the Information Age," 66 *Law & Contemporary Problems* 89 (Winter/Spring 2003); and about outer space (Brett M. Janos, "The Final Frontier: Incorporating Aspects of Culture and History in the Formation of a Workable, Legal Framework for Outerspace," *Selected Works of Brett Janos*, 2009, http://works.bepress.com/brett_janos/1/ (accessed December 4, 2009).

in arguments related to *res communis* and to important concepts of modern international law: the reasonable person; the freedom of the seas, property, and usufruct rights.

The Reinterpretation of the Roman Doctrine of *Res Nullius* in Kant

According to Roman law codified in the *Institutes of Justinian*, within the category of things (*res*) (as opposed to persons) there are some things that cannot be privately owned. These are things Justinian considered by force of natural law to be common to all and yet belonging to no-one (*res nullius*):

> the air, running water, the sea, and consequently the sea-shore … the public use of the sea-shore, as of the sea itself, is part of the law of nations … they cannot be said to belong to any one as private property but rather are subject to the same law as the sea itself, with the soil or sand which lies beneath it … Things which are sacred, devoted to superstitious uses, or sanctioned, *belong to no one,* for what is subject to divine law is no one's property. (*Nullius autem sunt res sacrae et religiosae et santctae: quod enim divini juris est id nullius in bonis est*) … (Justinian 1953)

Along with things unappropriated by anyone, such as the sea, sea-bed, and public use of the sea shore, the category of *res nullius* included sacred things dedicated to the gods. According to geographer Gillian Rose:

> *Res nullius* (in Roman law) were either things unappropriated by anyone, such as things common, unoccupied lands, wild animals; or things which cannot be appropriated: sacred things dedicated to the celestial gods; religious things dedicated to underworld gods; and sanctified things, such as the walls and gates of a city … (Rose 1984: 49)

Roman property law demonstrated an interest in the sorts of things that were outside the domain of private and public property. Even if these classical distinctions appear confused to modern legal thinkers (Buckland 1921)—*res publicae* (government-run navigable rivers and territorial seas) can overlap with *res communis* (the seas and their fisheries) and with *res nullius* (the high seas and ocean whales)—they suggest a worldview where common, public, and sacred properties had a well recognized place that lent private property robust, socially acknowledged limits.

According to legal historian Daniel Coquillette, interest in nonexclusive property begins to disappear in Western legal thinking by the seventeenth century with the growth of the enclosure movement, such that by the nineteenth century the American James Kent could observe that what was called "common property" was rapidly vanishing from American law (Coquillette 1979). In her treatment of modern applications of nonexclusive (common) Roman property law, legal scholar Carol Rose emphasizes that roads and other physical spaces required for mobility were developed by the Romans for military reasons, while Americans would rationalize the public nature of such domains as the backbone of commerce (Rose 2003). Together these sweeping statements concerning the Western history of the decline of commons and the rise of public domains in the name of commerce fail to tell the story of the violent dispossession from their commons-based livelihood of aboriginal and peasant populations across Europe, Africa, Asia, and the Americas. In the history of Western legal thought, common property systems lost the interest of scholars and the authority of normative and substantive law as part of the extensive *post facto* rationalizations in support of the liberal state. Regarding *res nullius*, the German philosopher Immanuel Kant provided logical arguments to extinguish the "confused" thinking behind Roman systems of nonexclusive property and usher in practical reasoning in support of the increasing power of the market, urban civil society and individual ownership. I offer the following discussion of Kant's detailed theoretical thinking about *res nullius* to emphasize that, alongside the assimilation of *res nullius* to *terra nullius* we see in colonial sovereignty, a corresponding move occurs in philosophy to make *res nullius* not a theoretical but a practical concept, such that it could be more easily detached from its theoretical lineage and embedded in quotidian practices.

In a key text of the European enlightenment, the *Metaphysical Elements of Justice*, Kant, philosopher and geographer, provides an argument against the legal category of *res nullius* by stating that according to the juridical postulate of practical reason, there cannot be a category of things belonging to no-one:

> (I)t is possible to have any and every external object of my will as my property. In other words, a maxim according to which, if it were made into a law, an object of will would have to be in itself (objectively) ownerless (*herrenlos* [literally: without a master]) (*res nullius*) conflicts with Law and justice. (Kant, *The Metaphysical Elements of Justice: Part I of the Metaphysics of Morals 1797*, 1965)

In order for someone to conceive of something as an object of his or her will, Kant says, it must be:

> something over which I have the physical capacity to make use, a use that is within my power (*potentia*). This capacity must be distinguished from having the same object within my authority (*inpotestatem meam redactum*) ('Brought under my authority.') The latter presupposes, not merely a capacity but also an act of the will. But in order to merely conceive of something as an object of my will, it is sufficient that I be aware of the fact that it is within my (physical) power. *Consequently it is an a priori assumption of practical reason that any and every object of my will be viewed and treated as something that has the objective possibility of being yours or mine.*

> This postulate can be called a permissive law of practical reason (*lex permissive*). It confers on us an authorization that we cannot derive from mere concepts of justice in general, namely, the authorization to impose an obligation on all others—an obligation that they otherwise would not have had—to refrain from using certain objects of our will because we were the first to take possession of them. *Reason requires that this postulate be taken as a basic principle*, and it does this as practical reason extending itself a priori by means of this postulate. (52–53, my emphasis)

Kant's critique of the concept of *res nullius* introduces the idea of a human will and its *dominium* as it dismisses the idea/category of sacred objects that are the *dominium* of the gods. Kant finds the Roman concept of *res nullius*, then, to contain a contradiction: it includes objects in one's power that cannot be possessed. Logically, Kant argues, if something can be used, it has the objective possibility of being possessed. Beyond being merely an argument for the "disenchantment of the world" and a ground for possessive individualism, Kant's argument erodes areas of Roman law that protected common property. For Justinian, a thing could be commonly used by humans without being in their *dominium*, without potentially becoming their property. In Kant this becomes a logical impossibility. *Res nullius* is thus reinterpreted to bring it into modernity following basic principles of practical reason and a claim that it follows the law of nature.

Thus in the founding legal and philosophical texts of modernity an argument begins to be formulated for the erasure of a legal category inherited from Roman law that is comprised of things which one might use but over which one cannot assert *dominium*. These are undominated things, things humans sometimes share with the gods. Sacred and sanctified things belong to a world that is neither law like nor entirely reasonable. Rather, in Roman law the world humans share with the gods is best understood in the stories of the gods and their interactions with humans. It may not be surprising that the authority of such myths lose their ground in modernity, but it does give pause to consider how the *dominium* of the gods in becoming objects of human will end up losing a legal jurisdiction that provided humans with mythical instructions on how to share things that could not be owned. In short, when the *dominium* of the gods—*res sacrae, religiosae et santatae*—is vacated to follow the dictates of reason, we see the creation of a legal fiction that authorizes humans to create common ground beyond "mere concepts of justice," as Kant says. That common ground beyond justice and beyond further human reflection is an *a priori* domain. It leads to a place without further negotiation or discussion. Because Reason reflected natural law, the foreclosure of the illogical also leads towards a naturalized right to private property.

A spatial imaginary supports Kant's argument. Making the world of objects "objects of our will" brings the world into line with a new paradigm of belonging based on the principle of noncontradiction. Reason, as Kant reminds us, dictates that our understanding of modern usable space be without contradiction. In *The Critique of Pure Reason*, Kant goes to great pains to maintain Reason as a space of noncontradiction but he is not entirely successful. Kant's argument to exclude contradiction from the domain of Reason relies on a spatial metaphor. In a passage where Kant is describing the position of the (culturally contaminated) imagination with respect to the self-sufficiency of the conceptual domain of pure understanding, we find the following analogy:

> We have now not merely explored the territory of pure understanding, and carefully surveyed every part of it, but have also measured its extent, and assigned to everything in it its rightful place. This domain is an island enclosed by nature itself within unalterable limits. It is the land of truth—enchanting name!—surrounded by a wide and stormy *ocean, the native home of illusion*, where many a fog bank and many a swiftly melting iceberg give the deceptive appearance of farther shores, hopes, and engaging him in enterprises which he can never abandon and yet is unable to carry to completion. (Kant 1982)

The metaphor of the ocean is used to explain the exclusion of the imagination from the domain of reason. In this passage, Kant puts himself in the contradictory position of using a metaphor to outlaw metaphor from the realm of truth.

In *The Philosophical Imaginary*, philosopher Michele Le Doeuff calls such metaphors "a dialectical presupposition of the theory." She notes that the metaphor of the ocean/island in Kant is "an allegory of the basic distinction between the legitimate (empirical) use of the understanding and its confusing (amphibological) use" (Le Doeuff 1990). The contradiction of Reason being imaginably constructed as a domain (island) that excludes metaphor (the ocean) lends Reason both an exclusionary and what Le Doeuff calls "amphibological" form. Reason may present itself as an exclusionary form of thought but, like an amphibian moving between land and water, Reason is also a domain that oscillates between two mutually exclusive jurisdictions: Reason and the imagination. The spatial imaginary supporting Kant's description of Reason appears in the metaphor of the ocean, a metaphor that persists in several areas of modern thought as a mark of the instability of the law of noncontradiction.

The ocean is part of the "epistemic imaginary" of Reason, the imaginal repertoire of the epistemic structure of Reason.[2] Michelle Le Doeuff claims that "philosophical texts offer images through which subjectivity can be structured and given a marking which is that of the corporate body" (19). In other words, certain metaphors important in the construction of philosophical systems may migrate to other modes of thought and enter a more general structure of subjectivity at an institutional level. This is what I think happens with the image of the ocean. In the institution of international law where subjectivity is a formation of sovereignty, the law of the seas functions as the model for how we imagine sovereignty in other quite different environments such as the atmosphere or outer space. These

2 I am grateful to Helen Watson-Verrans' essay, "Renegotiating What's Natural" (New Orleans, October 12–15, 1994) for introducing me to this term.

domains of modern sovereignty extending from their analogical base in the law of the seas constitute the modern global commons and suggest that we take a closer look at the role played by the sea in the way we imagine commonly shared space in modernity.

From a highly abstract point of view, just as Kant eventually labeled the metaphoric ocean in the epistemic imaginary of Reason mere illusion, the law of the seas describes its maritime domain as the functional equivalent of empty space: open access, nonexcludable, *res nullius*. In other words, international law as a structure of reasonable subjectivity/sovereignty conceptualizes the oceans as abstract, homogeneous interstate space rather than as heterogeneous nonstate space. But, just as the imagination continues to function within Reason in the architecture of Kant's system, nonstate heterogeneous space persists as an imaginal component in the laws that render the seas (and by analogy the atmosphere and outer space) homogeneous, abstract interstate space. As such, laws that maintain the high seas as nonexcludable, open access arenas have interstices where a different vision of the seas can be legally addressed, a topic I will address more fully in Chapter 5.

The ocean, then, is a foundational image in a now broader epistemic imaginary that informs modern legal thinking about common space. And the ocean is always the indicator of a contradiction inherent in the way we legislate these public domains. Over and over in legal texts related to the global commons we find statements explaining that the law is seeking to govern something that is, by its own definition, ungovernable. In legal reasoning, *res/terra nullius* refers to areas like the oceans and outer space that cannot be mastered (technologically) and thus cannot be effectively governed. Because states cannot effectively *exclude* others from such areas, they become *by default* a commons. Such a definition of commons creates an ineffective cultural basis for legislating and imagining shared space. But, because the ability to exclude is an essential characteristic of both Reason and the state as an institution of modern sovereignty, it is also true that the ungovernability of the modern commons, its maintenance as a space of nonexcludable open access *res nullius*, has long been less about a physical impossibility than about a willed inability that benefits certain institutions and certain social actors. *Res nullius*, then, is the name of this contradictory space in international law.

To summarize then, Kant's discussion of *res nullius* represents the formation of a modern spatial imaginary in international law. In Kant we see a paradigm shift from the Justinian concept of *res nullius*—a category of things which includes, along with stray and wild animals that may be caught and taken as private property, things belonging to no-one because they must be used by everyone and/or because they belong to the gods—to the modern legal concept of *res nullius* as things which belong to no-one but, like stray cats and wild animals, if brought within the scope of human will, may become private or state property. *Res nullius* comes to be reinterpreted in terms of human will. This means excluding the category of things that belonged to the gods, and making all "things" objects of Reason and thus either actually or potentially objects of the human will. In this way, modern space was conceptually *emptied* of prior (nonhuman) belonging and *opened* to (human) appropriation. The prior became the *a priori*. It was emptied of foundational myths with their fictional characters and contradictory plots accounting for why the world is the way it is. And it was opened to a new foundational spatial imaginary, a Euclidean, *tabula rasa* on which stood a new kind of common sense: postulates of practical reason. *Res nullius* moved from a heterogeneous to a homogeneous foundation for conceptualizing relations of sovereignty. The connection between emptied space and open space remains in the concept of *res nullius* to this day.

In addition to introducing homogeneous space and practical reason into a basic concept of international law, Kant's discussion of *res nullius* also provides a look into the contradictions of homogenous space and practical reason. Reason is both exclusionary and "amphibological," that is to say, both logical and fanciful. This contradictory structure forms the "epistemological imaginary" of Reason. And the figure of the ocean remains a part of the image repertoire of Reason, even though Reason may seek to denigrate its importance.

Wherever the figure of the ocean has migrated to legal institutions that describe the global commons, it also brings with it the problematic of empty and homogeneous space. Just as the ocean was the metaphor of the imagination as both constitutive of (our ability to conceptualize) Reason and exclusive of (the logic of) Reason, so the sea in modern international law becomes the allegorical domain wherein common space is conceptualized as both governable and ungovernable, both knowable and unknowable. That is to say, the analogy of the seas introduces a contradictory element into the rationalized arguments legitimating the use of common space in modernity.[3] This theoretical argument will be more empirically laid out in Chapter 5 when we look at specific cases involving the law of the seas. For now it is enough to see the rhetorical structure of the cultural logic that connects empty space, reason as a domain of exclusion, modern sovereignty, and the ocean as an actual and metaphorical foundation for the international law of shared sovereignty in space belonging to nobody.

Res Nullius, Res Communis, Res Publicae: The Modern Commons Emerging from Grotius' "Law of the Seas"

Before Kant provided the philosophical basis with which to equate natural law with Reason in regards to *dominium*, it was the sixteenth-century Dutch jurist Hugo Grotius who argued for the application of a theory of natural right with respect to *dominium* in international law. Many scholars consider Grotius, with his

3 This brief description of the problem of Reason's repressed connection to the imagination and the strange laws it produces in its quest to govern the ungovernable is very nicely worked out in Steve Tyler, "Post-Modern Ethnography: From Document of the Occult to Occult Document," in *Writing Culture: The Poetics and Politics of Ethnography*, ed. James Clifford and George Marcus, 123–125 (Berkeley: University of California Press, 1986).

early work on natural rights theory in relation to the law of the sea (*Mare Liberum* 1609) and his later work *The Law of War and Peace* (1625), to be the father of modern international law because in these works we find the first reconstruction of an actual legal system in terms of natural rights. This set Grotius' work apart from those who supported conventional monarchical systems of law based in the divine right of kings. Although not reflective of the dominant legal trend at the time of its writing, by the late nineteenth century Grotius' natural rights theories became the philosophical foundation of the law of nations (Tuck 1979).

In *Mare Liberum* (literally, freedom of the seas) Grotius provides the first articulation of common nonterritorial space in modern international law. The text is a discussion of the problems raised by colonial conflicts on the high seas. Grotius argues on behalf of his employer, the Dutch East Indian Company, that Portugal's claim of sovereignty over the Indian Ocean is unlawful and interferes with that company's trade in the area. The Spanish had at that time claimed sovereignty over the Pacific Ocean and the Gulf of Mexico, and Portugal had likewise claimed the Indian Ocean and the Atlantic Ocean south of Morocco. Grotius' task is to show that, according to the Law of Nations, the seas could not be the possession of any sovereign. They must be free and open to all nations. Trade on the high seas, Grotius argues, should be lawfully defended (by acts of war) if such access were denied.

Grotius' Theory of the Commons as Precursor to and Residual Form Surviving the Emergence of State and Private Property

To support his argument, Grotius develops a theory of the emergence of private (individual) and public (state) property based on acts of occupation or possession. Before such acts, Grotius argues, Roman law shows that the ancient world functioned as a commons. The emergence of sovereignty, according to Grotius' reading of the law of nations, was a slow process of occupying and then demonstrating possession over occupied areas. For Grotius, the seas represent a terrain that cannot be possessed, a residual form of the ancient commons (*res communis*). They cannot be possessed therefore they cannot become the sovereign property of any state.

But actually the argument is more complex and ambiguous. In Grotius' work, written in the Latin of his time, the seas are sometimes referred to as *res nullius* (something belonging to no-one) and sometimes *res republica* (something belonging to the state). At other times the seas are not *res* (things) at all but rather agents that possess humankind. A careful reading of Grotius' text shows how the arguments in a legal brief originally solicited to win trading rights for the Dutch East Indian Company came to form the foundation of the modern law of the seas and by extension the law governing the global commons as such.

Grotius begins his argument by noting that the sovereignty status of the seas is entirely ambiguous in international law. "In the legal phraseology of the Law of Nations," Grotius writes,[4]

> De mari autum prima sit consideratio, quod cum passim in iure aut nullius, aut commune, aut publicum iurs gentium dicatur. (Grotius 1916: 22)
>
> … the sea is called indifferently the property of no one (*res nullius*), or a common possession (*res communis*), or a public property (*res publica*).

The seas enjoyed this ambiguous description, Grotius tells us, because "… in (…) ancient times, all things were held in common." The analogy of the seas to an ancient form of commons (*res communis*) plays a strategic role in Grotius' argument. It sets up the spatial foundation of what can and cannot be considered property, what can and cannot be subject to claims of sovereignty.

How does Grotius describe this ancient common space? First, Grotius warns that our "modern nomenclature" gives us a different understanding than what the term (*communis*) had in "primitive law."

> Iure primo Gentium, quod et Naturale interdum dicitur, et quod pottae alibi etate aurea, alibi Saturni aut Iustitiae regno depingunt Commune igitur tunc non aliud fuit quam quod simpliciter proprio opponitur; dominium autem facultas non iniusta utendi re communi … (23)
>
> In the primitive law of nations which is sometimes called Natural Law, and which the poets sometimes portrayed as a Golden Age, and sometimes in the reign of Saturn or Jupiter … 'common' (*commune*) meant simply the opposite of 'particular' (*proprio*) and 'sovereignty' or 'ownership' (*dominium*) meant 'the privilege of lawfully using common property' (*re communi*).

In Grotius' understanding of Golden Age usage then, "commons" refers to the opposite of the particular (*proprio*). Even though commons (*commune* and *re communi*) is translated as "common property" in this 1916 English edition of Grotius' work, in Latin it is in fact the opposite of property (*propria*) just as it is the opposite of *proprio*—the Latin for "one's own" as well as the etymological root of the English word "property." Commons are not a form of property in either Grotius or in his understanding of Roman law. Further on, Grotius quotes Cicero and Horace to tell the reader that in this Golden Age there was no private property, since "Nature knows no sovereigns (*Neque enim potuit natura dominos distinguere*)." "Primitive men acquired everything in common and … Justice maintained a community of goods by means of an inviolable compact (*casto foedere*)."

4 Translations from the Latin are by Magoffin in the 1916 edition of "The Freedom of the Seas." I show the Latin text where necessary.

Grotius understands that the ancient commons is maintained by means of an "inviolable compact" among others. Communal rules and practices, Grotius implies, were worked out in the delimited ways suggested by *casto foedere* (translated in other texts of Grotius' era as "chaste union") with the connotation of divine sanction.[5] This is an important observation because the next set of adjectives Grotius offers gives a slightly different view of the ancient commons, one which is not delimited but rather boundless and heterogeneous:

> To make (my description of the commons) clearer, (the ancients) say that in those primitive times the fields (*campos*) were not delimited by boundary lines (*limite partitos*), and there was no commercial intercourse (*negant eo tempore campos limite partitos, aut commericia fuisse ulla*). (As Avienus says): 'The promiscuity of the fields had made everything seem common to all.' (... *promiscua rura per agros Praestiterant cunctis COMMUNIA cuncta VIDERI*). (23)

There are two important observations to make about this second description of the commons: this commons was boundless and heterogeneous. In the sentence which follows the above quote from Avienus, Grotius remarks that Avienus was right to say "seems" (*videri*) because he was speaking of the visual aspect of fields undifferentiated by marks of ownership. This implies that there are now two aspects of the ancient commons: one which is delimited (in terms of the user rules of the *casto foedere*) and another which is not delimited but rather *promiscua* (from *miscere* "mixed"), that is to say composed of heterogeneous sorts. It is important that the latter is known in a purely visual way. This passage suggests that Grotius had an understanding of an ancient commons which appeared visually boundless but only because of its intense heterogeneity. In sum, the ancient commons, Grotius implies, was a delimited space but its delimitations were not visually recognizable. What one saw there was simply boundless difference.

I emphasize the metaphors Grotius uses to describe the ancient commons, in particular those involving vision and delimitations, because they indicate a spatial imaginary in his thinking about how ancient commons must have been managed. Indeed Grotius' description of traditional commons turns out to be an appropriate analogy for the sea precisely because his abstract description of common fields looks more like the sea than the land: there are no visible delimitations on the high seas and that gives them the appearance of homogeneous space when in fact they are a domain of boundless difference.

Further on in Grotius, we find that the relation of the ancient commons to the state (*republica*) is similar to the relation between the state and the seas. For Grotius, the state as an institution emerges out of the ancient commons. This is a fundamental part of his argument, one that requires careful examination. Grotius shows that the confusion existing in international law of the seas over *res nullius*,

5 The term is found in ecclesiastical Latin texts to describe the kind of marriage that the Virgin Mary had with Joseph.

res communis, and *res publicae* is understandable because the seas are a residual part of the ancient commons that predate the emergence of the state. "At the time of their invention," Grotius writes, "(property [*propri*] and ownership [*occupatio*]) had to be wrested away (*divulsa*) from early ownership in common (*prima communione*)" (26). The division of the ancient commons into two groups—things that are public (the property of the people) and things that are private (the property of individuals)—occurred "at the same time … States began to be established (*Eodem autem tempore et respublicae institui coeperunt*)" (26). With the historical emergence of the state, then, property also arose, but there remained some form of space that resisted becoming either private or state property. This was *res communis*. Grotius explains it this way: property came into being through acts of occupation or possession.[6] After occupation had created two forms of dominium (states and individuals) then, Grotius writes,

> Contra autem Thucydides eam terram quae in divisione populo nulli obvenit, αόριστον hoc est, indefinitam et limitibus nullis circumscriptam vocat … (Thucydides I, 139, 2). (Grotius 1916: 27)

> the land which in the division falls to no nation (is called by) Thucydides αόριστον, that is, undefined, and undetermined by boundaries.

What happens to the land that "in the division falls to no nation"? Is it the form of *res communis* Grotius discussed as the ancient commons, a heterogeneous (*promiscua*) space that is boundless (only in appearance) and persists as a residual space in relation to the dominant? Or is it instead a new form of *res communis*, born out of a more dialectical relation of the ancient commons to the emergent state?

Let us pursue the second interpretation of *res communis*. What does it look like after "the division," after it separates from the ancient commons? Grotius quotes Thucydides on the post-state commons: it is undefined and without limits (*indefinitam et limitibus nullis*). So, in one respect, the new (post-state) commons looks very much like the ancient (pre-state) commons described by Avienus: boundless (*negant … limite partitos … fuisse ulla*) and heterogeneous (*promiscua*). Both commons are characterized by their boundlessness. But what happened

6 The oft quoted description of occupation or possession in Grotius is from this section of *Mare Liberum*: "this occupation or possession, however, in the case of things which resist seizure, like wild animals for example, must be uninterrupted or perpetually maintained, but in the case of other things it is sufficient if after physical possession is once taken the intention to possess is maintained. Possession of movables implies seizure, and possession of immovables either the erection of buildings or some determination of boundaries, such as fencing in (*Occupatio in mobilibus est apprehensio, in immobilibus instructio aut limitatio*)" (25–26). In English the adage is: possession is nine-tenths of the law.

to the heterogeneity of the commons? There is one clue as to what is going on with the spatial imaginary informing Grotius' text. A few pages after Avenius' description of the ancient commons, in a gloss of Seneca's description of the pre-state (ancient) commons, Grotius gives us a different image: "(in the ancient [pre-state] commons) there was a kind of sovereignty (*dominium*), but it was universal and indefinite (*universale et indefinitum*)" (24). The spatial images supporting Grotius' argument become clearer in this passage. Grotius has two definitions of the pre-state ancient commons: one is boundless (*negant ... limite partitos ... fuisse ulla*) and heterogeneous (*promiscua*) and the other is universal and indefinite (*universale et indefinitums*). At the level of their spatial imaginary, both these descriptions of the pre-state commons share one feature with the description of the post-state commons which Grotius, via Thucydides, describes as "undefined and without limits" (*indefinitam et limitibus nullis*): they all three share the common feature of being boundless or without limits. What they do not share is a reference to being either heterogeneous (*promiscua*) or universal (*universale*). These two characteristics of the ancient commons appear mutually exclusive: heterogeneous, on the one hand, universal or homogeneous on the other.

What happens to these two contradictory characteristics of the pre-state commons after what Grotius describes as the great divide, the emergence of state and private property? There are two ways to answer this question from Grotius' text. One might say that after the emergence of the state, the commons (*res communis*) is different. It is now only universal and boundless, its heterogeneity is universalized and made homogeneous. Or, on the other hand, one might say that after the emergence of the state, *res communis* begins to oscillate between a form of commons that can be used by the state (universal, homogeneous and boundless) and a form of commons that is more resistant to state capture because it still enjoys its residual heterogeneity which remains protected, as it were, in the authority of the ancient mythic picture of the Golden Age, an authorized truth which Grotius includes in his new category of Natural Law. Judging from nineteenth-century references to the law of the seas, the latter scenario forms the epistemic imaginary of the emergent international law with its confusing oscillation between *res communis* and *res nullius*. Once Grotius begins describing the sovereignty of the commons as universal and limitless he is heading in the direction of homogeneous space, what I have called "interstate" space. When he describes the commons as heterogeneous and boundless he is describing nonstate space. Grotius finds both spatial aspects of the commons in the ancient law of the seas.

Grotius' description of the pre-state ancient commons as boundless and universal is reminiscent of that other famous phantasmatic description of common space by John Locke. Locke is a student of Grotius' natural law theory. In our earlier discussion of Locke, we noted a strong connection between images of boundless homogeneous space, the emergence of the state, and the creation of property based on natural law arguments. The foundational image of undifferentiated expanses that Locke used in his description of the emergence of private property and the colonial state in the Americas is very much like Grotius' description of the ancient commons as universal homogeneous space. "In the beginning," Locke wrote in 1660, "all the world was America" (II.49.1). This projection of an undifferentiated, homogenous quality onto the heterogeneous (and unknown) terrain of the New World was the preamble, the spatial, epistemic imaginary behind the justification of European natural rights theory of property, the theoretical justification for dispossessing Native Americans of their land. The image of undifferentiated expanse functions politically in the same way as the metaphor of a *tabula rasa* (blank slate) in the extension of the dominium of Reason to nonEuropean minds: *tabula rasa* makes Euclidean space—everywhere the same, uniformly subject to the same laws, and abstract in the sense of being empty—the universal foundation of Reason. It is an originary abstract space that can serve as a foundation for the seizure of that space by the state or by individuals. Locke's strategic image of the vast homogeneous expanse of America may owe its force to Grotius' description of the communal "universal" quality of the seas once they had become *res communis* in relation to the state.

The important thing to note in both Grotius' and Locke's rhetorical strategies is the role played by the sense of sight. It is a visual quality attributed to vast fields and to the wide-open sea that mediates the boundlessness of common space into homogeneous space. In both Grotius and Locke, the ancient commons (either of the Golden Age or of 1492 America) is homogeneous space only in relation to the emergence of a theory of property. It is homogeneous space only on the cusp of its being occupied and possessed by individuals or by the state. In Grotius' natural law theory, the spatial imaginary of the modern global maritime commons is twofold: it is a dialectical product of the ancient commons transformed in the emergence of state and private property (homogenous/interstate space), and it is also a surviving remnant of the ancient commons with its mythic authority (heterogeneous space/nonstate space).

User Rights (Jus Utendi) in Pre-State and Post-State Commons: Law of Nations Fishing Rights and Natural Law Freedom of the Seas

How does this twofold description of the ancient commons (*res communis*) relate to Grotius' law of the seas? Let us return to the post-state land which "falls to no nation" (*populo nulli*) and has the qualities of being "undefined" (*indefinitam*) and boundless (*limitibus nullis circumscriptam*). It has none of the markings that would show occupation or possession. The discovery of this form of space is what leads Grotius to the following conclusion: "that which cannot be occupied, or never has been occupied, cannot be the property of any one (*nullius proprias esse posse*) because all property has arisen from occupation" (27). This argument then leaves Grotius with the task of showing how the seas cannot be properly occupied and thus cannot become the property of the Portuguese. But such a task is apparently not so easy to do. Are the seas in Grotius' work like Thucydides' and the Roman authorities' description of the ancient commons? Yes and no. Grotius begins building a legal description of the seas as commons:

> The question at issue is the outer sea, the Ocean, that expanse of water which antiquity describes as the immense, the infinite, bounded only by the heavens, parent of all things; the ocean which the ancients believed was perpetually supplied with water not only by fountains, rivers, and seas, but by the clouds, and by the very stars of heaven themselves; the ocean which, although surrounding this earth, the home of the human race, with the ebb and flow of its tides, can be *neither seized nor inclosed; nay, which rather possess the earth than is by it possessed* (*nequqe teneri neque includi potest, et possidet verius quam possidetur*). (37, my emphasis)

Here the seas are indeed infinite and boundless. Not only can they not be possessed, they are themselves agents who possess us. This description of the seas does not leave those waters as homogeneous, abstract space that can become an object of human will or possession. Instead this sea becomes a possessor in its own right, not as a form of human agency but as some other force with whom humans share the earth. A promiscuous and heterogeneous force indeed: not only is this sea not an object (*res*), it is not a subject. It is altogether heterogeneous and appears likely to possess humans rather than being possessed by them, recalling arguments found by today's environmentalists who are critical of Western law's species-centric description of the oceans as mere resources for human use. This argument is Grotius' strongest defense of the seas as *res communis*, a residual form of commons that was "left over," as it were, from the mythic division of an original land undifferentiated by either the state or by private property. In no way, Grotius concludes in *Mare Liberum*, can Portugal legitimately claim to possess this sea.

This is the sea of what the French philosophers Gilles Deleuze and Felix Guattari call "smooth space," a space without the striations or the marks of possession of the state. For Deleuze and Guattari, as well as the political theorists who have used their spatial concepts to think about sovereignty and property in emergent, postmodern spatial terrains such as the Internet and globalized capitalism, such space is itself an epistemic imaginary, a defining ground for the type of nonstate subject that can arise there. We will explore how the seas, outer space, and the radio frequency spectrum—spaces that move—offer theoretical and practical implications of this particular spatial imaginary for the law of the global commons in the next chapter.

Regarding Grotius and the picture he draws of how nations might govern the seas, there is a strong reminder in *Mare Liberum* that the state's striations in the seas are immaterial to truly possessing or occupying it:

> when (the Portuguese) divide up the world to the disadvantage of other nations, Grotius notes, 'they cannot even defend their action by showing any boundaries either natural or artificial, but are compelled to fall back upon some *imaginary line*. Indeed, if that were a recognized method, and such a delimitation of boundaries were sufficient to make possession valid, our geometers long since

> would have got possession of the face of the earth, our astronomers of the very skies.' (39, my emphasis)

The Tordesillas and other "imaginary lines" in the waters and in the skies cannot form the basis of legitimate claims of sovereignty, according to Grotius. But one could easily argue that in fact the power and effects of such "imaginary lines"—from the scientifically drawn lines of longitude and latitude that crisscross the oceans to the politically etched borders of nation-states—have been well recognized in law and they do become the *de jure* basis of the outline of states.

Furthermore, even Grotius' declaration of the seas as nonstate space is unstable. Grotius waivers in his definition of the high seas as nonpossessible. In *Mare Liberum* Grotius notes that if the sea could be subjected to national sovereignty, it could only be done by "(he) who holds in his power the nearest ports and the circumjacent shores" (43). But he quickly notes:

> even if a man were to have dominion over the sea, still he could not take away anything from its common use, just as *the Roman people could not prevent any one from doing on the shores of their dominions all those things which were permitted by the law of nations*. And if it were possible to prohibit any of those things, say for example, fishing, for in a way it could be maintained that fish are exhaustible (*potest pisces exhauriri*), but still it would not be possible to prohibit navigation, for the sea is not exhausted by that use. (43, my emphasis)

Here Grotius offers a prescription for two kinds of universal usufruct rights (*jus utendi*) corresponding to two kinds of space. The first user right comes from the ancient heterogenous commons. It is a residual right to commons related to subsistence, a right to take fish from the shores of Roman dominium. The right persists in natural law described as the law of nations because the shores are land from the ancient commons that, after the emergence of the state and private property, "falls to no nation" (*populo nulli*). The space of this usufruct right is thus set in the epistemic imaginary of a world, the commons, which preceded the invention of property. This commons persists in the now heterogenous space it shares with the state and private property, but it is not a property right. Rather, appearing in Grotius as a right to fish, it is a right to subsistence. Thus the right to subsistence derives from the ancient, pre-property commons and cannot be rightfully taken by any post-property entity, either state or private individual.

This first kind of usufruct right in commons is quite different than the theory of limited sovereignty that is generally attributed to Grotius, the theory of usufruct rights in nonexclusive, nonstate space (Green and Dickason 1988: 242). That right, referred to in international law as the *freedom of the seas*, is indeed the second kind of user right Grotius refers to in the above paragraph, the right to navigate the high seas. That second user right derives not from the law of nations (the law of Indigenous, nonRoman customs and practices) but from the law of physics and human reason, a secular school of the law of nature beginning to develop in the

European world at this time. Grotius was living through one of the bloodiest periods of European history, the Thirty Years War, when justification for massive bloodshed came predominantly from religious differences. Thus for Grotius and other natural law thinkers of this period, the discovery of universal, nonreligious principles as a basis for law was a hopeful move. Given a basis in human reason, Grotius could argue that it is illogical to think that navigating the seas is a right that could be exhausted by another's use. The seas are immense beyond the imagination and beyond the cartographic materiality of sixteenth-century Europeans. This second user right, the right to travel the open seas, becomes a foundational principle of international law by the late nineteenth century. Taking its name from Grotius' book *Mare Liberum*, this right becomes known as "the freedom of the seas". While merely a user right, its logic that the full exercise of one state's right on the high seas need not interfere with the full exercise of another state's right does not contradict the theory of full state sovereignty or private property. Contrary to many theorists of natural law, Grotius' concept of "freedom of the seas" does not provide a limiting principle of user rights in international law. It does not interfere with the logical premise of Western property regimes that derive property rights from possession. Rhetorically, it simply links inexhaustible use and nonexclusive use to the full power of the sovereign state and, importantly, to the idea of *res communis*.

But, as we noted, Grotius refers to another vision of *res communis* in the above passage, a commons related to fishing. Unlike the second user right (*the freedom of the seas*), this first user right does not have as a main criterion the exhaustibility of a domain. Indeed, fish are exhaustible—*potest pisces exhauriri*—as Grotius states. Neither is the first user right based on excludability or possession. Physically, Romans could have excluded nonRomans from fishing on shores throughout the Roman Empire, but they were not authorized to exclude others from the shores. According to Grotius, to do so would have taken away the first type of user right, a basic usufruct right to subsistence, a natural right that was inscribed in the law of nations. Fishing on all shores is permitted because the Roman law of nations classifies the shores as *res communis*. The seas were *res communis* under Roman law because, as Grotius explains it, the law of nations recognized the residual pre-property form of the ancient commons and a corresponding right, a *jus utendi*, for nonRoman peoples under the law of nations to their livelihood. Does the *jus utendi* regarding fishing from the commons introduce a sense of limits to the power of the state in international law? Absolutely. It sets a limit on actions of the Roman state but more importantly it creates an obligation of the state. The state whose territory includes the sea shores cannot inhabit that territory as a fully sovereign state. Rather, it holds those sea shores in trust for the fishing livelihood of all people—Roman and nonRoman. This principle of user rights is furthermore not based in human reason but in the mythos of the ancient commons and the variety of *casto foedere* that peoples devised to nourish themselves on all the shores of the earth. These *casto foedere*, these practices and rituals that contained know-how and principles of sharing common food sources, reside in the law of nations and form one strain of Grotius' understanding of natural law.

Thus Grotius' text offers several seemingly contradictory possibilities or principles in natural law to account for *res communis*:

1. *the fishing jus utendi*: the seas and shores belong to everyone (*res communis*) and everyone has a right to use them because they are the residual form of a pre-state, subsistence-oriented ancient commons protected by the law of nations and managed by *casto foedere* with territorial states (*res publicae* or *res privatae*) respecting peoples' user rights;
2. *the freedom of the seas*: the seas belong to no-one (*res nullius*) because they are physically incapable of being possessed, but everyone has a right to use them (res communis) because their use does not exhaust the seas and natural law supports this physical logic as a universal, natural right;
3. *might makes right*: the seas belong to no-one (*res nullius*) and therefore may be claimed by someone (*res publicae* or *res privatae*) if that someone can possess/occupy them; and
4. *the seas possess us*: the seas are not a thing, not an object of our will, not a res, and therefore not property; in these possessive seas we can have user rights but not property rights. Indeed in Mare Liberum the seas retain the same ambiguity that Grotius had set out to dispel.

Grotius in Modernity: The Power of Property Regimes and their Shadow on the Common Heritage Principle

Grotius' detractors, John Selden and other jurists of the day, held that the seas were susceptible of legitimate enclosure and could therefore be lawfully possessed by states (Selden 1652). The practice of Grotius' era was consistent with those passages of his writings in which the high seas were *res nullius*, open access but belonging to nobody and therefore susceptible to legitimate claims of sovereignty (possibility number three above). England used Grotius' arguments against claims of full sovereignty on the seas in order to counteract Spanish and Portuguese maritime rule. But at the same time England also claimed full sovereignty over the North Sea, the English Channel, and other ocean sites.

Legal historians who point to Grotius as "the father of international law" nevertheless emphasize that history turned to favor Grotius' reasoning on the matter of sovereignty over the high seas. They claim that by the nineteenth century, Grotius' concept of a natural right of *dominium* had bequeathed modern law the notion of a concept of limited sovereignty (what Grotius referred to as usufruct rights) that won out over his detractors' view of modern sovereignty as a right of *imperium*, an unlimited right of sovereignty over the high seas (Tuck 1979). Our reading of Grotius' work and its persistence in modern international law with respect to the global commons suggests otherwise. Contemporary legal historian Tuck notes, "Grotius was able to argue … that the sea was *not yet* private property in the modern sense, but equally that men did have rights of a kind over it and on it. What they enjoyed were the original rights of (analogical) *dominium;* they could take what they wanted, knowing that they had a definite right to do so" (61–62). From the perspective of our reading, there is a problem with this position. Grotius' theory of original usufruct rights applies not only to a "sea (that) was *not yet* private property in the modern sense" as Tuck states. It applied also to a sea that had resisted and then partially persisted in spite of the division of the commons into state and private property. Furthermore, the analogy to original rights, referred to by Tuck, does indeed stem from Grotius' analogy of the seas as part of the ancient commons. But which ancient commons? Is the analogy to an ancient commons which was universal and unlimited where human societies could take what they wanted, or is the analogy to the ancient commons as heterogeneous, boundless and yet governed by "inviolable compacts" (*casto foedere*)? The commons as interstate space that does not limit the full sovereignty of the state, or the commons of nonstate space where social contracts among users (which include nonstate entites) rule the day?

Theoretically, it was the view of the ancient commons as homogeneous, abstract interstate space, the commons as the dialectical result of the invention of the state and private property that won out in international law. This is the view of the high seas as a global commons in international law today. In such space, states have nonexclusive rights to use "resources" but very little legal sense of how to restrict or adequately limit that use. From a rhetorical perspective, these legal concepts necessarily fail to enact sufficient legal limitations because their proposal to govern the seas as (un)governable is haunted by mythic homogenous space which is "unlimited" and "universal." The striations of the modern law that covers the global commons thus tend to support the practices of full state sovereignty in the global commons. And yet, along with this conception of commons as interstate space, there remains nonstate space. The rhetorical oscillations between *res nullius*, *communis* and *publicae* in laws governing the commons today produce the contradictory conceptual terrain of both interstate and nonstate space.

In the late nineteenth- and early twentieth-century maritime law the seas were also conceptualized as open access *territoria nullius* carrying with them the colonial legacy of virtually no effective concept of limited sovereignty beyond those produced by war. The high seas were also conceptualized as residing both inside and outside the category of *territoria nullius*. Thus the seas were, like uninhabited lands and lands inhabited by Indigenous peoples, "open to acquisition and a reign of full sovereignty." And, as contradictorily noted in contemporary manuals of international law,

> the open sea, though *territorium nullius*, is not now susceptible of sovereignty, save in certain cases where prescriptive rights are claimed to sedentary fisheries on the sea-bed. (Lindley 1926: 80)

Thus, in the international law that supported imperialists of the early twentieth century, the open sea remained a problematic and unstable conceptual realm with respect to claims of full sovereignty. The high seas were placed in the category of *territorium nullius*, a category that elides with *res nullius* and has eventually come to include the atmosphere and outer space. This is a strange category. It appears to be ordered not so much theorematically—under the genus of a commons—but problematically, within the problematic of *terra/res nullius* which we have described as an oscillation or indistinction between *res nullius* and *res communis*, between interstate space and nonstate space.

Today the seas as *territorium nullius* continue to avoid limitations placed on the exercise of state sovereignty. They have developed into a competitive and nonexcludeable open access domain among nation-states with weak regulatory features. This arrangement has allowed for the current state of ocean waters as a global sink (for industrial scale garbage), a passage for multinational commercial vessels, a depleted source of fish, a site for national and international military maneuvers, and now a rising threat to coastal habitations around the globe due to climate change. Grotius bequeaths our current legal order the *de jure* understanding of limited sovereignty as "open access" (unlimited exploitation) and the contradictory *de facto* practice of states still imagining, professing, and acting out claims of full sovereignty in these spaces. In modern international law, the concept of freedom of the seas stands for open access, nonexclusive space while the concept of sovereignty refers to territorial, exclusive space. Still missing from this picture is the kind of limited sovereignty seen in the jurisdiction of subsistence user rights in fishing that Grotius also described with regard to the shores and seas.

What happened to Grotius' picture of an ancient commons that existed before the state and private property and yet persists even now after the state and private property have proceeded to cover the face of the earth? In 1967, the Maltese Ambassador to the United Nations, Arvid Pardo, made a famous address to the General Assembly concerning the high seas and the legal status of the sea-bed. Pardo was speaking at a time when countries were scaling up industrial production and the demand for mineral resources for energy and steel was looking well into the future. States were focusing on all potential mineral sites and, despite the technological difficulties of extraction, the seabed became a site of the industrialized world's attention. At the same time the developing countries of the global South began following the example of the United States and asserting territorial claims to the sea 200 miles out from their shores.[7] The traditional international limit and the political logic of this delimitation had been set in Grotius' era: three miles, the distance of canon fire that could protect the coastline of states in a wood-based economy. In the oil-based economy of the later twentieth century, new

7 The United States began the move to enclose the high seas in 1945 with the Truman Proclamation. I will return to the history of the enclosure of the ocean commons in the next chapter.

technologies permitting off-shore oil exploration and factory fishing triggered 200 mile extensions of state "economic zones." These extensions meant the enclosure of the earth's fisheries and ocean reserves, and until resolved by United Nation Third Law of the Seas Convention, initiated by Pardo in 1967 (and finally ratified fifteen years later), it meant the enclosure of key straits that impacted the right to freely navigate the high seas.

To stem the tide of enclosure of the seas, Pardo spoke to UN General Assembly on behalf of countries which lacked the technology and capital to mine the deep sea-bed. He referred to the sea-bed was the "common heritage of mankind," invoking a principle that gave all countries rights to its potential wealth and obligations to protect the deep seas from pollution and overfishing. Pardo proposed the creation of a trust fund that would receive the wealth of the ocean commons and use it to close the gap between the rich global North and poor South.

In several ways, the Common Heritage of Mankind Principle reflects Grotius' idea of a right in commons that preexisted and persisted through the cultural invention of state and private property. Several political theorists have argued that Pardo was not arguing for a property right in the notion of "heritage." The confusion arose, they say, in the translation of "heritage" into romance languages as *patrimoine* and *patrimonio* where it retains a strong association with possessory, property rights (Baslar 1998: 62). Like those passages in Grotius where the possessive, ownership interest is abandoned in search of a principle of user rights, Pardo's focus moves on to the appropriate management structure of the deep sea-bed commons and the equity issue of wealth distribution. While Pardo and his followers were disappointed with the results of the Third Law of the Seas Convention, primarily for its compromise regarding the 200 mile Exclusive Economic Zones, they point to the potential of the Common Heritage Principle to carry the notions of stewardship and trust management into the law of the seas where the law of property continues to dominate.[8] Decades of work by Pardo and others to create an international law of the seas based on commons principles failed. From a rhetorical perspective on the concepts and arguments that support this failure, not enough can be said of the power of the spatial imaginary behind the *res nullius* Roman category of property and the *terra nullius* doctrine of colonial sovereignty.

By the late nineteenth century, *res nullius* arguments are inseparable from the imperialist strategies of *terra nullius*. Some of the earliest legal arguments describing commons tenure in modern international law use the doctrine of *res nullius* to refer to spaces belonging simultaneously to no-one and to everyone. A key spatial figure used to construct this contradictory epistemology of domains

8 As noted in Chapter 1, so difficult is the task of creating a commons legal structure not tainted with the rhetoric and disabling concepts of private and state property, the Treaty Initiative for a Genetic Commons studiously avoided invoking the Common Heritage of Mankind Principle and using the term "heritage" in its definition of the gene pool as a global commons.

which are both excludable and nonexcludable is the metaphor of the sea. Through analogical reasoning, the seas bring homogeneous space to a modern legal imaginary whose (colonial) theory of property is built on the zero sign of *res nullius*.

Our reading of Grotius and Kant demonstrates that the metaphor of the sea has been an unstable tool to represent homogeneous space. The seas function rhetorically to produce spatial imagery which is both homogeneous and heterogeneous. If we are aware of this contradictory rhetorical function, it becomes easier to understand why the metaphor of the seas and, by extension, maritime law have come to dominate contemporary legal thinking on the status of the global commons. In modern international relations theory *res nullius* plays the same role as the high seas: the category of things that belong to no-one encompasses both interstate and nonstate space. On the one hand, it carries a notion of space as a degree zero, a clean slate on which (colonial) justifications of modern property claims can be launched, whether these claims are individual and private or whether they are centralized and statist. But on the other hand, *res nullius* also carries the sense that unknown potential could give way to self-organizing systems, that an unruly domain could be the basis for the innovation of new rules, new ways of knowing to emerge. This confusing juridical logic on the global commons was present in Grotius' arguments for a law to protect the freedom of the seas. And it is present in a newly confusing domain of the *res nullius/res communis* conundrum in international law, the radio frequency spectrum and its technological corollary, the Internet.

Radio Frequency Spectrum and the Internet: Postmodern Global Commons Foregrounding the Need for New Spatial Imaginaries to Protect Against New Technologies of Enclosure

> Since early in the 20th century, national governments have asserted sovereignty over the electromagnetic spectrum. These assertions were initially embraced as a way to control the monopolistic ambitions and offensive business practices of the Marconi Wireless Telegraph Company. They are still the basis of radio regulation. However, as wireless communication moves to higher and higher frequencies—into the range of infrared (heat) and free space optics (light)—it is becoming obvious that claiming sovereignty over radio frequencies makes no more sense than claiming sovereignty over colors of the rainbow. Is radio legally different from light? If not, might we someday need government permission to use certain colors of light for certain purposes, as with the invisible colors of radio? (Horvitz 2008)

Robert Horvitz of the Open Spectrum Foundation in Amsterdam noted at the 1st COMMUNIA Workshop on "Technology and the Public Domain" the ludicrous logic behind legal conceptions of one our more recent global commons, the radio frequency spectrum. Using the spatial analogy of "free space optics (light)," Horvitz asked whether these public airwaves were juridically thinkable in terms of current definitions of sovereignty in the international law of the global commons. Similar questions have been posed with regard to a related global commons domain, the Internet. In this section I examine spatial metaphors behind legal reasoning on radio spectrum and the Internet. Human communication relies increasingly on a global grid of wired and wireless telecommunications networks. The power to govern these global domains has been transferred from international agencies to nation-states that increasingly turn their licensing authority over to the private sector, allowing corporations to hold the power to create architectural standards for the governing protocols of the Internet. In this complex, inter-related arena of international law, an examination of key spatial metaphors and their historical connections to maritime domains of the global commons is instructive in understanding the successes and failures of commons-making today.

Because the digitally networked environment uses the electromagnetic radio frequency spectrum, it falls partially under the United Nations' jurisdiction of the law of outer space. Space law traditionally divides up frequency spectrum and, employing a centralized spatial imaginary, engages an international agency—the International Telecommunications Union (ITU)—to grant licenses to nation-states for their use. In a similarly centralized fashion, space law divides up and licenses the geostationary orbital routes for satellites. While the geostationary routes are an excludable commons— two things cannot occupy the same orbital space—the electromagnetic spectrum is not necessarily an excludable commons. Used to transmit the digital signals that enable all major forms of telecommunication from television and radio to the Internet, radio spectrum is not necessarily a limited resource like the earth's orbital pathways. Some 70 years ago, when the new technology of radio broadcast was finding its place in the legal commons, radio frequencies were licensed to allow a small number of large broadcast companies to send their signals to a large number of receivers without frequency interference. Today the situation has changed dramatically. The receiver equipment of Internet, cell phone, and local cable television network users is no longer passive. It can be configured to emit messages, even to emit them without interfering with other messages traveling on the same frequencies.[9] Despite this new situation where the electronmagnetic spectrum need no longer be viewed as a limited resource, the legal

9 In his study of the difficulties to overcome in building a commons legal structure for the digitally networked environment, Yochai Benkler cites a study sponsored by the National Science Foundation which funded a New Mexico school district to set up a network that allowed for communication between schools and direct access to the Internet. The school district's network used a part of the frequency spectrum that was already licensed to a private broadcast company but sorted out the signals in the receiving equipment. By using the frequencies as an "open road" instead of as a "toll road," the school saved thousands of dollars in Internet connector fees. Yochai Benkler, "Overcoming Agoraphobia: Building the Commons of the Digitally Networked Environment," *Harvard Journal of Law and Technology* 11, no. 2 (1998): 293.

organization of frequencies remains a centralized infrastructure licensing their use. Given the nonexclusive nature of this physical infrastructure, the recent movement for governments to auction licenses to corporations or individuals, in other words, to privatize the radio spectrum commons, is even more confounding.[10]

Despite proposed technological solutions—standardizing receiving equipment and agreeing on some general user rules, it does not appear that the law will shift its course from the decision to privatize. Both licensing and privatizing are centralized modes of property management. But why centralize management and propertize frequency when it is no longer considered a limited resource? How does the spatial imaginary informing the law of the digitally networked commons contribute to the dominant position of these arguments for enclosure? Are there spatial images that can grasp the complexity of this emergent technological infrastructure as a commons? Certainly the very nature of the space in question presents new challenges to our concepts of social space. In many ways, the moving space of radio waves and the virtual space of the Internet take us far from the tangible property distinctions we inherited from the Romans with their categories of *res nullius* and *res communis*. Or do they?

To answer these questions, I take a close look at the legal arguments made by one of our era's most prolific advocates for the creation of a digitally networked commons, the Harvard law professor Yochai Benkler. In a provocatively entitled 1998 article, "Overcoming Agoraphobia: Building the Commons of the Digitally Networked Environment," Benkler addresses some imaginal and conceptual problems of regulating the wireless communications infrastructure. Benkler notes:

> Our capacity to think about the truly central questions concerning regulation of wireless communications is obscured by the language we use to discuss the problem. When we speak of regulating wireless communications, we speak of managing 'a resource,' namely 'the spectrum.' Generally, we use market-based solutions for resource management, and therefore when posed with such a problem look for some*thing* to which we can affix property rights to be traded in the market. *But there is no such 'thing' as 'spectrum.' There is no ether out*

10 In the United States politically conservative organizations like the Heritage Foundation and the Progress and Freedom Foundation have advocated for exhaustive privatization of the right to control wireless communications capabilities. In the 1990s, US Senator Presslor introduced a draft bill that advocated exhaustive auctioning of perpetual property rights in spectrum. There is also advocacy for such privatization within the Federal Communications Commission. These groups push for the state to auction off frequency use rights in perpetuity to the highest bidder, treating the broadcast spectrum as if it were *res nullius* rather than *res communis*. The argument for privatizing the *res nullius* radio spectrum commons is a neoclassical economic one: the licensing system of a scarce public resource is inefficient and the best way to manage these commons resources is with the free-market mechanisms (see Benkler above).

> *there, no finite physical 'resource' that needs to be allocated.* (Benkler 1998: 289; my emphasis)

If spectrum is not a "thing," it should not fall into the Roman category of "res" and the baggage of property relations international law has inherited from Justinian, including the enlightenment reinterpretations of *res nullius* and the centuries of colonial sovereignty. Benkler argues that we should understand spectrum not as *res*, but as people communicating with each other, sending and receiving messages with equipment that uses electromagnetic waves to encode messages and transmit them wirelessly. Spectrum management should thus be about regulating how people use their equipment, Benkler argues, not about apportioning spectrum to governments and licensing or auctioning spectrum rights to private interests. When governments solve their spectrum coordination problems by prohibiting most people in society from operating radio transmitters and threatening to tear down their antennas and confiscate their transmitters if they communicate wirelessly without government permission, they are simply doing this, according to Benkler, "so that other people—broadcast licensees or spectrum 'owners'—can successfully communicate."

"The rhetorical effects of treating spectrum as 'a resource'," Benkler states, "obscure the more important choice to be made with respect to radio communications." The choice is really about whether wireless communication is framed as centralized control or as multilateral coordination. We need to understand that we are regulating equipment and not a resource. Benkler offers the analogy of how states regulate automobile traffic and networked computers:

> In the case of automobiles or networked computers, which involve similar coordination problems, our social choice has not been to give a small number of users an exclusive license or property right to control an input essential to the use of the equipment. Instead, in the case of automobiles, we have chosen to allow anyone to buy and use the equipment subject to certain "rules of the road" that allow equipment users to coordinate their use and avoid interference. In the case of networked computers, we have relied primarily on a public domain standard, TCP/IP, supplemented by industry and professional standard-setting procedures, and on competition in the equipment and service markets that rely on access to this standard. (290)

Benkler uses the spatial metaphor of the road—actual roadways and virtual superhighways—to explain how a conundrum of usage has been traditionally solved in modern societies. "Because roadways are operated as commons, anyone who can walk or has the wherewithal to purchase the necessary equipment (a car, a bike, or wheelchair), can choose when, where, how, and with whom to travel without needing permission from anyone else." Benkler notes that "non discrimination in pricing and service can no more substitute for individual control over communications than efficient train travel can replace the freedom of the open road" (Ibid.).

I want to focus on the metaphor of the road and what it contributes to an understanding of the global commons. Benkler's analogy is really an extension of the modern road metaphor into the virtual space of a global Internet highway. There are then two levels of the road metaphor to explore here: first, the more tangible road and second, the virtual Internet. The road metaphor allows Benkler to argue that international and national governance of the radio frequency spectrum can apply something like scaled up traffic rules to create a workable global commons in spectrum use. On the one hand, this spatial logic allows Benkler to emphasize user rules that allow individuals to enjoy the "freedom of the open road" (echoing Grotius and the "freedom of the seas"). The "freedom of the road" metaphor makes the government policy that allows state entities to sell off spectrum use to cable and cell phone companies so they can, in turn, sell these rights off to individuals look like highway robbery. On the other hand, there are areas of the road metaphor that Benkler does not go down: the American highway system was initially created for military as well as commercial use (a detour that would also fit the creation story of the Internet). Benkler does, however, focus our attention on another connotative level of the modern open road: its psychological dimension. There are two dominant psychological connotations of road use in modern industrial societies, freedom and fear. The title of Benkler's essay is "Overcoming Agoraphobia," referring to an illness afflicting those who develop phobic aversion to open, public space. Literally, agoraphobia means fear of the *agora*, the Greek work for marketplace. Benkler only uses the word agoraphobia once in the entire essay. Outside of its use in the title, there is no further mention of agoraphobia, but through ellipsis its rhetorical value hangs over the essay. With this sparse use, Benkler suggests that those who aim to enclose the radio spectrum are pathologically afraid of the open access nature of a virtual global commons with its freedoms and potential for self-governing structures. Following other connotative elements of the agoraphobia spatial metaphor in modernity, however, we would find ourselves back in the epistemological arena of empty space.

A historical look at agoraphobia demonstrates how empty space is part of its semantic field and, by way of Benkler's analogical use, part of the semantic field of our current understanding of the global commons of radio spectrum. Agoraphobia arises as a spatial disorder of modern industrial societies in late nineteenth-century Europe. The term itself was coined in 1873 by Dr Otto Westphal, who invented it to speak of the growing clinical presence in Berlin of young men who were unable to cross over the wide, gaping public squares that had recently been erected in European capitals. When faced with crossing these spaces of built emptiness, the patient would falter, break into a sweat, suffer wild heart palpitations and, if not frozen by anxiety, rush to the nearest wall or physical support. In the late nineteen-hundreds, agoraphobics characteristically learned to avoid these new massive, expanses of public space created by the violent destruction of the cities' narrow street neighborhoods and the removal of their resident working classes to the peripheries of urban centers. Throughout Europe's large cities, agoraphobia was noted in this period by the burgeoning field of psychiatry. Today, the psychiatric literature shows that agoraphobia is predominantly a women's disorder and its incidence has spread globally along with the international design principles of the Euro-American megalopolis. The clinical picture names as the sites of the contemporary agoraphobic's greatest fear the stultifying homogeneous expanses of urban freeway and, that other great architecture of modern isolation, the shopping mall.[11]

Agoraphobia has been used as a metaphor throughout the modern period to speak of the human (often gendered) fear of the felt emptiness of massive public space, the sterility of international style in modern city design, and the globalization of capital (Hirsch 2004, Bauman 1998). Benkler's analogy, not surprisingly, emphasizes the exhilaration of freedom in the expansiveness of the physical and digital open access highways of modernity. Invoking a robust and gendered American literary tradition of freedom on the open road, Benker uses agoraphobia as a metaphor for the fear of such freedom and the enclosure (through privatization) of that space.

To my mind, the metaphor is a telling one, mixed as it is through a suggestive ellipsis with the history of empty space in modernity. Perhaps outside the rhetorical strategy of its author, Benkler's metaphor of agoraphobia speaks less to Americans' fear of decentralized governance structures and more to the larger social lack of imagination we face with regard to how we think about globalized and virtual space. Why should expansive open space connote fear from the perspective of social psychology or a call to privatize from the perspective of classical economics? The answer, from a broader rhetorical perspective, may be in the deeply engrained cultural conception of such space as Euclidean, infinitely extended, homogenous space. This is the space that Locke referred to in his *tabula rasa* argument as the background of European personhood, something all humans—including Indigenous peoples once properly educated, could have in common. In previous chapters we have discussed how this spatial imaginary was connected to surplus value and private property. It is a space that, as Kant showed, supports no (overt) contradictions. With regard to the radio spectrum, a legal system that allows for allocations, licenses and some exclusive property at one end of the frequency spectrum and then open access commons—permitting cities to build open access WiFi infrastructures—at the other end, is a mixed legal model the imaginal supports for which seem to be out of the reach of our normative cultural codes.

In his essay, Benkler argues that "(b)oth owned infrastructure and the open road are essential to our relationship with the physical space in which we live." We should be able to think such juridically mixed space in our legal concepts

11 For a description of agoraphobia as a pathology of modern space, see Kathryn Milun, *Pathologies of Modern Space: Empty Space, Urban Anxiety, and the Recovery of the Modern Self* (New York/London: Routledge, 2007).

that govern the electromagnetic radio spectrum. This mixture of owned and open space is what Benkler has in mind when he speaks of treating spectrum as we do the Internet, as "a well-regulated commons" some of whose features would be privatized. The mixed commons Benkler and others call for here is noncentralized and partially nonstate space. It is odd that Benkler chose the metaphor of agoraphobia to speak of the fears invoked by this space. This heterogenous, mixed space is not empty space and it is unfortunate that another spatial metaphor is not readily available in our cultural imaginary to help us picture the complexity and potential of such dynamic space. Arguments for the creation of such a mixed commons in the radio spectrum are numerous but on the defensive. They speak of "a world where (licensed) 3G and (unlicensed) WiFi will work together, with recognition that they are complementary, not competing, technologies" (Norton and Ruth 2006: 281). But these calls for a mixed radio frequency commons entail a cultural repertoire of spatial metaphors that are not readily available in our modern *res nullius*-based tradition of international law.

The struggle for a similarly mixed ownership commons on the Internet points again to our cultural lack of spatial metaphors in support of a mixed commons domain. Legal arguments for the complexity of freedom on the world wide web need metaphors that steer clear of the powerful, hegemonic epistemologies of *res nullius* empty space. Indeed, the Internet does offer an analogy in support of such spatial thinking. Thus in addition to talking about spectrum as the unwarranted object of agoraphobic fear, Benkler could reach again for the Internet, this time as a metaphor for the kind of complex commons he envisioned for the international law of the radio frequency spectrum. "In the case of networked computers," he writes, "we have relied primarily on a public domain standard, TCP/IP, supplemented by industry and professional standard-setting procedures, and on competition in the equipment and service markets that rely on access to this standard," suggesting that TCP/IP was a robust figure of the public domain, a secure protocol well recognized by law, industry and markets (290). But a few years later, in 2002, Stanford law professor Lawrence Lessig writes what amounts to a dirge for the principle of net neutrality behind TCP/IP. Lessig, the legal innovator behind the worldwide Creative Commons licensing project and a vocal figure of the international movement for an Internet commons, was expressing his fears for how the key design principle of TCP/IP, the basis of the Internet's neutrality with regard to the data it moved from end user to end user, was under siege. At the bottom of this, Lessig noted, was an aversion among government and industry for the heterogeneous "space" that formed what Lessig called the mixed commons/property architecture of the Internet.

Referring more to the American context of Internet law, Lessig employs two metaphors to describe the Internet as a mixed commons domain.[12] The first

12 For a perspective on European law of the commons with regard to the Internet and radio frequency spectrum, see Cornelis Disco and Eda Kranakis, "New Industrial Commons in Europe Working Paper Nr. 2009-17," *Tensions of Europe/Inventing Europe*, May 27,

metaphor is architecture. The property system of the Internet, he writes, has three architectural layers. First is the physical layer made up of wires and computers. Owners have control over this layer which is governed as property. On top of the physical layer is a logical layer made up of the protocols that make the net run. These protocols are numerous "all chucked into a single box called TCP/IP." The protocols are created under a principle of network design called end-to-end that calls for the network itself to remain simple and neutral with respect to the third layer, the content. The content—blogs, wikis, emails, advertisements, YouTube—is the third level which the network will move from end user to end user. The equipment or physical layer can be smart, but the logical layer of the network itself will remain simple and neutral. This logical level was thus built as a commons, writes Lessig.

> … This feature of the network that distinguished it from all that had been built before—built this network into a commons. One was free to get access to this network and share its resources. The protocols were designed for sharing, not exclusive use. Discrimination, at the heart of a property system, was not possible at the heart of this system. This system was coded to be free. That was its nature.
>
> Thus on top of a physical layer that was controlled rests a logical layer that is free. And then on top of this free layer was a content layer that is both free and controlled. The free part is all the content that effectively rests in the public domain. The facts, data, abandoned property, undiscovered theft—this is the content that is open for the taking and that is taken openly. But it also includes a part dedicated to be open: open source or free software, dedicated to be free …
>
> This then is a picture of the complexity we call the Internet. At the bottom is a physical layer that is controlled: on top of it is a logical layer that is free: and on top of both is a content layer that mixes free and controlled.
>
> This complexity builds a commons. And this commons has been the location of some of the most extraordinary innovation that we have seen. (182)

Lessig's description of the Internet commons emphasizes its mixed, heterogenous nature. It is one part exclusive property, one part free/open access, and one part a mixture of private property and public domain. It is important to note that the free/open access part is not a static form. Its free, open nature cannot be protected by a

---

2009, (accessed December 15, 2009). For a discussion of global commons issues from an Asian perspective, see the paper "How Does an Asian Commons Mean?" presented at the Alternative Law Forum in 2008 by Lawrence Liang, Prashant Iyengar and Jiti Nichani online at: http://www.altlawforum.org/intellectualproperty/publications/How%20does%20an%20Asian%20Commons%20mean.pdf/view.

property rule, but rather through a liability rule. It is made of code, and code can be rewritten. Thus cable companies are enclosing the Internet commons by writing a layer of control onto the free logical layer. To avoid competition from online video, for example, cable owners place restrictions on the code of broadband users so that no more than 10 minutes of streaming video can be contract for at any time. When challenged in court, judges in the DC circuit have supported cable companies by saying that the code they write is a form of free speech, protected by the First Amendment. As broadband providers are allowed to discriminate, they dismantle the free, nondiscriminatory layer of the Internet. And, as Lessig laments, this enclosure is happening without a public outcry, without the understanding of Internet users.

To more fully describe how the commons is being enclosed, Lessig switches from the architectural analogy to a second metaphor: urban map-making:

> Because we believe 'the whole world is best managed when divided among private owners' we are changing the architecture of the net to enable it to be divided and controlled ... because we believe as our ideology says, we are remaking the Internet to fit this ideology. Without even pausing to understand it; without taking a moment to see how it might actually work. We are map makers who, upon finding the city doesn't quite fit our map—an extra building here, and river we didn't expect there—proceed to remake the city to make sure it fits the map. (183)

The "we" appears to be Americans blindsided by a belief that private property is the best map they have to manage how they move in the world. Americans are map makers, taking a tool (the idea of property) and using it to find their way in the world. When they encounter something in the built environment that does not look like the property on their map, they change the architecture to fit the ideological map. In this way, even the innovative mixed economic systems they build—like an open access free Internet commons—will be retrofitted to behave like a property system and the map—like the system of longitude and latitude that standardized the earth—will help create a world of homogenous space with regard to the law of property.

What we learn from Benkler's and Lessig's metaphors for the digitally networked global commons is that this commons is not the kind of "thing" found in the categories of Western property. (But then recall that Grotius, too, did not find the oceans properly categorized in Justinian's law; the oceans, Grotius argued, were also part of a primordial, *promiscua* or mixed commons, a residual persistence through the creation of the state and property.) Benkler's and Lessig's analogical thinking also describes a commons that is mixed—productively co-existing with property—but intolerable to the dominant categories of property. In terms of the spatial imaginary behind their thinking, both the radio frequency spectrum and the Internet are forms of heterogeneous space succumbing to the power of homogeneous space.

The Spatial Imaginary of the "Tragedy of the Commons" Thesis

Describing the reaction to a US Federal Communications Commission proposal that certain users at the higher end of the radio frequency spectrum be permitted to use the spectrum without licenses as an open access commons, Benkler notes how apologists for privatization and licensing invoked the "tragedy of the commons" thesis. They insisted, he writes, that a frequency commons without centralized control would bring chaos, "the spectrum will be overused and under-maintained … (and thus it) would suffer from the 'tragedy of the commons' effect" (294). The "tragedy of the commons" thesis is one of the most naturalized of all international relations arguments against noncentralized (nonstatist) forms of commons tenure. It is also an argument that is inherently supportive of the privatization of the commons and extremely influential in this regard.[13] The spatial imaginary it propagates and its relation to the history of *res nullius* and modern empty space is instructive.

In 1968, when environmental consciousness was coming to the fore of the Western world stage, the biologist Garrett Hardin published "The Tragedy of the Commons," an article that quickly became a "seminal" work of economic theory on how common property should be governed. In that article Hardin used a description of the premodern English commons framed by Hobbesian-inspired rational choice theory to explain why communally-governed land was inherently disaster prone. Thus Hardin described a classic tradition of an agricultural commons where pasturage is set aside as open access for public use. This system works well to the mutual benefit of those involved, Hardin claimed, as long as the number of cattle does not exceed the grazing capacity of the land. Once that happens, the inherent logic of the commons generates tragedy:

> The rational herdsman concludes that the only sensible course for him to pursue is to add another animal to his herd. And another … But this is the conclusion reached by each and every rational herdsman sharing a commons. Therein is the tragedy. Each man is locked into a system that compels him to increase his herd without limit—in a world that is limited. Ruin is the destination toward which

---

13 A colleague who teaches environmental law in the law school of a major American university told me in 2005 that he does not even allow his students to use the term "commons" when thinking about environmental law as the only reference they know with regard to the commons is Hardin's tragic thesis. In other words, a perfectly good term, "commons," is avoided in the teaching of environmental law because no normative use exists yet besides Hardin's thesis. Hardin's article has been reprinted over 50 times. Entire books have been devoted to exploring the meaning and implications of Hardin's memorable title. According to one global commons scholar, "The phrase 'tragedy of the commons' has slipped into common parlance at colleges and universities and is rapidly becoming public poetry. Discussion of the inevitability of such a tragedy is the lawful prey of economists, sociologists, philosophers and theologians" (Buck 1998: 46–47).

> all men rush, each pursing his own best interest in a society that believes in the freedom of the commons. Freedom in a commons brings ruin to all. (Hardin 1977: 20)

Hardin goes on to explain how the devastation of the English commons, caused by a flaw in human nature, was eventually resolved by the enclosure movement of the late nineteenth century. The historical analogy of the late medieval English commons is then offered as the reason for which all commonly owned areas must eventually be rescued either by privatization or by the external coercive management of the state.

While Hardin's theory has enjoyed a rich development in the political analysis of commons problems that begin from a premise of possessive individualism, its assumptions and its solutions have also been strongly challenged.[14] Feminists have asked whether herdswomen would have behaved in the same uncooperative way as Hardin's herdsmen. Others who find Hardin's view of human behavior to be "narrow, pessimistic, instrumental and indeed economistic" claim that his analysis simplifies the problem and does not allow for altruism. There are also those who point to the cultural assumptions inherent in this narrow rationalist perspective, claiming that it is based on an ideology of free market capitalism that has in fact helped to destroy so many of the traditional common property arrangements based on entirely different communitarian values[15] (Vogler 1995: 11–13). Since the publication of the *Tragedy of the Commons*, many scholars have pointed out that the logical argument Hardin makes masks the history of violence that has accompanied the enclosure of commons domains around the world (Linebaugh 2008, Liang, Iyengar and Nichani 2008).

While these critiques of Hardin's premise and solutions are important, I want to call attention to the historical inaccuracy of Hardin's description of the English commons. As many historians have shown, the premodern English commons was never a *res nullius*, nonexcludable, open access regime as Hardin described it. In the medieval English commons system, a villager was entitled by common law right either as a freehold tenant or through usage and grants, to pasture limited numbers of specific animals on the lord's waste. According to historian Susan Buck Cox:

---

14 Rational choice theory also informs the political thinking behind the notion of "the prisoners' dilemma" which gives a hypothetical demonstration of why rational individuals will fail to cooperate even when it is in their own joint interest to do so. With regard to the global commons, I owe the following summary of critiques of Hardin's work to Vogler discussion on pages 11–12. For a classical critique of the presuppositions behind Hardin's work, see the seminal work by Crawford Brough MacPhearson, *The Political Theory of Possessive Individualism: Hobbes to Locke* (Oxford: Oxford University Press, 1964).

15 For a description of successful commons management structures, see Elinor Ostrom, *Governing the Commons: The Evolution of Institutions for Collective Action* (Cambridge: Cambridge University Press, 1990).

> it is important to note that even from the beginning, the use of the common was not unrestricted. Common pasture of stubble and fallow was a feature of open-field husbandry from the start … and with it went communal control … the English commons was not available to the general public but was only available to certain individuals who owned or were granted the right to use it. Use of the common even by these people was not unregulated. The types and in some cases the numbers of animals each tenant could pasture were limited, based at least partly on a recognition of the limited carrying capacity of the land. (Cox 1985: 48)

There are many other examples in premodern Europe and around the contemporary world of successful local commons tenure systems which impose limitations on users. Even the current practice of a public right to access common space in national parks or deep-sea fishing is quite different than the original use of the term in premodern England. "The right of common," the commons historian Susan Buck-Cox writes, "was a right granted to specific persons because these persons had some prior claim to the land or because the actual owner of the land granted them that right in return for their services." Buck describes the legal right of common as:

> 'a right which one or more persons have to take or use some portion of that which another's soil produces … and is a right to part of the profits of the soil, and to part only, the right of the soil lying with another and not with the person who claims common.' This right is an ancient one: 'Recent archaeological and historical work indicates that in many places nucleated villages did not come into being until the ninth, tenth, or even eleventh centuries … But whatever their origins, the classic common field system probably developed with them.' … (cite) these rights were not something specifically granted by a generous landlord, but were the *residue* of rights that were much more extensive, rights that are in all probability older than the modern conception of private property. They probably antedate the idea of private property in land, and are therefore of vast antiquity. (Taylor in Cox 1985: 53, my emphasis)

There are many important descriptions of the normative and juridical rules that made up the tenure systems of the medieval English commons. What is most important with regard to Hardin's argument is that critics of Hardin agree that the decline of the English commons was not the result of unlimited access (which never existed), but rather the result of historical forces of the industrial revolution and agrarian reform. Hardin's argument was therefore not only historically inaccurate; it perpetuated a spatial imaginary of commons as unlimited, ungovernable, homogenous space. This metaphor of a space emptied of human rules and belonging is at the basis of rational choice theory and enjoys continued life as a political uncommons in the persistent arguments Benkler encountered describing the impossibility of protecting a fearful "chaotic" global commons for radio frequency spectrum and the Internet.

In addition to the metaphorics of empty space, another dominant metaphor for the Internet is "surfing." The analogy of the World Wide Web to the waves of the ocean ties the cultural picture of the digitally networked commons to the complex spatial thinking behind Grotius' problematic description of governability of the high seas. Even in Lessig's description of governance issues in the Internet's public domain we see an analogy with the mixed property, piracy and freedom Grotius described in his juridical picture of the high seas: "The free part (of the Internet) is all the content that effectively rests in the public domain. The facts, data, abandoned property, undiscovered theft—this is the content that is open for the taking and that is taken openly. But it also includes a part dedicated to be open: open source or free software, dedicated to be free ..." (Lessig 2002: 181). Just as Grotius offers a picture of a mixed, heterogeneous space as the site of original usufruct rights to commons along with the right to freedom of the seas, Lessig presents an equally heterogeneous virtual public domain of complex property relations mixed with calls for freedom of the Internet. Thus in digital space, the oceans continue to provide a metaphoric understanding of inhabitable, complex, heterogeneous space, the apparent antithesis of the uninhabitable, homogenous emptiness we find on the flip side of the ocean metaphor. On the other hand, Lessig's emphasis on "freedom" with regard to the Internet commons has drawn criticism. At the 2008 Asia and Commons Conference in Taiwan, participants discussed why it is that terms like "sharism" were more likely to gain widespread acceptance in Asia, in contrast to Lessig-esque terms like "free culture."

> The problem, as Liang pointed out, is that the words 'free' and 'freedom' have been irreparably polluted by American geopolitics and tainted by perceived agendas of regime change, making anything labeled with those words a hard sell in the developing world. Riffing off the expression 'free as in beer,' he remarked: 'free as in America is unhelpful.' There was a widespread sense among people in the room that an emphasis on 'public good' and 'sharing' will enable the movement to have a much deeper impact, ultimately. (MacKinnon 2008)

Freedom of the seas may be a concept in international law transferable by analogy to other global commons domains, but the extent to which it works for non-Western cultural subjects or even subjects not formed in the privileged context of a global hegemonic power is questionable.

When used as an analogy for the governance of global commons, the metaphoric seas can also entrain certain confusion. But this confusion can be explained, albeit in a highly abstract manner. The concept of limited (or mixed) sovereignty over commonly shared space has been influenced by the theoretical thinking, beginning with Grotius, of limited sovereignty on the high seas. When the concept of limited sovereignty is accompanied by the epistemic imaginary of the seas as universal, homogeneous unlimited space—as it was in for the most part in Grotius and generally afterwards in international law—the limitations placed on sovereignty appear rhetorically ineffective and nearly meaningless.

Such ineffective limitations provide the perfect evidence for the "tragedy of the commons" which foretells that commons domains will inevitably fall into misuse and chaos unless rescued by the sorts of limitations that only a centralized spatial imaginary can provide: only the state or a private concern can effectively manage space whose primary coordinates are given in Euclidean dimensions. Only state or private property can create ownership claims in domains of *res nullius.* Thus the spatial imaginary of international law is dominated by zero degree space. This is why Hardin's descriptions of the premodern English commons are ahistorical. They might as well be descriptions of the boundless homogenous aspect of the high seas.

Grotius avoided any mention of real historical commons tenure systems of premodern Europe in his work on the global maritime commons. When Grotius sought an analogy for limited sovereignty on a *res communis* sea, he did not turn to the landed commons of premodern feudal Europe. Instead he relied on an imaginary description of commons from a "mythic" age, a golden period of pre-state commons that he derived from Greek and Latin mythology. Indeed there is good reason why Grotius would want to avoid reference to medieval European commons traditions in his work. Primarily, Grotius' work sought an alternative paradigm to the legal arguments about property and sovereignty that were dominant in his day: it sought to replace the feudal model based in traditional commons and divine right with a legal system based on natural rights. Nature, in this new paradigm—this "first Grotian moment" as legal scholar Richard Falk has called it—had its own laws for maintaining balance. Nature mimicked the law of Reason. And reason was meant to inhabit the throne formerly occupied by God. The view of Nature obeying laws of reason is the underlying premise of neoclassical economic theory which trusted that the free market would always balance social welfare as long as it had open access to what it saw as an unlimited supply of nature's resources. And the seas, so apparently limitless, inexhaustible and ungovernable, provided the perfect spatial image for nature as an unlimited resource. The image of the domesticated pasturage of pre-modern England and continental Europe would not have lent itself to the open access policy which Grotius argued was a just manner of conceptualizing shared use of common space between the emergent nation-states of Europe. The high seas provide the perfect spatial imaginary behind a social economic paradigm new in the sixteenth century and continuing strongly today. Grotius' conception of the modern global commons as a nonexcludable, open access domain has provided the right spatial thinking for modern international law and policies of deregulated global capitalism. Its maritime spatial imaginary is consistent with the governance of the commons as ungovernable space, without restrictions to the boundless agency of free market capitalism and the exploitation of the state. Moreover, arguments for international law to restrict global commons by privatizing or centralizing the governance of commons space also rely on the same spatial imaginary which persists in the cultural logic of the tragedy of the commons.

Conclusion

In summary, the twentieth-century definition of commons in international law is marked by the philosophical and legal arguments that inform *res* and *terra nullius*. This means that the global commons is connected to a modern legal subject who is identified with the dictates of Reason and conceptualized in relation to empty homogeneous space (Kant and Locke). Furthermore, the common legal object of *res nullius* is conceptualized as boundless and empty, either by its association with nonstatist, often nomadic, peoples or by its association with the seemingly limitless expanse of the open seas. In the cases of nomadic lands and boundless seas, both spatial forms are eventually *res nullius* in international law because they are ungoverned (by a state). The logic of *res nullius* allows for two things: *res nullius* space may be captured by individuals or by the state in the form of property, and *res nullius* space may be conceptualized in international law as a global commons, *res communis*. In this later case, when *res nullius* becomes *res communis*, legal arguments oscillate between two types of global commons space: *interstate space* (which is regulated by centralized interstate agencies like the United Nations) and *nonstate space*, (which is ungovernable, nonexcludable, open access). The example of the radio frequency commons illustrates failures of this model for international law. The interstate commons governs with a centralized infrastructure. The nonstate commons is not recognized as governed because it cannot institute a centralized model. With regard to the radio frequency spectrum and the Internet, there is no robust spatial imaginary for a noncentralized, economically heterogeneous model of global commons regulation, even though, in the case of the Internet, the Creative Commons license system provides evidence of how such a disjunctive commons can work in practice. In the radio frequency spectrum, the real argument as to why it cannot be left as a commons, that is to say the real "tragedy of the commons" is not that it will produce chaos, but rather that it will produce something not readily understandable and/or too unruly to be controlled in familiar centralized modes that allow propertization and easy extraction of surplus value.

But the spatial imaginary behind global commons governance is much more complicated. One such complication is foregrounded by how global commons inherit a spatial imaginary from maritime law and with it a metaphorics of the seas as empty space. This means that descriptions of global commons are subject to the two rhetorical functions of empty space: first, their social infrastructure can be conceptualized from a degree zero, a clean slate of homogeneous, limitless Euclidean abstract space; and second, their social infrastructure can be conceptualized in terms of a "profoundly" empty space which is heterogeneous from the start, given to mixed, disjunctive arrangements whose limits will only be making themselves known as the social infrastructure is built.

These two aspects of empty space, these two rhetorical functions of its spatial imaginary, are not mutually exclusive. Theoretically speaking, as Deleuze and Guattari showed, we can speak of homogeneous space intensifying to a point where it no longer functions as pure extension but gives way to a complexity that is nonstriated, nonstate space. Practically speaking, the radio frequency spectrum was initially conceived to accommodate a large, centralized, state-licensed broadcast system but it has since developed into a myriad system of multilateral users that includes the Internet. These different yet nonexclusive spatial imaginaries show that what is now needed is a legal conception of the commons that can imagine space as in part centralized, in part open access, regulated and nonregulated. Most importantly, the drama of such diversity should not be conceived of as a tragedy of the commons. Rather the diversity must be imagined as the experience of limits that are productive, not reductive. Such limits are experienced when incommensurable systems are forced to communicate with each other, and they can only do so when they share a common space that is fundamentally disjunctive.

The legacy of a degree zero commons hampers the legal imagination as it seeks solutions to problems caused by the *de facto* unlimited sovereignty of nation-states in areas they share with other nation-states (the high seas, the atmosphere, and so on), with nonstatist Indigenous peoples (reservations, traditional forms of commons tenure, and so on), and with other living creatures (the earth as an ecosystem). To restate the problem for international law: when modernity is experienced as an increasingly vast, indeed globalized domain of homogeneous empty space, the experience of limits finds less and less reflection in or access to the laws that define the spaces we share with each other.

The next chapter takes a theoretical and practical look at the spatial imaginary informing the law of the seas and by extension the laws of outer space. It tracks how the two rhetorical functions of empty space noted above manifest themselves in the law that covers the oceans and the atmosphere.

Chapter 4
Covering *Res* that Move: Theory and Practice; Whales and *Res Divini Juris*

> As long as we limit our attentions to land areas and associate these together in terms of large land units, referring to the seas only as an afterthought, we inevitably etch deeper the impression given by our maps, that the seas are negative in human relations and hence form the great barriers between peoples … The fundamental error in poplar geographic thought is that of regarding the land masses of the continents as the basic divisions of the world. You and I know that this is false. Because the oceans are nearly empty, they do divide, but they do not separate. (Hartshorne cited in Steinberg 2001: 10)

Opening the High Seas to Include a Theory of Space as Motion

Social historians have noted that in practice the experience of the sea has provided concepts, technologies, modes of perception, and political frameworks that organize our living on the land. Describing one of the more decisive transformations of sixteenth-century Western Europe—the process by which the town overtook the country in terms of its economic and practical weight—urban historian Henri Lefebvre notes that:

> this was the point at which the town was conceptualized, when representations of space derived from the experience of river and sea voyages were applied to urban reality. The town was given written form—described graphically. Bird's eye views and (maps) proliferated. (Lefebvre 1991: 269)

Lefebvre draws our attention to the bird's eye view which, he claims, allowed for a particular sort of abstract space to take hold architecturally on a wide scale in the creation of modern urban space. It is easy to see how this aspect of the sea—its apparent homogeneity and the visual technologies that arose to striate it with lines of longitude and latitude in preparation of navigating its "no-man's-land,"—might be engaged in the production of modern urban planning. The rise of the gridded city and the metaphorical view of the land as an abstract expanse may well be indebted to the maritime experience of a striated sea, what Lefebvre calls abstract space.

Abstract, homogenous space often accompanied the extension of maritime law into various domains of modernity. In his discussion of the laws created to cover the Internet, Lawrence Lessig noted that concepts applied to the Internet were, sadly, like the abstract space applied by an ideologically set map-maker to the city:

instead of creating new tools to deal with the reality of a river or building not on his map, the map-maker proceeded to make a city that corresponded to his (ideological) abstract map. A similar metaphor of abstract, homogeneous space arose in Grotius' struggle to articulate universal, unlimited common space in international law. References to the maritime figure of a *res nullius* commons appear in the emergent commons debates surrounding biodiversity where arguments for intellectual property rights in genetic code are projected against a homogenous backdrop of *tabula rasa* empty space. The dominant figure of homogenous space is even folded back onto the picture of the late medieval English commons as we saw in Garrett Hardin's influential policy paper which reinterpreted premodern English commons as homogeneous abstract *res nullius* space. If indeed the maritime commons has become a prototype of global commons today, and if history shows us the material effects of the conceptual power of maritime spatial abstractions applied to life on land, the need is evident for a thorough understanding of the rhetorical power of this spatial figure so persistently informing our construction of global jurisdictions. In this chapter we begin by considering social theory that has reflected on the material and conceptual impacts of the spatial imaginary of the seas. What is the relationship between the seas and homogenous space? Do the seas impart other spatial conceptions that lead in other directions for the governance of common space in modernity?

Deploying the terms "smooth" and "striated" space, the French philosophers Gilles Deleuze and Félix Guattari have produced an influential ontology of space that places the seas in a key position.[1] In their influential work, *A Thousand Plateaus*, the authors name the sea as the model of "all striations of smooth space". The sea is "smooth" space par excellence and yet it was the first space to encounter the demands of increasingly strict striation. In the following passage, the authors describe how the smooth space of the seas becomes striated, homogeneous space for the use of the state:

> Maritime space was striated as a function of two astronomical and geographical gains: *bearings*, obtained by a set of calculations based on exact observation of the stars and the sun; and *the map*, which intertwines meridians and parallels, longitudes and latitudes, plotting regions known and unknown onto a grid (like a Mendeleyev table). Must we accept the Portuguese argument and assign (the year) 1440 as the turning point that marked the first decisive striation, and set the stage for the great discoveries? Rather we will follow Pierre Chaunu when he speaks of an extended confrontation at sea between the smooth and the striated during the course of which the striated progressively took hold. For

1 Deleuze and Guattari's work has been influential for contemporary social theorists describing globalization. See, for example, the works of Michael Hardt and Antonio Negri, *Empire* (Cambridge, MA: Harvard University Press, 2001); *Multitude: War and Democracy in the Age of Empire* (New York: Penguin Press, 2004); *Commonwealth* (Cambridge, MA: Belknap Press of Harvard University Press, 2009).

> before longitude lines had been plotted, a very late development, there existed a complex and empirical nomadic system of navigation based on the wind and noise, the color and sounds of the seas; then came a directional pre astronomical or already astronomical, system of navigation employing only latitude, in which there was no possibility of 'taking one's bearings,' and which had only portolanos lacking 'translatable generalization' instead of true maps: finally, improvements upon this primitive astronomical navigation were made under the very special conditions of the latitudes of the Indian Ocean, the elliptical circuits of the Atlantic (curved and straight spaces). It is as if the sea were not only the archetype of all smooth spaces but the first to undergo a gradual striation gridding it in one place, then another, on this side and that. The commercial cities participated in this striation, and were often innovators; but only States were capable of carrying it to completion of raising it to the global level of a 'politics of science.' A *dimensionality* that subordinated *directionality* or superimposed itself upon it, became increasingly entrenched. (1987: 479–480)

For Deleuze and Guattari, the sea is not only the archetype of all smooth spaces but the first to undergo the gradual striation of longitude and latitude. Commercial cities participated in this striation. As Lefebvre also noted, cities saw their gridwork spiral back as their own living spaces became geometrical living "quarters." But it was states that raised this striation to the level of a politics of science. That is why, for Deleuze and Guattari, under the influence of the state, the sea became the archetype of all striations of smooth space: the desert, the air, the stratosphere, and as we shall see in the next chapter, outer space.

The complex ontology of space described by Deleuze and Guattari requires further clarification. For Deleuze and Guattari, movement in space constitutes that space. And, importantly, space in this framework is a cultural creation. The mover, the "subjectivity," or the "sovereign power," creates space. But the subjectivity/sovereignty in question here is not that of the individual. Individuals do not create space any more than they create language or legal traditions. Individuals receive space just as they receive language and traditions of sovereignty. They become poets, city planners, and international lawyers in the cultural categories of a larger social order. Because of this larger connection between space and subjectivity with regard to striated and smooth space, a brief detour into Western psychology is necessary to fully grasp these concepts for the global commons.

In the West, space is often regarded as a kind of ground or "container" that holds us as subjects. Object relations theory in modern psychology, for example, describes mental space in this way. Human subjectivity, it postulates, is held in a container-like spatial imaginary that allows people to look out onto a world of perhaps fearful objects. It began with our first experience of space in our mother's womb, and then her arms, until little by little we learned to displace our container-needs onto "transitional objects," a toy rabbit, a car, and eventually an idea like the nation-as-fatherland, entities that could hold our identities in analogously comforting ways. Such formulations, in Deleuzian terms, are based on a *static* relation to *lack*: the lack of the original unity (mother/child) or the lack of the phallic usurper (the Oedipal father). In contrast, Deleuze and Guattari's anti-Oedipal model of subjectivity offers space as a relation of movement, of territorialization and deterritorialization. This relation is not based on the notion of lack, but of multiplicity. Lack and multiplicity are, in Deleuzian terms, two different kinds of "zero." The Oedipal zero is an originary lack that generates a series of substitutions. Zero in an anti-Oedipal system, on the other hand, is a "threshold of intensity," a moment where a level of intensity is reached that breaks up the aggregate into new forms or new multiplicities. From a psychological perspective, multiplicities, like subjectivities, are formations of the unconscious. But multiplicities are subjectivies that are inseparable from space and can therefore be understood at the larger social level. The *pack* is a form of multiplicity characterized by roaming nomadism (wolves or a swarm of bees being apt examples). Packs are related to smooth space. The *masses* are a form of multiplicity characterized by a static relation to striated space, masses being a form of collective identity that exists in relation to the state.[2]

These concepts of space as movement and stasis with corresponding subjectivities of nomads and states bring new theoretical tools to the cultural understanding of international law. Additionally, the corresponding idea of two kinds of zero—a zero which is conceived of as *lack* and a zero made up of *intensities*—is of singular importance to the cultural logic of empty space we have investigated in domains of the global commons. We can summarize our more complex understanding of Deleuze and Guattari's social theory of space thus far with another set of terms that capture the dynamic of intensity in relation to smooth and striated space: *extensio*—a term the authors use to refer to the Euclidean notion of a pure, infinitely extended space; and *spatium*—which describes the intensity of smooth space.

In *A Thousand Plateaus* Deleuze and Guattari note a pattern in the cultural logic of the striation of smooth space. In the aftermath of striations by the state, the authors tell us that two things can happen. The intensification of striation can lead in two directions. On the one hand structures of striation can reach a point of intensification where they break up (bifurcate) into something quite different from that which produced them. One example Deleuze and Guattari offer is what they call "retroactive smoothing." A megalopolis which expands the striations of its gridded networks ever outward might eventually produce shanty towns on its fringes, metropolitan extensions which are off the grid of electrical and communicative city flows and even beyond the territorializations of capital. Deleuze and Guattari describe it this way:

2 For a discussion of Deleuze and Guattari's spatial thinking with regard to urban planning and psychology, see Kathryn Milun, *Pathologies of Modern Space: Empty Space, Urban Anxiety, and the Recovery of the Modern Self* (New York/London: Routledge, 2006).

> In contrast to the sea, the city is the striated space par excellence; the sea is a smooth space fundamentally open to striation, and the city is the force of striation that reimparts smooth space, puts it back into operation everywhere, on earth and in the other elements, outside but also inside itself. The smooth spaces arising from the city are not only those of worldwide organization, but also of a counterattack combining the smooth and the holey and turning back against the town: sprawling, temporary, shifting shantytowns of nomads and cave dwellers, scrap metal and fabric, patchwork, to which the striations of money, work, or housing are no longer even relevant. An explosive misery secreted by the city, and corresponding to Thom's mathematical formula: 'retroactive smoothing. Condensed force, the potential for counterattack?' (481)

The cultural logic of empty space, following Deleuze and Guattari, defines a pattern whereby intensified striations may achieve retroactive smoothing. But the pattern includes another option for intense striations. They may produce something which mimics smooth space but which, like striated space, continues to organize flows within the parameters of the state apparatus. This is what Deleuze and Guattari call homogenized space:

> The more regular the intersection (of abstract, gridded spatiality), the tighter the striation, the more homogenous the space tends to become; it is for this reason that from the beginning homogeneity did not seem to us to be a characteristic of smooth space, but on the contrary, the extreme result of striation, or the limit-form of a space striated everywhere and in all directions. If the smooth and the homogeneous seem to communicate, it is only because when the striated achieves its ideal of perfect homogeneity, it is apt to reimpart smooth space by a movement that superposes itself upon that of the homogeneous but remains entirely different from it. (488)

Homogenous space shares features of what Henri Lefebvre calls abstract space but is more dynamic.[3] To picture this, I think of the rationality of the urban freeway system. Its aim with regard to urban planning is to make far flung parts of the city better "communicate" with each other: I can work downtown but live in a distant suburb, keep separate but also integrate my work life with my leisure and family life. But the more I extend this logic, the more I extend the freeway system, the greater the sprawl, the more hours on the road, the less time a parent has to tend to family life, and soon enough the suburb is no longer the ideal satellite of urban design. Highway rationality gives way to highway irrationality. But this irrationality is not necessarily of a different order than the original design. It is

---

3 Lefebvre appears to have recognized this function of homogeneous space in *The Production of Space*, even if he did not sufficiently deploy the concept in his historical analyses.

the product of it and remains tied to the original grid.[4] Homogenous space on the peripheries of the city, in this example, does not give way to smooth space as in the author's example of the slums that encircle Rio de Janero. They remain homogeneous space, communicating in an irrational way with the various parts of the city.

Smooth space in the Deleuzian schema is first of all presented as the seas, but this could be extended to all ecologically-complex systems. In *A Thousand Plateaus*, smooth space includes acephalous human systems like capitalism and the Internet, capable of worldwide reach. It also includes localized nomadic and other Indigenous tenure systems. Some have argued that the high seas as nonstate space is a form of smooth space, as it is a jurisdiction that permits all manner of political and singular entities—from NGOs to pirates and outlaws—to co-exist there (Kuehls 1996).

The point of this theoretical interlude is to provide new concepts with which to think about the spatial imaginary of the global commons in international law. Up until now, concepts like *res nullius*, *res communis*, homogenous and empty space, nonstate and interstate space, have served as analytical tools. Adding the concepts of smooth and striated space, and in particular the terms *extensio* (the space and logic of Euclidean extension) and *spatium* (the space and logic of motion and intensity) should allow us to examine more fully how international law extends itself to cover issues of *res*—space and things—that move.

For a work of social theory written in the early 1970s, *A Thousand Plateaus* presciently moved terms of social analysis such as subjectivity and sovereignty towards the spatial phenomena we more readily recognize in the Internet and other globalized formations today. With regard to the law of the global commons, the dynamic of homogeneous space described by Deleuze and Guattari can often be understood in terms of the legal concept of *res nullius* and its oscillating tendencies towards *res communis*. *Res communis*: a global commons which is set up for failure; a legal tool for early modern Europeans jurists to describe the open seas as a limitless domain for usufruct but not property rights; a domain that belongs to no-one and to everyone; jurisdictional realms which are created by international law as spaces which no law can govern. These would indeed be arenas set up by the striations of the state, creations of states that, because they obey a pathologically extended logic of states, will likely not function according to the rational rules of states. On the other hand, *res nullius* with no pretension to becoming *res communis* appears more like striated space that may or may not have the potential to intensify to smooth. *Res nullius*: a deeply a confusing category of property in Roman law that once encompassed the realm of the sacred on earth; a concept that could not be made to coincide with reason for Kant in his description

4 I owe these terms of highway rationality and irrationality to Michael Dear, *The Postmodern Urban Condition* (Oxford: Blackwell Publishers, 2000). For an excellent ethnography of this problem, see the documentary film (made by one of Dear's students) *Home Economics: A Documentary of Suburbia*, directed by Jenny Cool, 1995.

of justice and the secular state; the category of all things that could become the property of colonial sovereignty and thus the degree zero of modern international law; and finally, the name that capitalism gives to the public domain, a wasteland of all whose exchange value is not yet recognized by capital, a holding pattern for proto-property. The cultural history of *res nullius* recounts a legal pattern of making and unmaking homogenous space alongside the creation of global commons. All global commons struggle to defend themselves from *res nullius* even as they are thrown to their undoing in the popular understanding that they belong to everyone and no-one. "Radio frequency is not even a *res*," laments Yochai Benkler as he battles cable and cell phone corporations for the creation of a global commons regime in radio spectrum. Unless they can become culturally visible as something else, the domain of things belonging to everyone take on the burden of things belonging to no-one. This is the cultural logic of empty space, a spatial imaginary that carries the foundational fiction of a domain emptied of social relations.

The First Successful Practice of Global Commoning: The UN Convention on Whaling

In *The Global Commons, An Introduction*, Susan Buck offers whales as an example of something that would fall in the category of *res nullius* in Roman categories of property. Whales are wild animals that could become the property of whoever captured them. In later chapters of her book, whales reappear as a member of the only successful global *res communis*, the International Convention on Whaling. The journey from a *res nullius* to a *res communis* domain in international law is an important one for our study of the cultural logic of empty space. The oceans have long been the site of many attempts to create a global commons to control their degradation from garbage dumping, offshore drilling, and spills from oil tanker transport. But to this day the only successful global regime covering a commons resource is that which governs whaling, an industry whose economic vitality vanished long ago. But more than moving whales from an economic to an ecological sphere, the global commons surrounding whales found a way to recognize that these cetaceans had legitimate needs that went beyond current legal tools.

Before the mid twentieth century, an over-capitalized whaling industry enjoyed open access to whales for the lucrative whale oil business. By the mid 1940s the whale population was nearly exhausted. In 1946, 15 countries of a war-weary world created the International Whaling Commission. They agreed and decided on quotas and other restrictions for industrial whaling fleets. Their Convention on the Regulation of Whaling aimed to protect whales as a commercial resource. By 1962, however, industrial practices of whaling factory ships, explosive harpoons, and large deep-water stern trawlers continued to grow, and whale harvesting reached its peak with the recorded total take of 62,000 great whales. As whaling interests turned from the depleted oceans of the North (where conventions were drawn up between nations which were more or less abandoning the industry) to the unpoliced and unfished waters of the Antarctic region, the new technologies used by world fleets came to the attention of various environmental groups. When the whale population crashed in the 1970s, former whaling states like the UK and the US could afford to align themselves with NGOs and activist groups who sought to ban whale hunting. They enlisted the membership of other countries, such as Switzerland, which had never had an interest in such hunting, and by 1986 the Commission adopted a moratorium on whale killing that is still in effect today[5] (Buck 1998).

A moratorium is an odd legal forum for a commons. A moratorium is a delay or suspension of an activity or a delay of legal obligations to pay a debt. On save-the-whale websites, lawyerly friends of the whale are hoping that this moratorium will become permanent, a global commons structured as a permanent postponement. Juridically speaking, what are we waiting for? It is as if the international community does not yet have a legal category for this population of cetaceans. The moratorium has a provision for Indigenous peoples whose traditional forms of life are sustained by whale hunting, and another provision for scientists who study whales. These whales, coded by nonstate tribal societies and scientific communities, are killable. But for the true *res nullius* whale, the law is in a state of suspension.

The cultural imaginary played an important part in sending whales into this suspended legal state. By the time this first global commons regime reached an agreement on the moratorium, advances in underwater photography had also brought whales into the consciousness of large groups of citizens. In 1976, Jim Hudnall photographed live whales off the coast near Maui for the first time. Furthermore, the documentary work of Jacques Cousteau was bringing new images of the seas as a heterogeneous depth to many households. Likewise Greenpeace, in its anti-whaling campaign, offered television news programmers dramatic footage of whaling fleets using explosive harpoons on fleeing whales, while in between a manned inflatable dingy with the name Greenpeace emblazoned on the side protested the action. These were powerful images that created a briefly shared memory space for millions of viewers. In follow-up to these images, the noted US television news reporter Walter Cronkite cited a number of special traits which appeared to place whales and their cetacean cousins—dolphins and porpoises—in "a different moral category than other animals." Cronkite commented that there is something in humanity's ethical development "that is done violence to when men kill, without compunction, intelligent creatures which a growing number of people consider almost human" (Barstow 2001). In this period, then, popular culture began taking these giant mammals out of the category of economically identifiable species, and placing them in a fuzzy realm that was somewhere in between animal, teddy bear, and human. The International Whaling Commission itself advocated that whale-watching become a source of economic gain for former whaling communities. Once whales started to become like humans, they

5 See International Whaling Commission, *International Whaling Commission Homepage*, July 2009, http://www.iwcoffice.org/ (accessed December 21, 2009).

entered another category where the values of the *res nullius* market economy were insufficient to name their special status, as if that subcategory of *res nullius* Roman property law, *res divini juris* were reappearing in international law.

It is telling that when this area of international law tried to cover something that moved, it ended up in the strange temporal arena of a moratorium. Space and time are inseparable categories. The moratorium on whaling signals an ontological shift. It aims to take whales out of the category of natural resource, but it is unsure of where to place them. The seas, de-resourced with respect to the whale population, also change under this law. They are no longer the vast, static, homogeneous container for whales. They are a migratory home. In terms of Deleuze and Guattari's spatial concepts, the new law deterritorializes the seas from a striated series of zones which whales can get figuratively caught in and reterritorializes them as a dynamic arena reflecting the smooth space made by migratory animals.[6] The importance of the imaginary domain to the new environmental legal paradigm is without question.[7]

Environmentalists like Greenpeace routinely seek to circulate a counter image of the seas as a heterogeneous depth. They use global visual media—another analogous nonstate space—and simulcast their whale protection activities on the World Wide Web. In 2007, viewers across the globe watched the live online reporting of three Greenpeace ships that followed a Japanese industrial whaling fleet down to the Antarctic Whale Sanctuary to protest Japan's plan to kill up to 935 Antarctic minke whales and 10 endangered fin whales. Japan has ancient culinary traditions involving whale meat. While not a signatory of the Convention on Whaling, Japan was nevertheless in clear violation of the global commons convention despite its claim that it was killing whales for scientific purposes. None of the other signatories—not the US, nor Australia or the European Union—were traveling down to the Southern Ocean to stop Japan's unlawful behavior. The Greenpeace boats made the trip despite having their flags suddenly removed when their flag countries honored a request by Japan to deregister them (Japan, second only to the US in development aid, has a strong international arm). The Greenpeace ship had broken no law or regulation, but suddenly found itself out on the high seas without registration. Greenpeace travels to sites where international law,

6 Keuhls describes the Greenpeace whaling media campaign as an example of the smooth space of environmental politics, a new political space. See Thom Kuehls, *Beyond Sovereign Territory: The Space of Ecopolitics* (Minneapolis: University of Minnesota Press, 1996: 52–54)

7 In 2002, when a geographer working for the US Federal Government put online a map of the migratory pattern of caribou across the Arctic National Wildlife Refuge, an area the Bush Administration was trying to open to oil drilling, the geographer was promptly fired and his maps removed. The political cartoon Doonsbury recounted the incident in its syndicated comic, redrawing the maps for popular consumption (much to the dismay of the Bush Administration). See Lisa Getter, "Map Maker Fired Over Arctic Chart a Cult Hero," *Los Angeles Times*, May 19, 2001 (accessed at http://www.commondreams.org/headlines01/0519-03.htm; last accessed January 1, 2010).

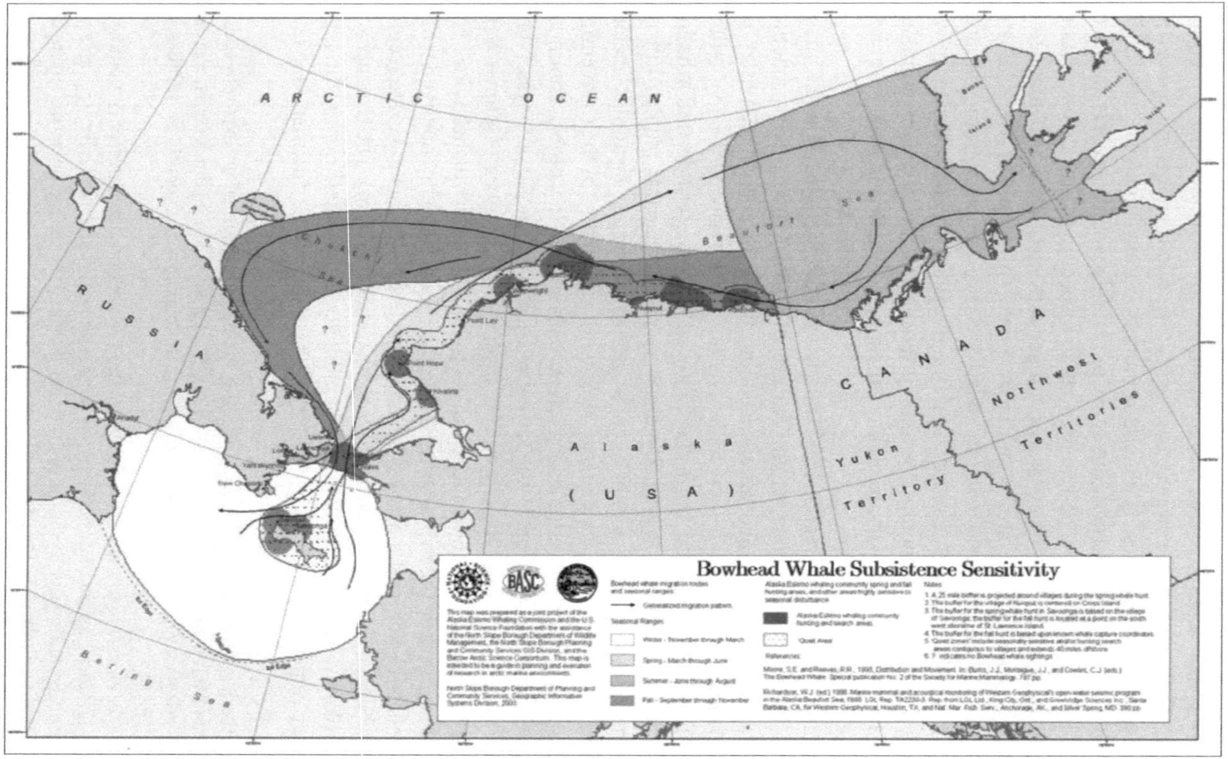

Figure 4.1 Map of whale migrations
Source: http://david-logan.com/General_HTML/GIS_HTML/WhaleMigrationMap.htm.

regulations, and treaties involving environmental protections are being violated and works to enforce the law. In the 2007 case, when the Greenpeace ship lost its flag, under international law any nation including the Japanese could attack and confiscate the ship at will.[8] The incident illustrates the "smooth" nonstate space of the high seas where outlaw and legitimate activity is indistinguishable. Japan claimed to be within the law, following the science loophole, but was clearly going against international norms and harvesting an endangered species with industrial scale techniques. No state would stop Japan. Only a nonstate, Greenpeace, would enforce the law. Greenpeace did have every right to be in international waters as the principles of the 1982 United Nations World Charter for Nature authorizes nonstate entities—non-governmental organizations as well as individuals—to uphold international conservation law, even in areas like the global commons which are beyond national jurisdiction. For Greenpeace, Japan's whaling fleets were criminal vessels operating in global commons. But since Japan had managed to get Greenpeace's statist allies to deny the use of their flag, Greenpeace was in the contradictory position of being both a pirate and a law enforcer. Globally shared commons jurisdictions have this complexity. They are nonstate, heterogeneous space giving legitimacy to entities that would, in territorial spaces, have none. These culturally constructed domains create a more diverse political economy. They permit *res communis* seas to function as a disjunctive commons with multiple and contradictory jurisdictions. And, despite the criminal activity of states and their flag partners, the *res communis* seas showed themselves perfectly able of being governed as commons, along with the migratory creatures that pass through them.

Zoning Ocean Waves and Capital Flows

Until the mid-twentieth century the sea was zoned into one vast *res nullius*, open access commons of non-excludable rival areas which states and commercial activities used on a first-come-first-served basis. Following the common law acceptance of Grotius' ideas (which triumphed over the more restrictive views of Portuguese and English), the ocean was fished, navigated and more recently laid with cables and flown over by aircraft, as nonsovereign areas open to the usufruct rights of all states. With the introduction of industrial techniques to maritime

8 Ironically, the engine of the Japanese fleet's whaling factory ship accidentally caught fire while under the gaze of Greenpeace's camera. One crew member died and the ship was stranded, threatening the pristine Antarctic environment with its vulnerable oil and fuel load. Greenpeace offered to tow it to safety but bureaucrats in Tokyo rejected the offer, calling Greenpeace a "terrorist" organization. See my report on the incident "Enforcing the Moratorium Commons: Of Terrorists, Pirates, State-Sponsored Industrial Criminals and Whales," *On the Commons*, February 21, 2007, http://onthecommons.org/node/1095 (accessed December 21, 2009).

resource extraction—whaling factory ships, explosive harpoons, and large deep-water stern trawlers—states extended their territories and depleted many ocean fisheries. As new techniques allowed for offshore oil and mineral exploration, states began to assert sovereignty over territorial waters and the continental shelf. The national moves towards enclosure of the ocean commons for purposes of mining and controlling fish stocks were spearheaded by the US Truman Proclamation in 1945 which claimed the natural resources of the continental shelf for the United States but still referred to the waters above as open access high seas. When Peru and Chile followed suit by proclaiming resource jurisdiction as well as sovereign rights over the seas extending 200 miles beyond their coasts, two United Nations conferences responded by attempting to reform and codify existing law of the sea. The *ad hoc* sovereignty extensions by many other countries of the global South finally threatened to turn 114 key straits of the ocean commons into territorial seas, thus making the seas unfunctional for interstate use. This was the context in which Arvid Pardo gave his celebrated talk to the UN General Assembly triggering a third UN Conference on the Law of the Sea. The sovereign assertions of this period resulted in the seas being divided into 200 mile Exclusive Economic Zones. Three zones, then, were sketched out on the worlds maritime mass: a first twelve-mile zone of territorial waters which border the coasts of nation-states; a second two hundred-mile zone for a sovereign state's exclusive economic use; and a third zone comprising the remaining areas of the high seas which would stay outside the jurisdiction of individual states. This third zone was the zone of open access, *res nullius* commons and it is the state of the ocean commons to this day.

In the 1970s and 1980s the division of the seas into "Exclusive Economic Zones," effectively enclosed 35 percent of the high seas, an area which according to scientists contained 90 percent of the seas' living resources. More recently, scientists are finding that they need to revise this picture of the high seas as a vacant desert, not only because of the role played by these areas of the seas in climate change, but also because:

> (i)n the deep-sea an even greater amount of species may be found than in all the other environments of the Earth together. The unsuspected high diversity of the deep-sea floor defeated the theory of *a desert-like environment*. This was supported by the overwhelming wealth of different habitats like seamounts, deep-sea trenches, reef-forming corals, submarine canyons, cold seeps and pockmarks. Especially the discovery of deep-sea hypothermal vents and their unique biological communities was one of the most important findings in biological sciences in the latter half of the 20th century. (Korn, Friedrich and Feit 2003: 9, my emphasis)

These new findings are bringing the deep seas under the scrutiny of jurists and activists. Coastal nation-states are engaged to police their own Exclusive Economic Zones with regards to fishing and garbage dumping while the remaining areas of *res nullius*, the high seas, have only very weak agreements governing garbage dumping and no policing agency to back up the laws. If social actors need to go outside the striations of the Exclusive Economic Zones of their states into the weakly-regulated international waters to dump garbage, they do so. Permits to dump come from the "flag state" (the state whose flag the ship flies, generally the same state in which the garbage is loaded). According to international law scholar, Vogler, there is no international inspection system for high seas dumping. States are supposed to give notification of the permits they issue for specific substances to be dumped, but very few in fact report these (Vogler 1995: 63). Finally, it is important to note that while all states have a *de jure* right to dump their wastes in the high seas, the *de facto* use of this right is much greater for the industrialized nations. The US and Britain, for example, were two of the more vociferous protectors of the right to dump their low-level nuclear waste from energy, medical, and military activities up until 1993 when, thanks to Greenpeace's steady campaign of direct and other action, an international regulatory treaty banned this practice (Vogler 1995: 62–64).

The zoning and garbage dumping allowed in the current law of the seas supports an exploitative regime that permits harms to move along ocean waves and currents while it directs profits flowing from open access use of space belonging to everyone to create wealth for citizens of the industrialized North. In the 1970s, at the height of the seas' enclosure, another zoning design was put forward to oppose the open access, free market high seas *res nullius* commons. As discussed in the preceding chapter, members of the United Nations known as the Group of 77, representing the countries of the global South, proposed to have the seas legally described as "the common heritage of mankind."[9] These nations of the less industrialized world put forth a new international policy that sought to make the profits and technology associated with the potential mining of the deep seabed more equitably distributed to the countries of the South. As with the earlier change in how international law covered whales, the context which triggered the new policy was the introduction of industrial techniques to maritime resource extraction, over-capitalized maritime industries and, coupled with the further enclosure of the seas into Exclusive Economic Zones, the fact that profits made from commons resources did not look like they would ever reach the southern states. While the attempt to create an alternative vision and political economy for the maritime commons eventually failed due to strong opposition from First World

9 In the International Relations community the less industrialized or "developing" countries of the global South are commonly referred to as the "Group of 77." The Group of 77 was established in 1963 by 77 nonaligned nations but its membership now exceeds 100 countries. The Group has dominated the United Nations General Assembly since the mid-1960s through its voting power. This alignment has shifted the power structure not only within the United Nations, but also in international negotiations in general. This was a large factor in the United States' denigrations of the United Nations during the Reagan Administration when Jeanne Kirkpatrick was the US Ambassador to that organization, and again in the first years of the twenty-first century when President George Bush took control of the White House and the US went to war in Iraq without UN sanction.

states—the final document (ratified some 20 years later in 1994) maintained the high seas as open access *res nullius*—it is worth examining these debates today as the Group of 77 finds itself in a similar situation with regard to the distribution of harms from rising sea levels due to global warming.

In the mid 1970s, the Group of 77 proposed that, under the Common Heritage Principle, a UN corporation called the Enterprise be established and funded by half of any private or state mining project entered into on the commons seabed. The Enterprise would assure the lesser developed countries of the capital and technology to continue their own operations and the profit would be divided among the member states (Webber 1983: 1436). After nearly two decades of negotiation, this treaty was ratified without the signatures of the USA, Britain, and West Germany who objected precisely to the Common Heritage Principle. The treaty that came into force in 1994 is a gutted version of the Group of 77's demands for a new commons regime, in effect preserving the "open access" policy of *res nullius*.

Given the relationship of resource extraction during colonial times, the global South sought a structure of commons governance that would allow compensation to flow from northern states should the South be forced to follow a less aggressive route to economic development due to environmental concerns. The same principle of historical retribution was at stake in outer space when states debated the potential of mining on the moon. In 2009, the Group of 77 was able to make small headway in the Copenhagen negotiations towards the creation of a fund that would direct countries of the global North to give financial and technological assistance to the South to mitigate the costs of clean energy practices and climate change refugees.[10] The same trust fund mechanism is being used (unsuccessfully thus far) in the Law of the Seed (Seed Treaty) to share with seed-saving farmers corporate profits from patents on plant germ, as discussed in Chapter 1.

The establishment of a trust mechanism to redirect capital flows coming from profits made through use of global commons points to a conceptual, if not yet actual, second Grotian moment noted in the Introduction to this volume. The trust mechanism frames nation-states as subjects with obligations attached to their use of global commons. Spelling out those obligations, the trust reframes nation-states' tenure in the global commons as that of a trustee, placing the global commons itself in the position of a public trust. The rhetorical possibilities for commons governance using a trust mechanism are paradigm-shifting. As global commons become public trust domains, trustees become stewards of these domains of the earth. And because these are domains that move, stewardship obligation can

10 The Tobin Tax, a tax on financial transactions, was supported by the Group of 77 and the European Union as a mechanism to fund the implementation of the Copenhagen agreement. The justification of a global tax on financial transactions that can be distributed to those in global need with regard to climate change is well on the way to understanding the financial system itself as a global commons.

expand as can the authority to predistribute flows of capital hopefully following principles of equity.

The legal institution of the trust is a unique one in international law. The concept of trust does not generally translate from English into romance language documents of international law because the institutionalized concept is unique to the common law tradition. In the Initiative for the Genetic Commons, for example, English, French, and Italian versions of the treaty all use the English word "trust."[11] Historically, the concept of trust entered English common law around the time of the Crusades, when soldiers leaving to fight in the Holy Land needed a mechanism to protect their land tenure while they were gone. Holding land, property, or assets for someone who is not there is a main function of the trust. Resolving problems that arise with regard to the management of the trust involves the use of equity law, unwritten moral principles of justice. (Equity law is another common law tradition without precise counterpart in civil law traditions where written code and strict categories of judgment take the place of the more flexible common law practice of precedent and analogy.) In US environmental law and laws that are emerging to govern the global commons, the idea of a public trust places governments in the position of trustees or stewards protecting the earth on behalf of all humankind, with humankind being a category of person that includes future generations.

Covering persons not (yet) present obliges law to extend its temporal imaginary. Since time and space are inseparable, the not-yet-present generations can only make their potential being known in a *res* that includes their potentiality. Philosophically, the idea of space that contains such potential or "becoming" was described in the writings of Henri Bergson and incorporated into Deleuze and Guattari's notion of smooth space as intensity. Becoming, as opposed to being, is associated with space as movement. If public trust law is to cover future generations, it introduces an active dimension into property law, a dimension that allows trusts to break orbit from the dominant sphere of property concepts. In this way, the law of trusts covers smooth space and the intensities or potentialities that arise there.

The legal concept of trust also exists outside of secular law. In *The Concept of the Common Heritage of Mankind in International Law* (1998), Kemal Baslar describes how various religious traditions contribute institutionalized notions of trust to the theoretical background of the Common Heritage Principle, in particular, the Islamic notion of *zakaat*, the annual contribution of two and a half percent of

11 "The Parties to the treaty … further agree to administer the gene pool as a *trust*"; "… de gérer le patrimoine génétique en tant que trust"; "administrar la dotación genética como un fideicomiso"; " amministrare il patrimonio genetico come un trust." For the French, Spanish and Italian translation of the treaty initiative, see The Foundation on Economic Trends, *Genetic Commons Treaty*, 2009, http://www.foet.org/past/GeneticCommons.html (accessed January 1, 2010). The concept of trust has some overlap with the Roman category of property of *universatis rerum*, or universalities in the civil law tradition. See Jane Ball, "The Boundaries of Property Rights in English Law: Report to the XVIIth International Congress of Comparative Law," *Electronc Journal of Comparative Law*, December 2006: 12–15.

one's wealth to charity. Baslar cites Judge M. Bedjaoui's understanding of how religious notions of compulsory charity take on the character of an institutionalized act:

> Why should the end of the twentieth century … not be equal to the ideas of the sixteenth century, during which jurists like Vitoria maintained that the Holy Scriptures designed the fruits of the earth as intended for the whole human race, be utilized by everybody and made available to all? And I am sure that in the powerful spirituality of India, there are sacred texts along the same lines. Why should not the twentieth century be equal to the spirituality of the seventh century when the revelation of the Koran proclaimed to all men that all riches, all goods belonged to God, and hence to all members of the community, hence in that consequence the '*zakat*' or giving of alms took on the character of an institutionalized compulsory act, a manifestation of solidarity among men … (Bedjaoui in Baslar 1998: 20)

The contributions of liberation theology and Buddhism also add to Baslar's expansive reflection on the "common heritage of humankind" principle.

Working out the political institutions of a global commons often leads political theorists to that very category that was dropped from Roman property law during the enlightenment, *res divini juris*. Some political theorists have proposed a reintroduction of the category in the context of a radical democracy. They propose instituting a *Res Divini Juris* License among the Creative Commons licenses instituted by Lawrence Lessig. Creative Commons licenses revitalize the public domain and offer legal support against the commodification of culture and privatization of meaning. The *Res Divini Juris* license would protect things that lie beyond the notion of human ownership, things that cannot be commodified or privatized. The project itself exists as a wiki page, part of *Wikipedia*, one of the most extensive knowledge commons to grow on the Internet. Visitors can contribute to the category by adding new wiki pages (Berry and Moss 2006).

The authors emphasize that while they are thinking of the "sanctity of life" and other qualities associated with the sacred, they are also thinking of how public law itself emerged in Roman law and the evolution of the "a radical democratic definition of positive community rights." Thus the authors claim they are part of a broader "humanist notion of a shared human capacity for love." And thus I am surprised to see that one of the principles that users of the *Res Divini Juris* license should agree to is this: "This license operates under a permanent state of exception. It is a result of radical democratic practices beyond the state." The authors are referring to the political theory of Giorgio Agamben whose theory of "the state of exception" we discussed in Chapter One. Considering this statement in light of the arguments of the *The Political Uncommons*, it is as if the power of the spatial logic of *res nullius* were asserting itself again. The state of exception is no other than *res nullius*, a category of the state created as its own outside where its laws do not obtain. It is not far from the jurisdiction of the permanent moratorium into which the whales, once hunted as *res nullius*, have now fallen for want of a positive law to protect them. *Res divini juris* are not outside the state or part of the state-created "state of exception." Neither are they part of the anthropocentric humanist tradition that, following Kant, made human reason the measure of all things. If anything they are residual forms of belonging that persist in modernity.

Conclusion: The Paradox of Interstate and Non-State Space

Deleuze and Guattari claim that the striation of the sea is the model of striation of all common space. In recent developments in the international law of the seas we have seen important aspects of the model which we can now elucidate using Deleuze and Guattari's vocabulary. In the juridically defined oceans, striation involves rendering common maritime space visible as nonstate, homogenous space, a degree zero for the legal infrastructure of rules that will maintain that maritime commons as an open access *res nullius*. Like all intensely striated space, open access *res nullius* has the potential to further intensify and become a paradoxical domain. Thus, on the one hand, even though legally it belongs to no-one, states have made the global commons function as homogeneous interstate space which tends to work to statist advantage. On the other hand, to the extent that it remains the domain of no state, it is nonstate space.

The environmental organization Greenpeace provides examples of how homogeneous interstate space can be converted (even if only momentarily) into smooth nonstate space and used to other, nonstatist advantages. In the case of the ban on whaling, Greenpeace used the nonstate character of the sea to de-resource it. It made the sea visible as a space for the pack movements of sea life and showed how the heterogeneous underwater space is in conflict with the striated space of *res nullius* as open access to marine resources. Greenpeace is one of the few agents who have been able to make themselves "visible" as a political agent in nonstate maritime space. When Greenpeace anchors its ships in the open seas downwind from nuclear test sites, it inhabits international waters as nonstate space even as the nuclear state power conducting tests in that site attempts to claim it for statist purposes. Here is how one international relations scholar, using a Deleuzian framework, describes Greenpeace's political strategies towards France's nuclear testing in the South Pacific:

> Greenpeace's protests … deterritorialize French territory. They bring out transversal effects of France's "sovereign" decision to test nuclear weapons. The consequences of the decision to test nuclear weapons are not contained by the striated space of state sovereignty. They occupy the smooth spaces of sea and wind currents, which carry the radioactive consequences of France's decision into other territories. They operate within a global ecology that cuts across national boundaries. This deterritorialization of French space is simultaneously a reterritorialization of not-state space. Greenpeace's presence in the South

> Pacific is not as a representative of a sovereign state in an international dispute with France, but as a nongovernmental organization with members from and connections to many sovereign states and other organizations. Greenpeace's activities reterritorialize in the name of a (potentially) global 'citizenry' that exists in no one place. (Kuehls 1996: 53)

The striations of the seas that enable states to exist as monadic units in a Hobbesian environment can also enable what Deleuze and Guattari call "lines of flight," transversal access to smooth nonstate space in the seas. Moreover, nonstate space may enable the environmental politics of Greenpeace as well as the multinational and unidirectional flows of capital. To the extent that the sea is a nonstate space, it is free of the boundaries that form the map of sovereignty relations: it is a space formed by migrating whales, for example, or by wind currents. When modern capital inhabits such smooth space it can avoid many statist restrictions (tariffs, for example, in off-shore financial operations) that would inhibit its realization of profit. But other agents, like Greenpeace, can also take advantage of this nonstate space.

Many of the observations made in this chapter concerning sovereignty relations at sea are repeated in international law as it extends *res nullius* ever upward. In Chapter 5, I examine the extended legal analogy of the law of the seas into the law of outer space. As we follow the rhetorical arguments and spatial imaginaries tied to the failures of international law to rise to the challenge of covering things that move, it is instructive to keep in mind the historical narrative of this failure. In 2000, a scientist concerned about the discovery of a new greenhouse gas which "molecule for molecule is 18,000 times more effective at trapping heat in the atmosphere than carbon dioxide," recalled that a similarly alarming rise in the atmospheric level of CFCs had prompted a successful international treaty (the Montreal Protocol) to protect the ozone layer. His plea was on the front page of the *New York Times*:

> Not too long ago, people thought we can dump anything we want in the ocean because it's so vast … It's the same thing with the atmosphere. It's just been seen as this huge sink. Now we can see it's not an infinite reservoir. People should realize that and start taking better care of it. (*New York Times* 2000)

How simple is the injunction to "see" the global commons differently. And yet this utterly banal connection between our spatial imaginary—the "vastness" of the oceanic and atmospheric spaces that "we can see"—and our legal realization of space—our normative rules for the occupation and use of that space—is both so obvious and also so profoundly challenging.

Chapter 5

The Law of the Sea Extended Vertically into the Law of Outer Space, and the Law of Outer Space Reterritorializing the Earth

> (W)ho ever reaches the Moon, Venus or Mars will not land there as a Russian, American, British or Frenchman, neither on behalf of Russia, the United States, England or France, but as a representative and on behalf of the Earth. (Valladao 1960)

> Joe and Sam are sitting on the Moon next to their spaceship enjoying a sandwich after having just planted the American flag on moon soil. 'Look Sam!' says Joe. 'The Russians have just landed and they're painting the moon red. What should we do?' 'Relax, Joe' says Sam. 'When they're done, we'll just paint "Coca-Cola" on top.' (Joke told to the author by a Bulgarian colleague in Hungary 1979)

When Sputnik was launched in 1957 international law entertained a brief dream of a new form of commons, a nonstatist, interplanetary law for outer space. By the time the US landed on the moon in 1968, however, international law projected an improbable nationalized imaginary onto the open skies. Since that time, sovereignty relations in outer space increasingly reflect transnational property interests. The question "Who owns outer space?" betrays one of Western law's most powerful rhetorical moves. The question has been asked of global domains of biodiversity, the high seas, the radio frequency spectrum, and the Internet. Each time we note the attendant cultural logic remapping space in terms of a propertied inside and a not-yet-property outside. Empty space has figured prominently in the epistemological imaginary of the arguments and counter arguments of these globally common domains and the same is true in the creation of the law of outer space.

In the early days of space travel, outer space appears at times a terrain for the infinite extension of scientific thinking and instrumental reason with its promise to eliminate the need for international law. At other times it presents a hopeful potential for extraterrestrial life and distant "local" cultures that will force innovations in legal thinking, a *jus novum*. In the end, international law helped create outer space as a vertical copy of the high seas supporting dominant military and property ventures. The cultural history of the spatial imaginary informing the law of outer space recalls Deleuze and Guattari's assertion that "the striation of the seas is the model for the striations of all smooth space."

This chapter explores the spatial metaphors jurists have used to render legal descriptions of outer space in the early years of space exploration, and to extend property and liability law into outer space in our contemporary era. *Res nullius* and *res communis* are applied to the furthest regions of outer space, producing improbable and at times pre-Copernican legal assertions. Empty space appears as a key spatial metaphor in these debates, but it accomplishes a diversity of rhetorical functions that vary from buttressing a new cross-cultural conception of global commons to supporting a "tragedy of the commons" thesis for the enclosure of outer space.

Empty Space, *Res Nullius*, and the Question of Who Owns the Universe

Leading up to the successful launch of Sputnik in October 1957 and throughout the 1960s and 1970s, an impressive body of international space law—a *corpus juris spatialis*—was created. It includes treaties, reports on the peaceful uses of outer space, declarations on legal principles, and conventions on liability and registration of space vehicles.[1] Legal descriptions of outer space betray the larger cultural paradigm of the ascendance of science in the industrialized West during the 1950s and 1960s. While the dueling space programs of the Soviet Union and the United States may have looked more like medieval tournaments played out against the heavens, they also reflected the paradoxical ideology that a successful exploration of outer space could be evidence that nationalist and cultural differences are obsolete in the face of the universal voice of reason behind scientific and technological progress (Silk 1964).

Some have argued that during the 1960s the international law of outer space was less about the vertical assertion of sovereignty and more about Western law's need to combat the declining authority of its humanist values—in particular the value of property—in the face of the rising authority of science and technology (Beebe 1999). Instrumental reason no doubt provided the bureaucratic imperative to spend vast amounts of national budgets on space missions during this period. But it was law (along with science fiction) that provided the terms to represent the unrepresentable, to represent outer space. In the early space literature, lawyers refer to outer space as "empty space." The debates of early space lawyers hammering out the terms of a global commons in outer space are noteworthy in demonstrating the power and pitfalls of the rhetoric of property as it stretches itself to cover empty space itself.[2]

1 For a general list of the documents comprising the body of space law, see Heidi Keefe, "Making the Final Frontier Feasible: A Critical Look at the Current Body of Outer Space Law," *Santa Clara Computer & High Technology Law Journal* 11 (1995): 345–371.

2 As one space law scholar notes, "the (space) treaties were perhaps one of the first real attempts at establishing a global community … The vision is good and the words are pretty ones, but the concepts have not been without their problems … consider the fact that among the words giving rise to difficulties due to lack of definition is the term 'outer space' itself. All of the activities governed by the five treaties purport to deal exclusively with activities related to outer space, and yet none of the treaties define outer space. Customary international law seems to have firmly established that outer space is the area in which

The following discussion offers a close reading of the texts making up the first, second, and third colloquia on the law of outer space that took place in the Hague in 1958, London in 1959, and Stockholm in 1960. International lawyers argued over the jurisdictional character and the terms of reference of the new space opened up by technology. Using the heritage of Roman property law, they debated whether outer space was *res nullius* and therefore open access like the high seas, or of a completely different nature demanding entirely new rules. Debating the property status of outer space seemed ludicrous to some, reasonable to others. It reflected a broader "who owns the universe?" discussion seen in popular and scholarly Western literature throughout the early years of space law. When US reporters famously asked Chairman Khrushchev a version of this question in 1959, he responded that he was too historically evolved to consider the issue.[3] The question of ownership in the West, notes legal scholar Barton Beebe, is a typical one which functions as a catchall for issues of extraterrestrial sovereignty, jurisdiction, property rights and so on. In the early space law debates it takes the form of a boundary question: where does sovereign airspace end and outer space begin? This question continues to elude space law to this day. In the early space law debates two positions arise with regard to this question. The first is held by those who argue that the law of outer space should be based on maritime law and its three political zones: territorial sovereignty, contiguous sovereignty and open access *res nullius*. The second position comprises those who claim that maritime law is an inappropriate model for the "legal vacuum" of outer space.

---

earth orbiting satellites move, and beyond. However, where do satellites move? While most satellites orbit the earth with perigees above 130 kilometers, there are a substantial number orbiting in the 110–130 kilometer range, and one satellite has been recorded as orbiting the earth with a low perigee of 96 kilometers" (Heidi Keefe, "Making the Final Frontier Feasible: A Critical Look at the Current Body of Outer Space Law," *Santa Clara Computer & High Technology Law Journal* 11 (1995): 346–7).

3 Krushchev responded to a US reporter's question concerning the whether the impact of Luna 2 on the surface of the moon signaled a Soviet intention to claim possession. Krushchev answered:

> "I do not want to offend anybody, but we represent different continents and different psychologies, and I would say that this question reflects capitalist psychology, of a person thinking in terms of private ownership.
>
> But I represent a Socialist country, where the word 'mine' has long receded in the past and the word 'our' has taken its place, and therefore when we launched this rocket and achieved this great thing, we look upon this as our victory, meaning the victory not only of our country but of all countries of all mankind."

Texts of Khrushchev Speech at National Press Club and Questions, *New York Times*, Sept 17, 1959, 18. Cited in Barton Beebe, "Law's Empire and the Final Frontier: Legalizing the Future in the Early Corpus Juris Spatialis," *Yale Law Journal* 108, no. 7 (May 1999): 1759.

At the First Colloquium on Outer Space, speaking to the confusion surrounding how high above the land the property arrangements of earthly law could (or should) be extended, the Hungarian born Stephen Gorove noted "Roman law distinguishes the air (*aer*) that we breathe from the air space (*coelum*) super adjacent to the land. The air," Gorove reminded the audience, "just as the ocean and the flowing water of a natural stream, was considered *res communis* and was not susceptible of private dominion." Gorove offered the following history of this problem in international law:[4]

> On the other hand, Roman law protected public and private rights in regard to space above the land whenever and as to such height as was deemed necessary for the occupation and use of such space. The frequently asserted Latin adage '*Cujus est solum, ejus est wsque ad coelum*' (he who owns the land, owns it to the skies) has not been found to occur in this form in the Roman texts but has been traced back more directly to a gloss from which the common law seems to have borrowed it, as evidence by Coke's and Blackstones' language.

International law's assumption that Roman law supports the vertical extension of private property is an invention of English common law, Gorove shows. The maxim has been repudiated under the impact of aerial navigation and modern communications. Even the US Supreme Court, he notes, has stated that "the doctrine of extending common law ownership of the land to the 'periphery of the universe' had 'no place in the modern world'."[5] Despite all of this, Gorove finds it odd that "Whatever enlightened thinkers may say … the idea of complete and exclusive sovereignty of a state in the 'air space' above its territory has become a firmly embedded principle of both international and internal law." The idea of an upward extension of sovereignty is indeed a popular one among space lawyers and the general public. Gorove argues that this position is untenable and states a view shared by many of his colleagues at the 1958 colloquium:

> the earth's rotation and the difficulties of exercising control over far distant regions make the proposition that sovereignty should be extended upwards indefinitely an impractical if not an impossible and meaningless abstraction. (Gorove 1959: 72)

4 Professor Gorove studied at Yale and taught space law at the University of Mississippi School of Law, helping to develop their National Center for Remote Sensing and Space Law which publishes the "world's oldest journal dedicated to the topic," the Journal on Space Law. The Center's website at http://rescommunis.wordpress.com/ is entitled Res Communis.

5 This adds more evidence to those who claim that English law dominates international law.

Gorove's comments reveal several problems that arise in post-Sputnik debates on sovereignty in outer space: first, space lawyers have difficulty locating categories of Roman property law in a post-enlightenment era, and second, enlightenment (that is, rational) thinking on property/sovereignty becomes irrational once it achieves the intensity of extra terrestrial heights. In other words, the prospect of law in outer space gives jurists pause as to the limits of the enlightenment enterprise. Outer space is not (yet) Euclidean space because it does not support a linear, vertical extension of rationality. Thus the political rationality of natural rights-based sovereignty may not be infinitely extendible as it was for Locke. This pause, however, is only momentary in the history of space law. Even in 1958, it co-existed with geocentric arguments to model the law of outer space on the law of the sea.

Those who argued for a maritime model for extraterrestrial space need to explain how outer space is like the high seas. The metaphor of "empty space" often occurs in the literature to describe the most outer extension of vertical space. Thus another jurist at the first colloquia, the American John Cobb Cooper, proposed that outer space be divided into three zones of jurisdiction following the Chicago Agreement of 1944 which set international regulations for air navigation by dividing up atmospheric zones following the three jurisdictional zones of the seas. In Cooper's proposal, outer space, like the atmosphere, would contain three zones above national territory: the first zone extending to aircraft would be considered "territorial space"; the second zone would stretch to an altitude of 600 miles and be referred to as "contiguous space"; a third space above this would allow freedom of passage for all—or open access *res nullius*, not susceptible to claims of sovereignty (Cooper 1959: 39).

Many participants at the conference defend the schema of the upper extension of the law of the seas. Nonetheless they sometimes admit the paradox presented by the third zone of outer space, as did the following Argentinean commentator:

> (t)he air, therefore, would be the element enabling us to delimit the zone of exercising sovereignty. The empty space, however, has no material element which could render a basis of delimitation. (Sera-Vazquez 1960: 141)

When pushed to defend the idea that outer space is like maritime space, however, jurists like Vladimir Koppal of the USSR respond that:

> against the institution of the contiguous zone objections have already been expressed by some authors, referring to the difference of natural conditions (and) aims followed by a similar sea zone. These differences, however, are not serious and do not exclude the existence of the contiguous zone with a different purpose as well as contents in the outer space. (Koppal 1960: 112)

In this way space lawyers made the larger claim that outer space is not defined by its contents or by the purposes for which it is delimited. In other words, they are claiming that "the empty space" operated like Euclidean space.

A defender of the vertical extension of maritime law, Vladimir Koppal defends the sea metaphor in outer space:

> outer space, the space located above the airspace, be its frontier later on defined anywhere and anyhow, is and should remain freely accessible under equal conditions to peaceful research and exploitation by all countries. Similarly to high seas the outer space, too, should be considered as *res omnuium communis* governed by the principle of freedom of navigation which is excluded from the sovereignty of individual states. (110)

Such proposals for common property in outer space were generally accompanied by some statement of "equal access" noting the principle of the freedom of the seas. None of these proposals for equal access, however, suggested that profits or resources from outer space be shared equally with all countries of the international community. Rather they simply asserted that all countries have equal access to outer space as a global commons.

The preceding arguments then are typical of those who support the sea as a model for the understanding of sovereignty in outer space. Those who oppose the extraterrestrial extension of maritime law also raise several interesting issues. First, several jurists dismiss outright the use of the law of the sea in outer space. One reason given is the problem of zoning. In outer space, "the concept of contiguous space based on the analogy of territorial waters," says Gorove, "is incorrect, unnecessary and not susceptible to implementation" (1959: 73). Another speaker, the German Welf Heinrich, finds that "(i)t is already a strange pretension to attribute physical reality to the space in general and above all, particularly to the empty space" (Heinrich 1959: 29).

For these jurists, not only is delimitation impossible, but more generally our physics are in question in outer space. Here empty space is not homogeneous. It is unknown and, quite simply, other.

The Argentinean Modesto Sera-Vazquez laments that all our legal thinking about space is for naught. Echoing the argument of Yochai Benkler with regard to the radio frequency spectrum, Sera-Vazquez writes, "space is not a thing (*res*). Therefore it cannot be the object of a law. We may quite certainly say that the space cannot be attached to any category of things known. It pertains to another new category. Those," notes Sera-Vazquez:

> ... who qualify the space as a *res nullius*, and those who qualify it as a *res communis*, and even those who call it a *res communis omnium* render an arbitrary qualification because they proceed from the principle that space is a *res* and then attempt to qualify this 'res' according to the effects due to this qualification itself. They did not ask themselves whether this space is a *res*.

> At the beginning of this error, there is perhaps an ego-centric (or rather terra-centric) conception which makes our planet the center of the universe. The earth however, should be considered from a more objective point of view, i.e. that the earth is not the center of the universe but an insignificant part of it. (1960: 140)

Sera-Vazquez points to a characteristic of global commons we saw in Grotius' analysis of the seas: namely, its strange agential character which allows it to "possess us" rather than become an object possessed by us. Sera-Vazquez is in fact addressing the Kantian framework in which *res nullius* as an Enlightenment legal category resides. If outer space is not a *res*, it cannot be an object of our knowledge or our laws since both presume the knower or lawmaker as a subject who apprehends objects of Reason. When space cannot be apprehended as an abstraction with delimited qualities, when it is loosed from its "ego-" or its "terra-centric" moorings, it begins to resemble what Deleuze and Guattari termed "smooth space."

In 1958 it was still possible at a foundational conference on space law to suggest that outer space, conceptualized as Euclidean empty space, was a geocentric idea that lent an absurd ground to any law of outer space. Even those who supported the vertical extension of maritime law could remark that, "We now need a kind of 'geography of space'—what we might call *spatiography*. This field refers, of course, only to the empty space itself" (Koppal 1960: 112). In this suggestion, empty space may be non-Euclidean but it only hints that a new order of legal thinking is called for. The non-Aristotelian basis of such a new order is suggested by a Portuguese colleague at the conference, Eurico Fonseca, who notes:

> there is an urgent need to substitute the classical criterion, derived from Maritime Law and based on a geometrical and practically static concept, for a new Space Law based upon dynamic considerations. (Fonseca 1960: 25)

The new conception of empty space in law then would be non-Euclidean and based on movement not stasis. Here again we see the major attributes of what Deleuze and Guattari call "smooth space," but no sense of the corresponding model of sovereignty for the inhabitants of a world that included such space.

Finally, the Brazilian jurist Haraldo Valladao restates the position of those who would support a form of sovereignty in outer space based not on pure but on practical reason. Suggesting a kind of universal common sense, Valladao refers to the idea of a basic subsistence right contained in the Roman category of *res communes omnium*. More interesting for our purposes is Valladao's comment that the law of Reason has nothing to do with the law of the seas which he sees as "an open field for war." Valladao's remarks are worth noting in length:

> (Outer space is) similar to that of the air, the water flows or the seas, it being a natural right of man … Juridically therefore, the interplanetary space is not '*res nullius*'; its not a space subject to occupation by anybody whether individual

> or association, thus becoming *res privatae*, or by any state thus becoming *res publicae*. The Roman law following the Natural Law admitted the existence of the *res communes omnium* which are at everybody's disposal and the use of which is a 'natural faculty for all men to supply the needs of life, and against which no law can be invoked.' Hence as such things do not belong to anyone, they become unsusceptible of appropriation and being non exclusive their use is free for all. In interplanetary space, however, we go further: it is *res communis omnium Universi*; it is a common good not only for all nations of the Earth, but for all nations of the Universe … (I)interplanetary space, being wide, limitless, indefinite, extraneous to the earth, serves not only the Earth's men and states, but also to the rational beings that may exist in all the planets and their satellites.
>
> … (However) *the high seas and their law*, appearing a theater of war and military power in the XVth and XVIIth Century, under the sign of conquest and enslavement, still based on sovereignty, in a real anarchic state—*neither can nor should supply any definite subsidy for the new, truly and wholly unique and humane interplanetary Law.* In the present law to the high seas, each State is, at the same time, a contending party, police and judge, while the high seas themselves are an open field for war … Little improvement has been made in the law of the high seas, after the Geneva Convention on the matter, held on April 29, 1958. (1960: 160–162, my emphasis)

Valladao's comments raise an essential contradiction about maritime law. The law of the seas, on the one hand, claims to base sovereignty on natural rights theory, which finds its post-Kantian legitimacy in Enlightenment notions of Reason; to this end the law of the seas divides the oceans into three rational zones: a zone of sovereignty, a zone of contiguous sovereignty and the high seas, a zone protected from full sovereignty claims because of its ungovernability, but enabling claims of limited sovereignty in the form of open access usufruct rights. But in fact what happens in the third zone, the zone of "empty space," is that the ungovernability brings a paradoxical and irrational dimension to bear on the rational order. Like the modern urban highway system, a rational project extended to ever further sprawling and eventually dysfunctional suburbs, the third zone of empty space supports an irrational life world: nuclear testing and radioactive garbage dumping. It is an unregulated global commons where usufruct rights in *res communis* are rights of equal access without equity in the technological wealth of users. Since states are not technologically equal, there will be unequal extraction of what should be the commonly owned resources of the third zone. Thus the third zone claims to be both *res communis*, belonging to everyone, and *res nullius*, belonging to no-one. It is a zone that supports war and pillage. As Valladao noted, the maintenance of this third zone creates an "open field for war." In maintaining a war zone, a nonstate space which states can inhabit to communicate violently with each other or from which they can monitor each other for military purposes, the law of the seas no longer supports a rational regime but a paranoid one. In this respect, Valladao reminds us that the function of the third zone has not changed much since its inception in the fifteenth and seventeenth centuries.

The projection of the three maritime zones into outer space foregrounds the nature of space that is at stake in the sovereignty arrangements supported by the law of the seas. Jurists at the 1958 convention referred to this zone as "the empty space." For those who supported the upward extension of maritime law, the third zone was a Euclidean space, uniformly present and static "homogeneous space." To employ the framework of Deleuze and Guattaris, "the empty space" is epistemologically *extensio*, an intensely striated space, facilitating its occupation by the state. On the other hand, jurists opposed to maritime models in outer space use "the empty space" to refer to a space without abstract delimitations and static positions. Here is an empty space closer to Deleuze and Guattari's definition of *spatium*. This empty space, note jurists like Valladao and Sera-Vazquez, undermines any sovereignty arrangements on the part of nation-states. Once the spatial dimension of sovereignty is named as "empty space," it begins to oscillate: empty space is the foundation of both state and interstate territories and it is the foundation of nonstatist, disjunctive commons with (as yet) unimaginable forms of governance.

Strangely enough, Grotius had already pointed us to the contradiction we are discussing here by his assertion that the ungovernable seas were also governable. Likewise, Kant's spatial metaphor that explained the exclusive domain of Reason ended up by finding in the ocean a contradictory space that placed Reason in a nonexclusionary relation to its other, the imagination. If we were to speculate on what renders these two systems of thought (law and philosophy) unable to stop the oscillation between one thing (the governable and reasonable) and its asymmetrical other (the ungovernable and the unreasonable) we would have to point to the image or metaphor of the ocean and the role it plays in constructing the conceptual foundation of juridical and philosophical thought. The ocean lends itself to (visibly) homogenous space and to heterogeneous or smooth space. As it takes on the shape of empty space it becomes a figure in modern law and in philosophy that directs our attention to a question resonating throughout modern social forms: what is the form of subjectivity or sovereignty required by (an imagined and materialized) empty space?

This question appears to be of special interest to the Latin American jurists reflecting on space law in its early days. What is the form of subjectivity or sovereignty required by empty space? Historically, empty space is a fictional projection of Western law. It has always been a space emptied of social relations. It is *terra nullius*, a space that refuses to recognize certain ways and forms of life. Extended to outer space, the kind of subjectivity and sovereignty the law can recognize in empty space is deeply related to the legal status of extraterrestrials. And indeed the topic of the treatment of extraterrestrials was one that absorbed many Latin American jurists of early space law. Their concern over outcast subjects and sovereignties takes the shape of a concern for the description of the empty space in which such entities arise. The Argentinean Sera-Vazquez, we saw above, called for a new, non-geocentric law that would correspond to the empty space that was not *res nullius* or *res communis* because it was not even a *res* to begin with. Similarly, the Brazilian Valladao was concerned with creating a new code of interplanetary law that would in no way reflect the terrestrial law of the seas, a site of warfare, a space where law was set up to fail. In his 1999 essay on early space law, Barton Beebe notes that Latin American space law scholars of this period famously take a special interest in the legal status of extraterrestrials. From the perspective of postwar decolonization, dependency, and even liberation theology, it makes sense. For jurists who are members of formerly colonized spaces on the earth, space law needs a spatial imaginary that can stand as the backdrop for law to project not the *terra nullius* clean slate of colonial sovereignty, but unknown worlds greatly different than the earth, worlds where law would be called on to protect, not eliminate, difference.

Latino jurists joined other space lawyers thinking about the kind of subjectivity and sovereignty that the new interplanetary metalaw would support. Andrew Haley, a leading popularizer of space metalaw in the 1960s, wrote that "(t)he indefinite projection of a system of anthropocentric law beyond the planet Earth would be the most calamitous act man could perform in his dealings with the cosmos." Haley proposes a new categorical imperative for the metalaw principles of outer space: "Do onto others as they would have done unto them. To treat others as we might desire to be treated might well mean their destruction. We must treat them as they desire to be treated" (Haley 1963: 395). Commenting on the work of these early space metalaw theorists, Beebe notes, "legal commentary on extraterrestrials expressed the full ambition of law's empire. It projected the rule of law and lawyers into the cosmos, and sought to establish legal knowledge over the unknown and the unimaginable. There would be *no blank spaces* on the law's map of outer space, no unregulated commons ..." (1999: 1769–70, my emphasis). Among the scholars of this branch of space law was William Hyman whose work *Magna Carta of Space* included as Article 18 "the peoples of the earth do hereby declare that they recognize the rights of sovereignty, ownership and control of any other planet by the inhabitants thereof" (Hyman 1966: 304).

Latin American and other metalaw space theorists were rightly suspicious of the vertical extension of the law of the seas into the law of outer space. Mapping the three maritime zones onto outer space and labeling the empty space as a kind of oscillating interstate/nonstate, *res nullius/res communis* space, partakes of a logic well known to postcolonial cultural theorists. By drawing the boundaries of what is inside and outside, the cartographer determines what is property and what is not yet property. Asking "who owns the universe?" is a similar cartographic, rhetorical move to create from what could be a global commons, a universe of proto-property. Commenting on the early years of space law, legal scholar Barton Beebe notes that for the most part "space lawyers envisioned outer space as a finite commons, already overcrowded with 'sooners,' that required strict borders, clear rules, and property-based incentives for efficient exploitation. Notwithstanding

Krushchev's idealism, early space law in the West insisted on viewing outer space as a potential 'tragedy of the commons'" (1999: 1763).

In this era of space law, empty space emerged from its subliminal work as the spatial imaginary behind colonial sovereignty and property law and was foreground as the problematic, unstable epistemic imaginary behind *res nullius* and *res communis* on the global stage. In popular culture empty space did the same: as the motherless backdrop for the new photography of the developing fetus on the 1965 cover of Life magazine, and as the lonely background for spaceship earth in the first photos of our whole planet taken from Apollo 17 in 1972, outer space was imagined as the place without others and without social relations. As a social imaginary, empty space at once moved the West toward an almost religious expectation of science and ignited a global environmental movement to live differently on the earth. The seemingly infinite background, then, when viewed as homogenous space of Euclidean extension, functioned as a rhetorical device for its opposite: a "tragedy of the commons" argument for enclosure by nation-states. When viewed as the unknown potential for other ways of life, empty space became the rhetorical invitation for a *jus novum*.

Paradoxes of Sovereignty in Postmodern Outer Space: Militarization and Commercialization

While the form of global sovereignty appropriate to extraterrestrial space was fully debated in the first colloquia on the law of outer space, by the 1980s it was clear that no new form of world government was to emerge.[6] There is still no international agreement on the subject of territorial zones in outer space, but that did not stop American foreign and domestic policy from favoring laws that protected the increased militarization and nationalization of outer space throughout the 1980s and 1990s (Goldman 1996). Strange territorial boasts defying the rotational movement of the earth came from the White House during this period of the second peak of Cold War politics when former US Vice President Dan Quayle divulged some wishful, albeit pre-Copernican, thoughts on the need for the US to develop an anti-satellite capacity. "Eventually," Quayle said in his capacity as head of the National Space Council, "we will probably see agreements to establish self-defense zones in space that will actually divide up space between the Soviet Union and the United States, and other nations. If others come within our zones, then in fact they would be infringing on our territory" (Hitchens 1990: 78). In 1997 the US military reported that ground-based laser weapons had hit an orbiting satellite target 260 miles away with record accuracy. In 2007 the Chinese successfully used a ballistic missile to hit a satellite target 500 miles above the earth. Following

6 As many commentators at these early conferences noted, the moves to nationalize outer space were already well entrenched. See Leon Lipson, "National Sovereignty of Outer Space," *Harvard Law Review*, April 1961: 1154–1167.

the law of the seas, these anti-satellite weapon trajectories mark the territorial equivalent of the canon fire that gave us the three-mile territorial zone of national sovereignty into the seas. But of course such territorial analogies make no sense in space that moves.

The Outer Space Treaty (1967) establishes outer space as a global commons.[7] The extension of national sovereignty into an outer space which modern physics has not yet been able to describe much less zone is more readily pictured than made into law.

Figure 5.1 US Space Command's Star Wars advertisement

7 The Outer Space Treaty (1967) was signed by all space-faring countries, including the US. It is formally known as the Treaty on Principles Governing the Activities of States in the Exploration and Use of Outer Space, including the Moon and Other Celestial Bodies. It represents the basic legal framework of international space law. Among its principles, it bars States Parties to the Treaty from placing nuclear weapons or any other weapons of mass destruction in orbit of Earth, installing them on the Moon or any other celestial body, or to otherwise station them in outer space. However, the Treaty does not prohibit the placement of conventional weapons in orbit. Recent attempts to expand the treaty to include a ban on all weapons in space instead of only nuclear and weapons of mass destruction, has not had the support of the US. Nevertheless, the treaty does appear to prohibit the kind of militarized actions proposed in the US Space Command's pamphlet. See United Nations, *Outer Space Treaty* (1967), http://www.unoosa.org/oosa/SpaceLaw/outerspt.html (accessed December 1, 2009).

In a pamphlet showing a space-based laser weapons project commissioned by the Pentagon's US Space Command in 2001, a red rocket ship is dwarfed by the enormous curve of the earth's surface and the vast depths of galactic space.[8] Only by projecting a barely, albeit sublimely, visible US flag in the empty space above the fragile looking machine can the poster communicate the sense that outer space can be mastered by some national force. The pamphlet's motto is "Master of Space"—a caption that ironically recalls the French translation of outer space as *territorium nullius*, "territory without a master". A 1996 publication of the US Space Command, "Vision for 2020," has a colorful depiction of terrestrial targets being hit by a laser rocket orbiting above. The pamphlet's first page notes how the US Space Command is "dominating the space dimension of military operations to protect US interests and investment." It places its mission in a historical context by noting that "military forces have evolved to protect national interests and investments—both military and economic. During the rise of sea commerce, nations built navies to protect and enhance their commercial interests … Likewise, space forces will emerge to protect military and commercial national interests and investment …" with "full spectrum dominance." The pamphlet demonstrates its broader economic mission by projecting a future world where the resource and wealth accumulation of some will need protection from those who are without. "The globalization of the world economy," the pamphlet explains, "will also continue with a widening between 'haves' and 'have-nots'." By having the ability "to control space" and from space, "to dominate" the Earth below, the US Space Command spells out a use of outer space that certainly runs counter to the peaceful vision of the Outer Space Treaty.

When territorial nationalism isn't asserting the operative terms for the legal description of the space commons, the private marketplace is. In 1998 at the 41st Colloquium on the Law of Outer Space held in Melbourne, Australia, one company sent its lawyer to present a paper defending its plans to land on and declare ownership of an asteroid (Doyle 1998). The company plans to challenge the commons status of outer space in international law and push the issue of property rights over resources in outer space. While this claim might appear to stretch precedent beyond the bounds of current legal imagination, it should be remembered that it was in the 1990s that Monsanto successfully asserted their property claim over plant genetic material. Also, the recent melting of the Arctic icecap and opening of Arctic waters for navigation and oil extraction has propelled a scramble of underwater flag planting and an inciting "who owns the Arctic?" debate on the cover of the popular national US *Time Magazine* (October 1, 2007).

Despite new technologies and a post-Cold War mood among space powers, maritime law has underwritten both the nationalist and the commercial aspects of sovereignty in outer space. The appropriateness of an analogical maritime dominion was still debated for outer space in the late 1950s, but some thirty years later the

8 Published by the US Space Command in 2001 to announce its multimillion-dollar contract with TRW and Boeing to build a Space-Based Laser Readiness Demonstrator.

matter settled in the legal doctrines that interpret the Outer Space Treaty and other regulatory documents concerning commerce, exploration and debris emanating from outer space. "In many ways," writes international relations theorist Vogler in his regime analysis of the global commons, "outer space may be regarded as equivalent to the high seas" (1995: 100). In the following cases, the impact of the dominant maritime analogy is both evident and challenged in the practice of the law of outer space.

Outer Space Law Falls Back onto Earth: Three Cases from the Contemporary Law of Outer Space

Radioactive Contamination by Falling Nuclear Satellites: Liability in Space Law vs. Ground Law

In 1978 the nuclear-powered Soviet spy satellite Cosmos 954 accidentally re-entered the earth's atmosphere and crashed in Canada. The reactor broke apart, spewing radioactive debris over a large part of the Northwest Territory. The Soviet Union paid Canada three million dollars to help with clean-up costs because, as a signatory to the 1967 Outer Space Treaty, it was liable for any damages caused by a space vehicle launched in its territory. On the other hand, when the nuclear reactor at Chernobyl exploded in 1986, the Soviet Union paid nothing to any of the countries lying in the transnational path of the radioactive cloud of debris that settled in Asia, Europe, and North America. While Chernobyl's destruction was of a far greater magnitude than that of Cosmos 954, the fact that the Soviet Union was financially liable to Canada while in the Chernobyl accident it was not liable to anyone is significant. What makes space law a better protector than current international environmental law concerning transboundary radiological pollution?

Laws covering transboundary environmental disasters on land and in outer space are different.[9] The Outer Space Treaty, for example, holds states responsible for the actions of non-governmental organizations within its control or jurisdiction while terrestrial international law does not. The 1972 Liability Convention and subsequent space law provide that states pay victim states compensation for damages caused by any nuclear powered satellite (private or public) emanating from their territories[10] (United Nations 1972). Neither customary international law

9 My information on these two cases comes from David Goren, "Nuclear Accidents in Space and on Earth: An Analysis of International Law Governing the Cosmos-954 and Chernobyl Accidents," *Georgetown International Environmental Law Review* 5 (1993): 855–895.

10 "The Liability Convention states that the launching state is absolutely liable for damage caused by a space object on the surface of the earth. International environmental law should follow suit and establish strict liability by treaty. In the Chernobyl accident,

nor existing treaty law provide the same joint liability principle for land-based nuclear accidents that release toxins. In present international ground law, operators alone are liable.[11] Even on the high seas, it is the operators of nuclear powered vessels who are themselves liable, rather than states.[12]

In the Cosmos 954 case, absolute liability was imposed by treaty, whereas in the Chernobyl case only general provisions of international law were available to determine and enforce liability claims against the Soviet Union. In several other areas—notification, registration, technical standards, definitions of damage—space law treaties appear to provide better mechanisms to prevent accidents and

---

this would have meant that independent of whether the engineers who began the failed experiment were negligent, the Soviet Union would be liable." David Goren, "Nuclear Accidents in Space and on Earth: An Analysis of International Law Governing the Cosmos-954 and Chernobyl Accidents," *Georgetown International Environmental Law Review* 5 (1993): 892. As of 1 January 2008, 86 states have ratified, and 24 have signed the Liability Convention. Importantly, in the Liability Convention states must agree to pay damages in order that the polluted area is restored to its pre-accident status, thus providing room for environmental clean-up claims. "Ground law" at present has no provisions for such restoration costs. Goren notes that legal precedents in international law use a concept of "limited" damages, defining damage as "loss of life, personal injury, and loss or damage of property. Thus "limited" damage to property is generally understood to mean diminution of value or the difference in market value before and after the accident. Thus, the "limited" damage does exclude the cost of repair or restoration" (889).

Subsequent space law includes: The Moon Treaty (See United Nations, "Moon Treaty: Agreement Governing the Activities of States on the Moon and Other Celestial Bodies," *United Nations Office for Outer Space Affairs*, 1979, http://www.unoosa.org/oosa/SpaceLaw/moon.html (accessed December 1, 2009). The Moon Treaty was ratified in 1984, but not signed by any major space powers. As of 1 January 2008, 13 states have ratified, and an additional 4 have signed the Moon Agreement; and the Principles for Nuclear Power Sources, a report drafted by the United Nations Committee on the Peaceful Uses of Outer Space in 1991 and sent to the General Assembly. While the NPS principles cannot have the effect of a treaty because the General Assembly lacks the authority to make law, there is a strong argument that they may be considered customary international law if they are unanimously approved by the General Assembly (Goren 881). See United Nations Committee on the Peaceful Uses of Outer Space, "Principles Relevant to the Use of Nuclear Power Sources In Outer Space," *United Nations Office for Outer Space Affairs*, 1991, http://www.oosa.unvienna.org/oosa/SpaceLaw/nps.html (accessed December 1, 2009) (NPS).

11 There is some disagreement here. Goren remarks that "the general principles of customary international law enunciated by the *Trail Smelter* and *Corfu Channel* cases make states liable, even for activities of non-governmental organizations. However, the proposed Vienna, Paris and Nuclear Ship Conventions make operators of nuclear facilities liable." (887).

12 Goren wonders if this is because at the time the applicable international law was created only states were operators whereas today commercial entities are also operators (876).

to compensate injured parties in cases of transboundary pollution. There is reason, then, to see international environmental law revised based on the law of outer space.[13]

The Cosmos 954 case is about environmental clean-up, but the comparison with Chernobyl and land-based law raises further questions. How might the spatial difference of outer space provide a new epistemic imaginary for legal reflection on transnational problems on earth? In terms of the vocabulary Deleuze and Guattari provide for analytical reflection, outer space is like the high seas and can thus function as *smooth space*: it has no precise limits; and despite the military and commercial successes discussed previously, notions of property, enclosure, and measure are dramatically different in outer space. When nation-states and corporate vehicles travel in outer space they must reinvent rules for getting along together. Given the nature of this space, the rules for movement may be quite different than the rules for moving in geocentric space of earth. Satellites draw their own jurisdictions as they cast their mobile shadows across the land. "Nomadic *nomos*," as Deleuze and Guattari would say, the laws corresponding to space that moves. In the case of extraterrestrial liability, laws falling back to influence environmental law on earth echo the theory of "retroactive smoothing." Thus terrestrial laws that protect "static" organizations of sovereignty and liability could undergo an indirect sea change from outer space, gaining a new flexibility more in line with environmentalist paradigms that describe the dynamic of life.

Space law is indeed caught between static and nomadic *nomos*. Despite the legal rhetoric to extend national sovereignty into (empty) outer space, international space law incorporates dimensions of smooth (nonstate) space. From the perspective of an environmental paradigm, there is the possibility that concepts of sovereignty issuing from space law are more effective than those grounded in earth law. The Cosmos 954 case suggests that states can become responsible in outer space in a way they can legally refuse on the ground. As their laws become disentangled

13 Goren underlines the importance of factoring costs of clean-up into calculations for liability in environmental law. If international law had a provision like the clean-up cost principle of the NPS Principles, the Soviet Union would have been liable "not only for the direct costs of destroyed produce and livestock, but also for the costs incurred by states in searching for radioactive contaminants on their territory and removing those contaminants." (890). This goes a step further than the "polluter pays" principle which has in practice worked as a mechanism of free-market environmentalism. "A market system gives power to those most able to pay. Corporations and firms, rather than citizens or environmentalists, will have the choice about whether to pollute (and pay the charges or buy credits to do so) or clean up. Tradable pollution rights mean that permission to pollute is auctioned to the highest bidder. Very polluting or dirty industries can stay in business if they can afford the pollution charges or can buy up credits." Sharon Beder, *Global Spin: The Corporate Assault on Environmentalism* (Chelsea: Green Publishing Company, 2002: 104). "The market, far from being free or operating efficiently to allocate resources in the interest of society, is dominated by a small group of multinational corporations which aim to maximize their private profit by exploiting nature and human resources" (105).

from geometric notions of territory, states become different kinds of agents in outer space. The practice of states in outer space may be forcing space law to articulate new contours in what was generally accepted as empty homogeneous space. We see this, for example, in the way space law continues to distinguish between airspace and outer space, when in fact the sovereignty questions that arise with spacecraft launches and descents, as well as satellite transmissions and remote sensing, defy those spatial categories.

In summary, states appear to assume greater responsibility in international law for transboundary environmental disasters descending from far above the earth than they do from earth-based disasters crossing state boundaries. While Outer Space Law's "polluter pays" principle is not the way most environmentalists would like to see states handle their transboundary responsibilities to citizens and the environment, states at least are legally bound to monitor the commercialization of space in a more responsible fashion than within their terrestrial borders. Liability for transboundary pollution was built into space law at the very outset because of the transboundary nature of the space that the law was framing. Space law deals with the responsibility of those who use a nonterritorial global space commons.

The Common Heritage Principle in Outer Space

In 1999 the United Nations General Assembly voted to reaffirm the Outer Space Treaty and its provision that space "shall be used for peaceful purposes." In the attempt to reestablish the treaty, the Chinese delegate called for outer space to be considered "the common heritage of human beings." Only the US and Israel abstained from supporting this update. Perhaps even more than the commitment to peace, the US found untenable the commitment to commons (Grossman 2000).

"Common heritage," as we have noted in preceding chapters, is a code word for a very long argument in international law over the description of global commons. The principle generally holds that defined territorial areas and elements of humanity's common heritage (cultural and natural) should be held in trust for future generations and be protected from exploitation by individual nation-states or corporations. While Arvid Pardo is credited with introducing the concept in the United Nations in the 1960s as a new term of political economy for the global commons on the high seas, many commentators note that the concept is first ratified by all major nation-states in Article One of the Outer Space Treaty which states that "(t)he exploration and use of outer space, including the moon and other celestial bodies, shall be carried out for the benefit and in the interests of all countries, irrespective of their degree of economic or scientific development, and shall be *the province of all mankind* (my emphasis)."

The US was an early signer of the Outer Space Treaty in 1967. But there is no economic development of the concepts of commons or heritage in that Treaty. Indeed it seems to me that the first use of Pardo's Common Heritage Principle in international law comes with the Third Law of the Seas Convention, a treaty that the US was also one of the few not to sign. Indeed all treaties using the terms "commons" with regard to global domains are treaties the US does not sign, including the 1979 Moon Treaty, Article 11 of which declares that "(t)he Moon and its natural resources are the common heritage of mankind." So, while states have tried to bring the commons principle from the law of the seas to the law of outer space, the most powerful space-faring nation has consistently refused to participate. There is a concerted care on the part of lawyers defending the perceived interests of the US that outer space remains *res nullius* and not *res communis*. This is evident at the administrative level in the US refusal to ratify. It is also evident in the spatial metaphors describing domains of international law as commons. What spatial metaphors form the epistemic imaginary of the Common Heritage Principle and how do these metaphors operate in domains the US promises to defend and not to defend as global common? To answer this question we need a fuller understanding of the operation of the Common Heritage Principle in the various domains where it has been proposed in international law.

Recalling our discussion of the Common Heritage Principle in previous chapters with regard to the law of the seas, biodiversity, and the atmospheric commons, the principle covers mineral and genetic wealth and environmental harms by subjecting states to a predistribution duty.[14] With regard to the ocean commons, after two decades of negotiation, states of the over-developed North refused to support the Common Heritage Principle portion of the Third Law of the Seas Convention that would have worked out a regime based on Pardo's concept of common property. In the end, economic enterprise zones enclosed the oceans (capturing 95 percent of the world's fish catch without instituting any effective means of thwarting over-fishing and the collapse of the world's fisheries) and placed an additional 35 percent of the seas under national control (Baslar 1998: 229). Thus res *communis* oceans were effectively governed as *res nullius* oceans. The very same drama was played out in outer space in the negotiations over the Moon Treaty.

The Moon Treaty, initiated by Earthmen's first steps on the moon, came on the heels of the Outer Space Treaty but never saw the same level of support. Both treaties offer a description of the legal status of outer space, but only the 1967 Outer Space Treaty went on to be ratified by all countries with space programs

14 See Peter Barnes' discussion of "predistribution" from John Rawls, *Theory of Justice* (Belknap 1971): "Rawls distinguished between pre distribution of property and re distribution of income. Under income re distribution, money is taken from 'winners' and transferred to 'losers.' Understandably, this isn't popular with winners, who tend to control government and the media. Under property pre distribution, by contrast, the playing field is leveled by spreading property ownership before income is generated. After that, there's no need for income redistribution; property itself distributes income to all. According to Rawls, while income re distribution creates dependency, property predistribution empowers. But how can we spread property ownership without taking property from some and giving it to others? The answer lies in the commons—wealth that already belongs to everyone. By propertizing (without privatizing) some of that wealth, we can make everyone a property owner." Peter Barnes, *Capitalism 3.0; A Guide to Reclaiming the Commons* (San Francisco, CA: Berrett-Koehler Publishers, 2006: 118).

(and some without). The Moon Treaty (1979), while popular with several countries of the global South, was not signed by any space powers.[15] Northern industrialized countries do not support the Moon Treaty because it proposes that mining on the moon be organized to share profits and technologies with countries which do not have space programs. According to one space law expert, "(t)he Moon Treaty has not been accepted broadly, however, because of the inclusion of the common heritage principle … As in the Law of the Sea, the industrialized nations disagree with the common heritage principle, but the less developed countries consider it essential" (Heim 1990: 834). An American space lawyer further explains that opponents of the Moon Treaty in the United States raised objections to those provisions seeking to establish an international regime to regulate mining activities on celestial bodies by claiming that the international regime would resemble the Law of the Seas' regime and thus "expropriate so much of the wealth that private and even national investment in space commerce would be stunted." Furthermore, they claimed, "the provision (would) create … a *de facto* or even *de jure* moratorium on space mining" (Goldman 1996: 90). Recalling the events of creating a global commons regime around whales, declaring a moratorium is an apparent first step in clearing the foundational degree zero *res nullius* from legal concepts that should be instituted to govern the domain as a commons. With regard to whales, the moratorium remains in place until the law finds a new ontological category (a new epistemic imaginary) for the object it seeks to govern.

Turning to the rhetorical power of the different metaphors used to describe commons domains in the successful Outer Space Treaty and the failed Moon Treaty, it is clear that the differing spatial imaginaries play an important role. As noted previously, the first article of the Outer Space Treaty declares: "The exploration and use of outer space, including the moon and other celestial bodies … shall be the *province* of all mankind." The Moon Treaty, on the other hand, stated that the "moon and its natural resources are the "*common heritage* of mankind" (Art. II.1). While the terms "common heritage of mankind" and "province of mankind" have specific legal meanings, it is interesting to note that in reference to outer space, the industrialized North's preference for the term "province" over the global south's preferred term "heritage" carries other meanings. Generally speaking, "province" refers to an administrative division of a country or state. It stems from the Latin term *vincere*, to conquer, and was used by the Romans to

15 Vogler notes that "Although the Carter administration signed the Treaty, ratification was overtaken by some of the same arguments and actors involved in opposition to Part XI of the Law of the Sea Convention. The Reagan administration withdrew it from consideration by the Senate and it has been ratified by only a relatively small number of the Lesser Developed Countries" (1995: 103). International law professor David Goren notes that, "(t)he United States has opposed the Moon Treaty because it declares the Moon and its natural resources to be the common heritage of mankind, and establishes an international regime to control the exploitation of those resources. (This treaty would prohibit) nongovernmental organizations (from) … hav(ing) any property interest in the surface or subsurface of the Moon" (Goren 1993: 880).

designate a country or territory outside of the Roman countryside but under Roman dominion, administered by a governor sent from Rome. "Province" is a term historically connected to the military extension of empires. "Common heritage," on the other hand, besides being close to the notion of a commons, refers to outer space as "heritage," property that descends to an heir … something transmitted by or acquired by a predecessor or through legacy or birthright. While both terms denote forms of property, the former (province) suggests a spatial relation to a center (Rome, central administration) while the later (heritage) suggests a temporal relation to a past. The term "heritage" thus brings to international law the possibility of recounting the bitter history of appropriations and expropriations among "mankind" and therefore the political project of reparations—exactly what the Group of 77 drew on by invoking the Common Heritage Principle in 1967. The term "province," on the other hand, seeks to organize outer space with respect to the centralized power of "humankind," a humankind whose identity is linked to a nonhistoricized present.

There have been numerous proposals to make outer space—including the geostationary orbits, radio frequencies, and celestial bodies—a *res communis* commons where profit- and technology-sharing would result not in the free market ideology of a pre-affirmative action "equitable access", but rather in predistribution of resources among citizens of the earth. Instead, the treaties that exist continue to describe outer space as an "open access" regime. This "first-come-first-served" system creates important political and ethical issues. Despite the discussions of the early 1950s where outer space was imagined by international jurists as *res communis* or *res communis universalis*, international law continues to treat the common heavens as *res nullius* in the nineteenth-century imperialist sense.

Remote Sensing

Further legal contradictions facing the nature of sovereignty and global commons in outer space involve the practice of remote sensing. In the early days of satellite technology, remote sensing concerned spy satellites and infringements on state sovereignty. Today it is about commercial rights to sell high resonance images that capture goings-on in all manner of private, state and public space. In the 1960s, the contradictions concerned how sovereign state coverage of adjacent airspace could be reconciled with satellite reconnaissance violation of that airspace;[16] and the

16 A Soviet participant at the Fourteenth Colloquium on Law of Outer Space in 1971 spelled out the contradiction: "The national legislation of the majority of states proclaim the principle of full and exclusive sovereignty of a state over the superjacent air space above its territory. This principle has been given written expression as an international legal norm international multinational and bilateral agreements on aeronautic activities. This universally recognized principle is a sum total of full and exclusive rights of each state to regulate within its territory all air navigation, the commercial activities of air transport enterprises … (etc). At the same time the states agreed on, signed and ratified the 1967 Space

further contradiction that the Outer Space Treaty zones outer space for peaceful practices, but satellite spying is an act of aggression to a sovereign country.[17] These contradictions drew international attention and were just as promptly overlooked. In the early days of satellite spying the United States enjoyed solitary use of the *res nullius* skies, what US policy referred to as their "open skies" policy (Goldman 1992: 248). The Soviet Union emphatically challenged this practice as a breach of the Outer Space Treaty and an invasion of state sovereignty. Once the USSR had its own satellite systems in orbit, remote spying was mutually tolerated but admittedly illegal. Thus international law scholar Richard Falk could write in the late 1960s that:

> Espionage possesses the peculiar quality of being tolerated while it is, at the same time, treated as illegal. This odd status, *comparable to prostitution* in many European countries, encourages a practice whereby states engage in espionage but do not come forward and defend an agent who is caught by enforcement techniques … the satellite program represents a novel pattern of espionage activity that renders obsolete many of the enforcement concepts that were developed in the course of dealing with traditional espionage … If we grant that outer space is 'outside' national territory, it is still quite tenable to reason through analogy to practice in contiguous zones on the high seas that a state may make extraterritorial claims to regulate to the extent that these claims are reasonably necessary for its national security. There would be no need to claim sovereignty up to the heavens in order to show that Soviet enforcement of its espionage laws in outer space was legally well-founded. (Falk 1970: 253, my emphasis)

The metaphor of prostitution Falk employs to address the ambivalent legal status of the new technological uses of outer space is an odd analogy. It compares the arbitrary disregard of law that powerful states enjoy among themselves when

---

Treaty, containing the main principle of freedom of space activities of all states. According to this principle … every state has the right to exercise space activities by launching of spacecraft (which can remotely enter national airspace through sensing technology), in compliance with international law, on the basis of equality and without any discrimination." Vahan G. Emin, "Spaceflight and the Problem of Vertical Limit of State Sovereignty," in *Fourteenth Colloquium on Law of Outer Space*, ed. Mortimer D. Schwartz, 201–203 (New Jersey: Rothman & Co, 1972: 201).

17 In discussing state practices involving satellites, international space lawyer Nathan Goldman cautions that "since 75 percent of all satellites are military in their designation, one should never forget that in practice space policy is predominantly military policy" (Nathan C. Goldman, *American Space Law: International and Domestic*, 2nd, San Diego, CA: Univelt, Inc., 1996: 226). Although Goldman will not categorically say that the practice of remote sensing by spy satellites is illegal, he rightly notes that the Outer Space Treaty bans the use of extraterrestrial space for aggressive military purposes. Many United Nations principles have been drafted over the matter of the legality of remote sensing but all remain, to my knowledge, nonbinding resolutions.

contradictions arise regarding their actual practices to the arbitrary disregard of law that powerful states enjoy with regard to the weakest among them, those subsistence-dwellers who are driven to sell their bodies because they have no access to legitimate forms of wealth-creating property. More interesting than what it says about state power and the law, the prostitution metaphor is a symptom of the state's political unconscious, its underside of unjust property relations benefiting the haves and punishing the have-nots. Equally interesting is Falk's argument for sovereignty assertion that is interest and function rather than territory specific. Thinking sovereignty in a (outer) space that moves, Falk claims that international law has found a better way to think about sovereignty as such, one better suited to the decentralized legal order emerging from post-World War II global decolonization. Falk's argument echoes what we found with liability law covering radiological pollution from nuclear accidents: space that moves opens the possibility of creating international laws better suited to the technologically produced realities of late modern global life. Like many hopeful jurists writing international law for a new era of globally shared space, Falk's 1970 treatise on international law decried the enclosure of the global commons in the sovereignty extensions being made at the same time by the US and several Latin American states 200 miles into the high seas.

As it turned out, the seas were eventually enclosed by national Exclusive Economic Zone jurisdictions and outer space was increasingly nationalized, militarized, and commercialized. Remote sensing became a fact of late twentieth-century statist being in the world. The information it provides on troop movements, weather conditions, agricultural yields, geological formations, and wildlife movements support a profitable industry of data interpretation useful for betting on the stock markets, controlling water resources, predicting weather patterns, managing wildlife sanctuaries, and extracting oil and mining minerals; all of this without resolving the illegal character of remote sensing as territorial trespass.

Now that satellite technology is a fixture of extraterrestrial space, the sovereignty debates arising from remote sensing of foreign states have receded and the issue of access to and profits from remotely sensed information has taken center stage. Beginning with Reagan-era privatization of the US satellite industry in 1984 (which included continued public subsidies and eventual re-nationalization in 1992), multinational ventures have made satellite financing, construction, and launch, a mixed bag of state and private initiatives. Gathering and disseminating remotely sensed information is a highly lucrative market that includes international agencies' tracking geographical changes to monitor global warming, and private car owners using GPS dashboard technology to find their way home. Importantly, all these social actors are enjoying user rights to globally common space as defined and protected by the Outer Space Treaty. And while this outer space is less empty than it was 40 years ago, its principles remain loosely defined in law, as does its relation to our fictive and increasingly arbitrary delineations of sovereignty on earth.

Of Prostitution, Subsistence Rights, and Space Law Kicks

Referring to the 1969 televised lunar landing, an American professor of government at Georgetown University recently posted this story about his childhood encounter with the Outer Space Treaty:

> As a 10-year old child, I watched this momentous event on our little black-and-white television set. And at some time during the coverage, I remember (what) might have been the first reference to international law that I can recall. One of the commentators noted that when the American flag was placed on the moon that did not indicate that the United States was claiming sovereignty over the moon. Rather, the commentator noted, there was a treaty that prohibited states from making territorial claims to the moon. Indeed, there was—the 1967 Outer Space Treaty. (Arend 2009)

"Forty years later," he notes "the Outer Space Treaty has generally served the international community well." States have not placed nuclear or other weapons of mass destruction in orbit or on the moon, neither has any state claimed sovereignty over the moon or other celestial bodies. All of this was prohibited by Article IV. But, he wondered, since our use of outer space has so changed over these past years, is it time to update the treaty to reflect new technologies and military strategies?

UCLA Corporate law professor Stephen Bainbridge responded to this post by arguing that "human space exploration in the West increasingly will be privatized" and that this private exploitation of outer space has gone far beyond the terms of the Outer Space Treaty. In support of his position, he cites space law expert Heidi Keefe interviewed in the *American Bar Association Journal*:

> 'The current system works if nations accept a détente in space and all the resources are only used for the benefit of all mankind,' Keefe says. 'If that's the case, then there will never be commercialization of space and *there will be little benefit for mankind*. I know that's a cynical capitalist viewpoint, but I think if everyone is afraid to launch a venture because they might not be allowed to profit from it, then nothing will happen.' (My emphasis)

Recalling the prostitution metaphor employed by Richard Falk, Keefe notes that space entrepreneurs plan to launch their space ventures whether the law is ready for them or not. Confident in the sanctioned disregard of the law enjoyed by those with enough investment capital, they would "rather beg for forgiveness later than ask for permission now, and that is what may be needed to give space law a kick" (Bainbridge 2009).

For his final argument in favor of further privatization of outer space, Bainbridge invokes the "tragedy of the commons" thesis: "to encourage private exploration and exploitation of space and to address tragedy of the commons, I propose that a new Outer Space Treaty create a regime for creating and enforcing private property rights in space." Private property rights work as commercial incentive and to prevent the "tragedy of the commons," Bainbridge argues, offering as evidence the following rhetorical question and answer from a publication of the pro-free market, libertarian think tank the Cato Institute entitled "Resolving the Tragedy of the Commons by Creating Private Property Rights in Wildlife":

> Why was the American buffalo nearly exterminated but not the Hereford, the Angus, or the Jersey cow? Why are salmon and trout habitually overfished in the nation's lakes, rivers, and streams, often to the point of endangering the species, while the same species thrive in fish farms and privately owned lakes and ponds? … In all of these cases, it is clear that the problem of overexploitation or overharvesting is a result of the resource's being under public rather than private ownership. The difference in their management is a direct result of two totally different forms of property rights and ownership: public, communal, or common property vs. private property. Wherever we have public ownership we find overuse, waste, and extinction; but private ownership results in sustained-yield use and preservation. Although it may be philosophically or emotionally pleasing to environmentalists to persist in maintaining that wildlife, the oceans, and natural resources belong to mankind, the inevitable result of such thinking is the opposite of what they desire. (Smith 2009)

Aside from the historical inaccuracy embedded in the rhetorical question—buffalo and salmon were well-managed by sustainable cultural practices of Indigenous peoples until they were exterminated respectively by the US Army in mass shootings and by the US Corps of Army Engineers through dam construction that blocked access to spawning sites—Bainbridge's dream of oceans and outer space well-managed for humankind by private property regimes leaves aside the historical record of natural resource exhaustion under free-market capitalism and colonial exploitation of the rights of subsistence resource users.

The work of Professor Elinor Ostrom, recipient of the 2009 Nobel Prize in economics, debunks the "tragedy of the commons" thesis and provides evidence of successful resource management by common property regimes based in small scale commons tenure systems embedded in a diversity of Indigenous and modern cultural forms, both subsistence and profit oriented (Ostrom 1990). Following the work of Ostrom and other commons economists, extraterrestrial or maritime mineral extractions in global commons hold a key element of wealth creation ignored or undervalued by the economic thinking in Bainbridge's essay.[18] Apologists for privatizing the global commons fail to acknowledge that, as long as we protect the commons-creating clauses in international law, common assets

---

18 For a discussion of the wealth-creating potential of humankind's common assets, see Peter Barnes, *Capitalism 3.0; A Guide to Reclaiming the Commons* (San Francisco, CA: Berrett-Koehler Publishers, 2006). Barnes discusses the potential of and legal mechanisms for this wealth to close the earth's poverty gap.

belonging to all humankind (including future generations) are a potential source of subsistence wealth for many of the earth's citizens. The creation of common asset trusts and United Nations Authorities for predistributing the funds have been proposed in all areas of the global commons, the ocean sea-beds, outer space, the gene pool, and the carbon-carrying capacity of the atmosphere. From minerals mined on the Moon to carbon credits sold to industrial CO_2 emitters; fish harvested in the ocean waters and data gathered with satellites using the geostationary orbit, all of these wealth-creating private property schemes use assets of the global commons and enjoy legal protection in international law. In the case of the Seabed Authority established by Common Heritage Principle in the Third Law of the Seas Convention, developing countries were eventually excluded from decision-making roles and the profit sharing capacity was undermined (Vicuña 1978). The failure of the Common Heritage Principle was not the lack of effective commons economic mechanisms. It was the greed and power of private industries taking more than their fair share of globally common assets.

In the early years of debate over the proper law for outer space, the Argentinean jurist Haraldo Valladao argued that Roman law had a category for *res communes omnium*: things "which are at everybody's disposal and the use of which is a natural faculty for all men to supply the needs of life, and against which no law can be invoked" (Valladao 1960). Valladao, a founder of globally common property rights, was referring to a natural law, a global birthright for subsistence livelihood—"the needs of life"—similar to the natural right Grotius pointed to with regard to Roman law protecting shorelines for fishing in the law of nations. Recall that in the Introduction to this volume we discussed early theorists of modern property law, John Locke and John Winthrop, who also referred to natural law in support of private property rights. The early modern Englishmen built their natural right theory of property on a rhetorical figure of empty space: *vacuum domicilium*, a spatialized argument used to justify the taking of land from Indigenous peoples who produced mere subsistence and not surplus value from the land. The English colonialists were building on a tradition of property law that included *res nullius* and *terra nullius*, legal concepts informed by the same spatial imaginary. When the Latin American jurist Haraldo Valladao addressed the First Colloquium on the Law of Outer Space with the concept of *res communes omnium*, a category of property that referred to the most basic "needs of life," it is as if Western law needed the great distance from the earth that Sputnik brought in order to find another spatial metaphor in Western culture that could become a ground for the value of subsistence in common property. It strikes me that outer space—that most expansive form of global commons, exceeding the dimensions of the oceans, the atmosphere, the radio frequency spectrum, the World Wide Web, and the biodiversity of the earth—was the distance we had to go from Western notions of property to find a *jus novum* in which to ground a new economic order based in a right to subsistence ("the needs of life") with wealth generated from the assets of globally common property.

Conclusion

In previous chapters, I have examined the rhetorical value of an epistemic imaginary—static, Euclidean, homogenous, empty space—used to bolster arguments for dispossession and private property in international law. The experience of the ocean's vast expanse has always provided a counter-image to static, Euclidean space and, by analogy, to Western notions of possession, property, and governance. The oceans offered another picture of empty space in the West, but not different enough to escape the gravitational pull of what Deleuze and Guattari called striated space. "The striation of the seas is the model for the striations of all smooth space," these philosophers told us. Will the striation of outer space, the extension of centralized national agendas backed by weaponized spacecraft, lead the rationalizations of international law? What kind of property formations are we witnessing in the scaled-up and intensified striations of a rational legal system that can, on the one hand, bifurcate into the singularities of the Internet with its Creative Commons Licenses that inscribe diverse commons regimes throughout the earth but can, on the other hand, collapse into irrational systems that build new laser weapons capable of targeting Afghan villagers in the most remote regions of the earth? From the perspective of the theoretical model of striated and smooth space, a model deeply attuned to the history of Western legal and philosophical thought, outer space brings the return of the smooth to reterritorialize the earth. The theory offers useful concepts with which to think about this technologically accessed earth: there is state and nonstate space corresponding to two kinds of empty space, *extensio* and *spatium*, stasis and intensity, property and potentiality. These concepts have helped us consider a deep cultural logic informing the development of the global commons in international law.

In the final chapters of this book, I follow a more anthropological train of thought. I ask what common space might look like in Western law if we were to get rid of the epistemic imaginary of empty space. I have argued that the doctrines of *res nullius* and *terra nullius* are the carriers of empty space in international law. They are the degree zero of the system. So what would the system start to look like if we were to do away with the legitimacy of these longstanding doctrines, the very ground of private property and colonial sovereignty in the modern world? In the next two chapters, I examine the affects of the revocation of the doctrine of *terra nullius* in Australia and the Western Sahara. I consider the persistence of the residual, non-Western, non-statist land tenure systems that are suddenly authorized by statist law to speak in Western courts. What kind of shared space is this and what can this further excursion into the life of empty space tell us about the domains we share in the global commons?

PART II
Two Cases of the Revocation of *Terra Nullius*

Introduction

In the last three decades two landmark cases, *Mabo v. Queensland* (Australia 1992) and the *Western Sahara* case (International Court of Justice in 1976) have revoked the doctrine of *terra nullius* and retroactively delegitimized a form of colonial land acquisition in places inhabited by Indigenous peoples. In both cases the decisions cleared the way for Indigenous traditions of land tenure and sovereignty to be incorporated into Western legal cultures.

The reversal of a basic colonial concept by the highest national and international courts, along with the problematic introduction of Indigenous title into a Eurocentric legal system, raises important issues about modern sovereignty. The introduction of Indigenous sovereignty through the reversal of *terra nullius* signals a different process of decolonization than that begun by the United Nations following the Second World War. It is different in that it introduces a notion of limited sovereignty into a legal order that was formed to enhance and protect the full sovereignty associated with the modern nation-state.

The United Nations resolution of 1960 proclaimed the independence and full sovereignty of all countries under colonial administration. But the *de jure* ritual never occurred for many Indigenous peoples. While the number of nation-states increased precipitously during this period (there are now 192 sovereign states, 140 more than when the United Nations was formed) creating what was then called the "Third World," the status of the earth's Indigenous peoples remained unaddressed, casting this diverse population into a "Fourth World."[1]

1 Around 350 million people worldwide are considered to be Indigenous, according to the International Working Group for Indigenous Affairs (IWGIA), an independent group that holds consultative status with the United Nations Economic and Social Council (ECOSOC). IWGIA defines Indigenous peoples as "the disadvantaged descendants of those peoples that inhabited a territory prior to colonisation or formation of the present state. The term Indigenous is defined by characteristics that relate to the identity of a particular people in a particular area, and that distinguish them culturally from other people or peoples." See International Working Group for Indigenous Affairs *Indigenous peoples – who are they?* http://www.iwgia.org/sw641.asp (accessed December 15, 2009).

Granting full sovereignty to the former colonies has never amounted to their becoming sovereign equals of the powerful nation-states which came before. As international law scholar Siba N'Zatioula Grovogui has argued, the notion of full sovereignty offered as a model to African states is not a universalizable one. For many reasons, foremost among them being that acceptance of independent statehood was contingent on disavowal of reparations for the harm suffered under colonialism, the full sovereignty which the Third World was offered only catapulted them into a set of international relations with institutions like the International Monetary Fund and the United Nations which assured the former colonial agents' continued dominance. Grovogui's discussion of the notion of full sovereignty in international law, its conceptual history, and its actual practice, goes far in demonstrating the Eurocentric bias of the international legal order (Grovogui 1996).

The recent cases overturning *terra nullius* point in a different direction. The discrediting of *terra nullius* is part of a larger destabilization of the full sovereignty enjoyed by the most powerful nation-states. As many globalization scholars have pointed out, the creation of the World Trade Organization, the growth of multinational corporations, the threat of climate change and environmental disasters on a global scale, the new geography paved by multimedia telecommunications and the post-Cold War deterioration of state security as biological and nuclear weapons enter the hands of nonstate groups with different agendas; all of these quickly-changing boundary formations point to limitations on the sort of full sovereignty and stable boundaries which modern international law was made to protect. As the international becomes a global order, the micro-political study of places where full sovereignty encounters new limits and seeks to incorporate these limits into its framework becomes all the more indicative of the shape of a new world order, the second Grotian moment.

The global commons has an important role to play in an impending second Grotian moment. The December 2009 United Nations-sponsored meeting of states, nongovernmental groups, Indigenous peoples, and activists in Copenhagen to create a binding treaty for the regulation of greenhouse gas emissions into the global atmosphere was an important, albeit failed, centralized approach. Many scholars and activists place hope in other, decentralized legal tools like liability and public trust doctrine to do the job nation-states shirk. Social actors with claims to limited sovereignty will need to test their authority to make the law of nation-states work for them and their local collective needs. If modern international law has been built around state sovereignty empowered by a cultural logic of empty space, as I have argued in this book, then we can learn about the global shape of emergent legal frameworks by studying cases where the logic of empty space is challenged and a limited authority formed in relation to an earth not grounded in the foundational emptiness of modernity is recognized by the modern state. Chapters 6 and 7 examine such cases.

Chapter 6
The *Western Sahara* Case: Genealogies Captured by the Census

Introduction

The 1975 International Court of Justice dismissal of *terra nullius* as the legitimating doctrine of colonial sovereignty over the Spanish Sahara lead to the recognition of the Western Sahara as the last nation-state to emerge from colonial Africa. Declaring that the western region of the Sahara had never been empty space, the Court opened the door for other historical agents to speak in the codes of international law to determine the self-governing status of the region. The result is a complex legal situation where a combination of pre-colonial, nomadic, diasporic, and refugee forms of relation to the land are given expression within modern legal frameworks of the territorial nation-state.

The *Western Sahara* case involves the assertion of ancestral claims to land by the Sahrawi peoples. The Court used a Spanish census of the region conducted in 1974 to locate the voices of the historical agents who could vote in a referendum on how the territory should be ruled. The 1974 census put the size of the overall Sahrawi population in the Western Sahara at just under 75,000. The census showed no indication of Moroccan settlers in the territory. Morocco disputed the census and took military action to avert the UN referendum. Today Morocco occupies the territory of the Western Sahara. The Sahrawi are displaced throughout the occupied area and into refugee camps in neighboring Algeria. The United Nations maintains a peacekeeping mission in the region with the hopes of advancing the referendum process some day.

While this chapter addresses the referendum as a tool of international law used to hear the voices of genealogical memory, it recognizes that what really appears in the western Sahara with the revocation of *terra nullius* are phosphates.[1] Phosphates

1 Ninety percent of phosphates mined in the world are used to produce fertilizer for industrialized agriculture. Phosphate rock is a nonrenewable resource, its reserves highly geographically concentrated. The Western Sahara is one of the largest reserves in the world along with the US and China. (China has imposed a 135 percent export tariff on phosphate rock to secure domestic supply.) Western Europe and India are totally dependent on phosphate imports. The US has approximately 25 years of reserves remaining. Morocco has handed out phosphate mining (and oil exploration) licenses in the Western Sahara to multinational (French and US) companies, in defiance of United Nations rulings. The UN has condemned the importing of phosphate rock via the illegitimate authority of the Moroccan occupied Western Sahara. See Dana Cordell, "8 reasons why we need to rethink

are one of the most highly traded commodities in the world. The majority of the world's industrialized agricultural fields rely on fertilizers made from inorganic minerals such as phosphate. The Western Sahara holds one of the largest of the scarce phosphate deposits on the earth. The entry of the Sahrawi population into statehood corresponds to the global history of industrial agriculture and its need for phosphate-based fertilizer. This chapter cannot tell that story, but it recognizes its force behind the legal fictions, war zones, landmines, diasporas, refugee camps, and claims of statehood in the Western Sahara.

Revocation of *Terra Nullius* in the International Court of Justice Case (1975)

In the United Nations resolution of 1960 which proclaimed the independence of all countries under colonial administration, the General Assembly agreed that the former Spanish Sahara be designated a "non-self-governing" territory and thus subject to decolonization, a process which was to be carried out by means of a referendum (United Nations General Assembly 1966). The administering power, Spain, as well as Morocco, Mauritania, and "any other interested party," were to be consulted in setting up the referendum (McDougal and Reisman 1981).[2] While Spain finally agreed to this arrangement in 1974, it was contested by both Morocco and Mauritania, both of whom had recently attained statehood and were now claiming rights of sovereignty over the region. The referendum, which would have allowed the Indigenous peoples of the region, the Sahrawi, to express their opinion on their future, was quickly ignored in what followed.

Shortly after Spain agreed to hold a referendum, Morocco—fearing perhaps that the Sahrawi would not support its claim—asked the General Assembly of the United Nations to first request that the International Court give an advisory opinion in the case. Morocco wanted the Court to answer two questions: first, "Was the Western Sahara (Rio de Oro and Sakiet El Hamra) at the time of colonization by Spain a territory belonging to no-one (*terra nullius*)?" And, if the answer to the first question is negative, then a second, "What were the legal ties between this territory and the Kingdom of Morocco and the Mauritanian entity?" (International Court of Justice 1979: 4).

---

the management of phosphorus resources in the global food system," *Global Phosphorus Research Initiative*, www.phosphorusfutures.net (accessed December 1, 2009).

2 Sources for this history of the Western Sahara case include: Myres McDougal and W. Micheal Reisman, *International Law in Contemporary Perpsective: The Public Order of the World Community* (1981) 639–669; John Mercer, *Spanish Sahara* (London: George Allen & Unwin Ltd., 1976); David Lynn Price, *The Western Sahara* (Beverly Hills/London: Sage Publications, 1979); Suresh Chandra Saxena, *The Liberation War in the Western Sahara* (New Delhi: Vidya Publishers, 1981); V. Thompson and Richard Adloff, *The Western Saharans; Background to Conflict* (New Jersey: Barnes & Noble, 1980); Yahia H. Zoubir and Daniel Volman, ed. *International Dimensions of the Western Sahara Conflict* (Westport/London: Praeger, 1993).

Morocco's apparent aims were to see whether it could be proven that the area was never *terra nullius* but rather a region over which the Kingdom of Morocco had at one time exercised sovereignty. If this were the case, then Mauritania would automatically be eliminated as an interested party and Spain would be obliged to restore the territories to Morocco without holding any referendum. Mauritania, which initially had a similar strategy, eventually dropped its claim over the entire region, opting instead to split the two territories between itself and Morocco. Algeria entered the debates on the side of the Sahrawi. Algeria had no territorial claim to the area but rather an interest based on the fact that the nomadic population of the territory spent part of each year in Algeria. Furthermore, as a stateless people, the Sahrawi (who speak Hassaniya, a dialect of Arabic that is also spoken in Mauritania) had no standing and could not be recognized in the International Court.[3] Thus Algeria spoke on behalf of the Sahrawi and their representatives, the Popular Front for the Liberation of Saquiet El Hamra and Rio d'Oro (popularly known as the Polisario).

The Court's opinion stated that Saquiet El Hamra and Rio d'Oro (the former Spanish Sahara) were in fact not *terra nullius* at the time of occupation by Spain (1884). The Court called for a referendum of the Sahrawi people to determine the form of government their new state would take. The Court observed:

> The request specifically located the question in the context of 'the time of colonization by Spain,' and it therefore seems clear that the words 'was Western Sahara … a territory belonging to no-one (*terra nullius*)' have to be interpreted by reference to the law in force at that period. The expression '*terra nullius*' was a legal term of art employed in connection with 'occupation,' as one of the accepted legal methods of acquiring sovereignty over a territory. 'Occupations' being legally an original means of peaceably acquiring sovereignty over territory, otherwise than by cession or succession, it was a cardinal condition of a valid 'occupation' that the territory should be *terra nullius*—a territory belonging to no-one at the time of the act alleged to constitute the 'occupation' …
>
> Whatever difference of opinion there may have been among jurists, the state practice of the relevant period indicates that territory inhabited by tribes or peoples having a social and political organization were not regarded as '*terra nullius*.' (International Court of Justice 1979: 31–21 and 64)

Unlike the High Court of Australia in the *Mabo* case, the International Court made no statement in the *Western Sahara* case as to the discriminatory racial

3 At the time when the United Nations asked for the advisory opinion, one representative—from Kenya—spoke against Morocco's request, complaining that "the United Nations was being asked to treat (the Indigenous peoples) as chattels and not as people." Myres McDougal and W. Micheal Reisman, *International Law in Contemporary Perspective: The Public Order of the World Community* (1981) 639–69.

issues at stake in the colonial doctrine of *terra nullius*. Nonetheless, at the time many advocates of a newly forming worldwide Indigenous community saw this decision as a landmark case. It was hoped that the dismissal of *terra nullius* would provide "an analogous application to the question of Indigenous peoples' land everywhere" (Daes 1989: 46). A further difference between the dismissals of *terra nullius* by the International versus the nation-state court (Australia) is that in the *Mabo* case the problem of political representation was resolved by making the Indigenous peoples Australian citizens first, subject to the sovereignty of the Crown and authorized to articulate their claim in the terms of the state. This was not an option in the *Western Sahara* case where the Sahrawi remained stateless and thus "speechless." The mode by which the Sahrawi spoke in the framework of international law was by referendum.

Immediately after the decision of the International Court of Justice, Morocco moved its military into the contested region and the Sahrawi people split up. Some fled to refugee camps in Algeria, others joined the guerrilla group Popular Front for the Liberation of Saguia el-Hamra and Río de Oro (Polisario) that took up residence in the desert, and still others stayed on in the disputed region. From the early 1970s until the UN-brokered cease-fire in 1991, Polisario lead a guerrilla war, first against the Spanish, then against Mauritanian and Moroccan occupiers.

The Political Geography of the Western Sahara some 30 Years Later: Moroccan Occupation and Algerian Refugee Camps

The status of the Western Sahara today is uncertain. Morocco continues to deny the existence of a separate state for the Sahrawi peoples. Enjoying support (military and financial) from the United States, Morocco persisted for years in pursuing a military solution to bring the Sahrawi and the rich mineral reserves of their lands under the power of the Sultan. Morocco's strategy has been to create a settler state in the region. It moved thousands of Moroccans into the territory and began treating the area as a special development zone and by spending vast resources expanding agriculture, industry, and infrastructure (housing, roads, and so on) in the area. Morocco refers to this area of Western Sahara as their "Southern Province." The policy of population redistribution lead to a situation where, after one decade, Moroccan settlers outnumbered Indigenous Sahrawi by at least three to two (Scargill 1991: 165). In the 1980s Morocco constructed a series of defensive walls around the Western Sahara stretching over a distance of 2,720 kilometers. With the final section of the wall completed in 1987, Morocco had consolidated all the areas held from the north to the south. The wall (or berm) was built with substantial military and financial assistance from the US and Israel and has been fortified with an estimated one to two million anti-tank and anti-personnel landmines manned by one to two hundred thousand soldiers (Smith 2004). The wall seals off all the major towns, water sources, good pasturage, and the abundant fisheries off the Saharan coast, which were attacked repeatedly by Polisario guerrillas during the

1980s (Scargill 1991: 164). The largest city in the Western Sahara is El-Ayoun near the Moroccan border with roughly 200,000 residents. In the 266,000 square kilometers that make up the Western Sahara state, there are around 383,831 inhabitants as of 2008, the majority of whom are resettled Moroccans (Human Rights Watch 2008: 28).

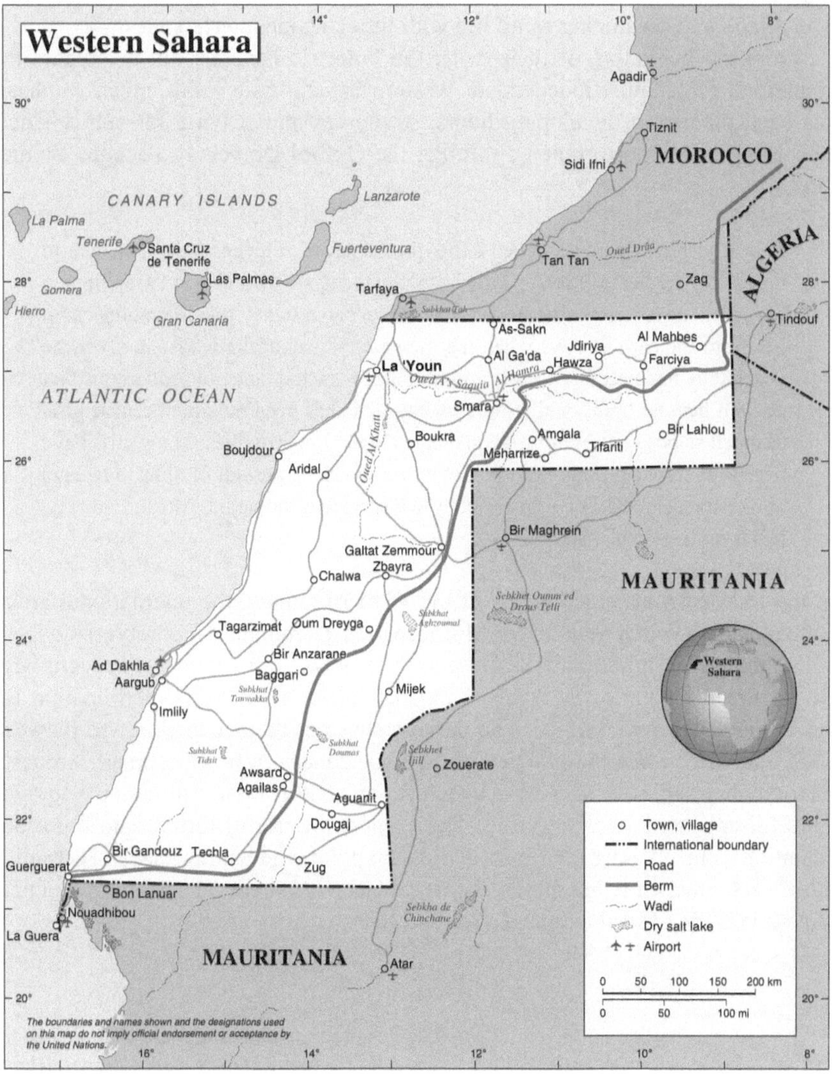

Figure 6.1 Map of Western Sahara showing Morocco's wall
Source: United Nations Map No. 3175 Rev. 2.

The Sahrawi Democratic Republic, the government-in-exile of the guerrilla group Polisario, claims to represent the majority of the Sahrawi in the Western Sahara. They run the Tindouf refugee camps set up 100 kilometers across the border in the neighboring state of Algeria. Like the vast majority of refugees in the world, the Sahrawis in the camps are mostly made up of women, children, and the elderly. The main difference in this case, however, is that thanks to the willingness of their Algerian hosts, the Sahrawi refugees themselves have been the ones running their own affairs and organizing camp life with little outside interference.

From the beginning of their exile, the Polisario have set out to prepare the population for a future independent Western Sahara. As a result, much emphasis has been placed on developing human resources and striving for self-reliance. According to a report prepared through the Oxford University Refugee Studies Centre:

> in nearly thirty years of forced exile, the Saharawi refugees have managed to practically eradicate illiteracy, which stood at ninety-five per cent in 1975. Women have also made impressive strides. They have played a key role in running camp life from the earliest days when the men were away at the warfront. Over the years, they have acquired skills and training in a wide range of professions that go well beyond traditional female realms. This has been possible because girls as much as boys have enjoyed equal educational opportunities. Many girls have been sent abroad on scholarships, sometimes for long periods of time, to receive university degrees. For a historically conservative, nomadic, Muslim society, this is quite radical. (Smith 2004)

In the Moroccan occupied zones of the Western Sahara, the international group Human Rights Watch reports that Morocco uses a combination of repressive laws, police violence, and unfair trials to punish Sahrawis who advocate peacefully in the occupied territories in favor of independence or full self-determination for the disputed Western Sahara.[4] The darkest phase of the occupation was between 1975 and 1991 when the practice of 'disappearances' was widespread. Amnesty International and Human Rights Watch report that at least a thousand Sahrawis were 'disappeared' in that period. They report the use of torture and notorious detention camps. Under the Moroccanization policy the Sahrawi speak Hassaniya mostly at home, while in schools, the workplace, and streets, the Moroccan dialect of Arabic is the official language (Smith 2004).

---

4 For information on the current status of Sahrawi population in the occupied zones and the refugee camps, see the 216 page report by Human Rights Watch, "Human Rights in Western Sahara and in the Tindouf Refugee Camps (Morocco/Western Sahara/Algeria)," *Human Rights Watch*, December 12, 2008, http://www.hrw.org (accessed December 1, 2009). See also, Colin Murphy, "Permanent Resistence in the Western Sahara," *Le Monde Diplomatique*, December 12, 2008, http://mondediplo.com/2008/12/12sahara.

Various international efforts have been made to settle the situation of the Western Sahara, but no solution has been reached as of this writing in 2009. In 1991 a cease-fire between Morocco and the Polisario stopped the fighting on the premise that a referendum would take place in 1992. The referendum never happened. In 2003 a UN Security Council resolution adopted a new peace plan that would turn Western Sahara into a semiautonomous region of Morocco for five years, after which a referendum would be held to determine independence, autonomy, or integration into Morocco. The Polisario agreed to the plan; Morocco refused to consider it. No country recognizes Morocco's rule in the Western Sahara. The United Nations still maintains a peacekeeping mission in the contested area. The long awaited UN referendum, now also sponsored by the Organization of African Unity, appears to be the most promising way to avoid renewed armed struggle in Africa's last colony.

Genealogical Nomadic "Identity" versus the Census Form

As part of any referendum a census must be taken to determine who can vote. This leads to a thorny question: who are the Sahrawi and can they be numbered? In the initial UN referendum discussions, Polisario claimed more than 165,000 Sahrawi refugees were in the Tindouf region of Algeria; Morocco claimed fewer than 47,000 refugees with only 30,000 "originating" from the Western Sahara. One commentator claimed there were "thousands of drought victims from Mauritania and the Algerian Sahara" in these camps, suggesting that Polisario was using these peoples to inflate their own population to gain more votes in the (always) upcoming referendum.[5] The arguments over who "counts" as true Sahrawi are tied to the fact that the identity of the Sahrawi people is so recently tied to a territorial space. As nomads, they passed through various state territories. Their "identity" was given in tribal affiliations tied to genealogical (biotemporal) structures rather than spatial structures like states. Ever since states have been trying to determine who they are, the Sahrawi have proven themselves uncountable.

According to documents submitted to the International Court of Justice, the Sahrawi consisted of some 100,000 people of Berber and Arab background who traced their history in the region back two millennia from the Neolithic 'Caspian' culture (whose chariots are still to be seen engraved on the rocks of this region) to the Almoravids whose conquests extended from the Ghana to the river Ebro in Spain around the eleventh century AD (Mercer 1976: 498–505). The linear accounts of the Sahrawi in this these documents relate a patrimonial history of battles won and lost. While this story of the continuity of Sahrawi identity won the nomads a future referendum from the World Court, it has proved useless in deciding who can vote in that referendum.

5 These figures come from D. Ian Scargill, "The Decline of Pastoral Nomadism in the Western Sahara," *Geography* 76, no. 2 (April 1991): 331.

The United Nations-sponsored census would establish Sahrawi identity based on genealogical memory. According to anthropologists, in the nomadic societies of the northwest Sahara, people traditionally define themselves in terms of tribal affiliation (Caratini 1997). The identity of the tribe is based on a founding myth about a person, generally someone from an elsewhere (Arabia or Yemen) who was prestigious in Muslim history, and who has passed on their genealogy to contemporary descendants. This unique origin (either real or fictive) is given by a man (the founding ancestor) and is passed on from generation to generation by men, or more precisely, by the blood of men. In this bloodline ideology, a child will be born into a particular masculine lineage, into a particular tribe (Caratini 1996: 116).

Beyond its function of group identity, mythic history legitimates a tribe's territorial control and social rank. The original myth is part of the tribe's oral history, a flexible legitimation discourse that gives the tribe room to reinterpret its history with each generation. Thus each child is told a chronology which allows him or her to place themselves in the world and in their society. Since nomadic mobility in time and space worked against the creation of fixed territories, pre-colonial nomadic society relied on genealogical memory to maintain their group's relation to the lands they traversed. This history, then, will be a combination of stories of the Muslim tradition (the life of the Prophet and his companions), the founding father, and local events retained by collective memory going back four or five generations. The combined stories of genealogical memory could thus "fill in," as it were, those spaces not covered by foundation myths.

According to anthropologist Sophie Caratini, who lived and worked with the Saharwi, when asked about his identity, no nomads of this region would spontaneously answer "I am from such and such a place." Rather, they would say "I am the son or daughter (i.e. the descendent) of such or such an ancestor" (1997: 44). This means that they are also related to all the descendants of the lineage to which that distant ancestor belonged, giving them a host of "cousins" they have never seen just as they have never seen many of the distant or nearby places referred to in the stories that make up their genealogical identity. Nonetheless, the nomad imagines these places and these relatives, making the work of the imagination fundamental to nomadic representations of space and time. These representations create links to an inexperienced somewhere or someone, links which according to Caratini can be translated into a precise set of rights and reciprocal responsibilities whenever such a "cousin," from no matter how distant a place, is encountered. In another culture they would be strangers, here they are "brothers."

In Islamic law, land crossed by nomads was called the Arabic equivalent of dead land.[6] These lands were not subject to privatization. Only land that had been made to "bear fruit"—agricultural lands and built spaces like houses and

6 Personal correspondence with anthropologist Sophie Caratini who worked in the camps with Sahrawi. See also Sophie Caratini, *Les Rgaybat (1610–1934)* (Paris: L'Harmattan, 1989) and Sophie Caratini, *Les Enfants des nuages* (Paris: Seuil, 1993).

gardens—could become private property. In this respect nomadic lands in Islamic law were not *terra nullius* open to claims of possession. Water and grassy areas for pasturing animals were, we might say, "regulated" by genealogical codes and rival acts of violence that provided for modes of access to members of various tribes.

Nomadic Identity Successfully Moving in State Law

Up until the time of their independence more than three decades ago, the Sahrawi had devised a number of strategies to get around the state borders imposed at the end of the nineteenth century by the colonial regimes of France and Spain. They would carry several identity cards, for example, so that they could be "Spanish" when they were in "Spain," "Mauritanians" when they crossed over to "Mauritania," "Moroccans" or "Algerians" if they found themselves in the north. Defying the identities of space, the Sahrawi stayed rooted in those of genealogical time: they continued to be the descendent of their ancestors (Caratini 1997: 45).

This ancestral identity with its investment in temporal (genealogical) over spatial (territorial) identities, thus served the Sahrawi well until the time of the decolonization of the Spanish Sahara begun in the 1970s. With the attempted creation of the Western Sahara as a nation-state, space (territory) suddenly gained precedence over time (genealogy) as the Sahrawi struggled to lay claim to a national territorial identity in the international domain. Indeed, the armed struggle declared in 1973 by the Polisario Front (first against the Spanish colonizer, then against Morocco and Mauritania whose troops occupied the Western Sahara in 1975) has gone hand-in-hand with the project of turning the nomadic inhabitants of this region away from their tribal identifications and towards a national unity called the "Sahrawi People." According to Caratini, this less externally public aspect of Sahrawi statehood is well recognized in the refugee camps. Outside the camps, it may be noted in the initial tracts that declared the group's revolutionary intent in terms of the Eurocentric slogan "mobilization of the masses." Inside the camps, however, the youthful leaders of the revolutionary movement have been developing an active anti-tribal campaign since the early 1970s. In the refugee camps, slogans denouncing tribalism as a crime against the nation could be seen on the walls and in the schools. Everyone was encouraged to "forget" that they belonged to a "tribe" but to recall that they belonged to a people, sometimes presented as one big "tribe" (Caratini 1996: 116).

The idea of a national territory as the ostensible primary referent for Sahrawi identity offers an extensive imaginary to the temporal continuity of genealogy. And yet, as Caratini notes, in the Sahrawi's relation to this land something of the paradoxical nomadic relations between time and space persists. For while the idea of national territory, so foreign to a nomadic culture, has permitted the unification of individuals, families, and tribes of this region, from the refugee camps it remains an imagined homeland associated with the myth of return. The camps themselves are organized into four large camps called wilayas, each wilaya named after a main town in Western Sahara. Occupied by a foreign enemy for the last thirty years, this "country" stands in a hesitant, multiple, and dynamic relation to the "Sahrawi people" and their self-representations.

Identity in the Ever Upcoming Referendum: A Census Based on Tribal Affiliation

Oddly enough, with the proposed referendum on self-determination, the place of time in Sahrawi representations is once again being reversed. In order for their right to this place to be recognized, each Sahrawi must take part in the United Nations' sponsored census to determine whether or not they can vote in the upcoming referendum. For the census they must each claim their tribal genealogy which can in turn be linked to particular areas of pastoral space in the Western Sahara. This has enormous problems.

The original UN decision stated that only those Sahrawi on the Spanish census of 1974 could take part in the referendum. This solution apparently pleased no-one. That census counted the tribes (the families and lineages) that were in fact present in the Spanish territory in 1974, but it did not take into account the pastoral territories where many tribes were stationed at that moment. Indeed, no tribe was entirely present year round in the territory of the Spanish Sahara. Thus the general complaint that not everyone was there in 1974 is true. The President of the Sahrawi Arabic Democratic Republic in 1997, for example, was not on that list. Neither was El Ouali, the first secretary of the Polisario Front and a great martyr of the struggle for liberation.[7]

During the 1990s, negotiations over the census included plans to count tribes whose pasturing areas fell in what is now the state of Western Sahara. This opens up another set of problems concerning who should vote in the referendum. There are "Mauritanian" and "Moroccan" tribes, small groups who did indeed pass through the area of the Western Sahara to pasture their animals. But in such a count, Morocco would be able to use the non-Sahrawi peoples of the entire tribe to cast a vote against the Sahrawi. Under these rules, Morocco could also try to get people on the census who claim to "originate" from the region of the Western Sahara. But since all the Arabs of Morocco passed through the Sahara since the seventh century, and since many Moroccans claim an Arab ancestry when in fact most of them, according to Caratini, are Berber, the discussion seems to have no end. The rights to pasture animals in various areas were also extended to tribes which were given "protection" to use the land commonly known to have "belonged" to another tribe. The complexity of these genealogical relationships, relationships which the Polisario sought to do away with to create a Sahrawi identity for a new

7 Caratini, personal correspondence.

state, risk reawakening ancient rivalries within the Sahrawi people, something that Morocco has used to its advantage in the past.[8]

The Census Form: Placing Rights in the Category of *Rex*, *Regis* and Registration

Benedict Anderson notes that British colonial census-makers from the late nineteenth century produced "identity categories" which were at first "superficially arbitrary" and hodgepodge. Eventually the complexity of religious affiliation was ferreted out and the categories were further rationalized and reduced to racial types (Anderson 1991: 164). In the Western Sahara case, the categories of the census are not racial categories. Furthermore, they are not supposed to come from colonial or even international regimes. The list of tribal affiliations derives from categories Indigenous to the Sahrawi themselves, categories of genealogical identity. This "identity" is far more complex than I could begin to describe here but even given this cursory description, it is clear that genealogical identity cannot lead to a clear vote that would establish a national identity for the people of this region. Suddenly, a number of terms do not seem useful to the description of what is happening in the post-*terra nullius* Western Sahara. Are genealogical affiliations "identities" in the sense that they are being asked to function in this census? Are genealogical affiliations, or as they are more commonly known in English, "tribes," even categories in the Aristotelian sense? They seem more like Wittgenstein's example of a categorical forms: family resemblances. Is this some resistance of "Otherness" to the structures of identity that come hand in hand with Western institutions? Furthermore, the census presupposes that the usufruct rights of genealogical identity can be translated into the political rights identified with citizens of a nation-state. This raises the question of whether "rights" can be understood outside of the context of *rex*, *Regis*, and registration.[9]

Furthermore, how are we to understand genealogy in this situation? According to anthropologist Steve Tyler,

> (the issue of genealogy) was never resolved in the good old days of kinship studies. The great argument was whether systems of kinship terminology could be understood by means of a universal grid of genealogical connection defined as blood, affinity, descent, etc. We could analyze kinship terms with great sophistication using the idea of genealogy as a kind of universal matrix

8 According to Caratini (personal correspondence) no solution is to be found in trying to base a census on the cultural and linguistic boundaries that separate the sedentary Berbers of south Morocco and the Arab-speaking Bedouins of the Sahara. These groups do not fall into an easily bounded area.

9 I want to thank Steve Tyler, Professor of Anthropology at Rice University, for this elegant formulation of my argument here.

> of notation, but it was never possible to demonstrate that this was anything more than a play with notations and had, in the language of by-gone days, no 'psychological' reality for the 'natives.'[10]

The UN census, whenever it is finally taken, is supposed to help rationalize the move from nomadic peoples to citizens of a nation-state. But the Polisario had already done that over the last decades with its campaign to eradicate genealogical memory. Nomadic relational structures come back in the picture with the census and add their own havoc to the transition from colonial to postcolonial state.

This uncontrollable outcome of an initial plan to rationally govern is not new. In 1946 the Indian Claims Commission was founded by the US Congress. Initiated in part in response to the Nuremberg Trials, the founding of the United Nations and its declaration of the inherent rights of self-determination, and the United States' guilt with respect to its native population, the Indian Claims Commission was envisioned as part of the package to terminate Indian tribes and their reservation lands; in short, to end the contradictory property system of sovereign Indian reservations within the sovereign borders of the United States. To this end the Indian Claims Commission sought to settle all remaining complaints American Indian tribes had against the federal government, pay off those who could convince the tribunal, and then leave the violent history of US-Indian relations behind in the dustbin of history, so to speak.[11] But in fact the opposite happened. Indians used their court cases to write tribal histories. In researching these they developed new relationships with anthropologists and historians (and produced a generation of Indian lawyers and Indian academics). The academic field of ethnohistory grew out of this collaboration; indeed the journal *Ethnohistory* was first published in 1954 as a forum for anthropologists to examine historical sources to determine whether specific tribes had occupied specific lands and whether they had received fair value for those lands at the time of "cession." A new forum for pan-Indian relations developed as Indian tribes began comparing notes on their histories of federal government abuse, histories which had been up until that time mostly local knowledge. The Commission, inaugurated in 1946, was originally meant to last five years. It heard its last case in 1976 and fueled the growth of the American Indian Movement.

This is not to suggest that the Indian Claims Commission was a success for Native American peoples. After all, of the 852 total claims submitted to the Indian Claims Commission, 80 were completed and only 15 involved awards. Rather, the

10 Personal communication with Tyler 7/20/98.

11 I am grateful to Randel Hanson for the historical information on the Indian Claims Commission. In his Ph.D. Dissertation, Hanson notes that the Termination Act of 1953 ended the official status of 109 Indian nations (or elements of Indian nations) by the late 1950s, although a number of these terminations were reversed in the 1970s. Randel Hanson, "From Bads to Goods: Marketing Nuclear Waste to American Indian Tribes" (Minneapolis: PhD Dissertation; University of Minnesota, 1998: 20).

point is that the unleashing of tribal histories produced more than the state had ever imagined. The government had initiated something that then could not be controlled. In the Western Sahara case, too, calling on genealogical or tribal memory (in the census) to establish a right to vote exceeds the intentions of the state-granting institutions. Tribal histories, it seems, do more than a state can manage.

Bio-Figurative 4 Generations History of S./Phosphates Tribe's Oral History

The anthropologist Marilyn Strathern has remarked on the struggle over identity that pits kinship-based relations against national citizenship. The distinction between literal and figurative works differently in the kin versus national economies, Strathern points out. Kinship systems make equivocal the frontier between proper, or what the West would term "biological," and the figurative family. Such equivocation is what allows the moral economy of kinship, based as it is on the communal, to operate (Strathern 1992).

The bio-figurative extended family of the Sahrawi is found in the flexible form of genealogical memory that includes several generations of oral history shaping who the Sahrawi are today. This would include the storied shape of nomadic life in the Saharan Desert formed in its relative distance during the nineteenth century from the European division of Africa as ratified by the 1885 Berlin Conference. The Berlin Conference that legitimized the use of *terra nullius* in Africa ratified Spain's holding of the Canary Islands and its protectorship over the nearby coastal areas of the Western Sahara. Given the Spanish confinement to coastal areas, the Sahrawi were relatively free to continue their nomadic existence.

Today's Sahrawi youth would be the bio-figural generation who had likely heard stories of their grandparents' and great grandparents' generation traversing the desert and dealing with European colonists. Those would be the Sahrawi who, during 1940s, suffered Europe's discovery of the world's biggest high-grade phosphate deposits in the Western Sahara. When the Sahrawi formed their own wing of the region's broad-based anti-colonial Army of Liberation that struggled against the French and Spanish, they did not form a nationalist movement. The primary concern of the Sahrawi in 1956 was to drive out foreign rule in the region rather than to build a nation. Later in the 1950s and 1960s, Spain's mission to exploit the mineral wealth of Western Sahara did lead to crucial changes for the grandparents of many Sahrawi living in the occupied and refugee regions of the Saharan Desert today. At that time large numbers of Sahrawis were forcibly settled and urbanized as cheap labor to work in the phosphate mines and to expand the colonial infrastructure. "Sahrawis of different tribes and castes alike were living and working together in the growing towns of the territory and were being subjected to the same conditions of oppression and exploitation. These various processes, by the late 1960s, had sparked renewed anti-colonial sentiments and had created the conditions for the emergence of a Sahrawi identity that went beyond traditional kinship ties" writes Dana Smith in her history of the refugees of the Western Sahara (Smith 2004).

Today's Sahrawi youth are formed in kinship ties that include the genealogical (bio-figural) histories of the new alliances that were forming in the 1960s among their grandparents' generation, some of whom were Sahrawi students studying at the Mohammed V University of Rabat,

> … influenced by radical student politics in Morocco, the rise of Third-World liberation movements, and the events in Spanish Sahara. Seeing themselves as the nucleus for a new liberation movement, they began recruiting Sahrawis within Morocco and beyond, in Spanish Sahara, and from the Diaspora in Mauritania and Algeria. Initially, they also sought the support of the Moroccan government in their quest to end Spanish rule, but this changed after anti-Spanish demonstrations, staged in southern Morocco in 1972, led to widespread arrests. This incident, along with contact with former members of the Harakat Tahrir who sought independence rather than integration with Morocco, took the Rabat group in a more strongly nationalistic direction. The new centre of activity shifted to Zouerate in Mauritania, and on 10 May 1973, the Polisario Front declared its birth. It also aimed to build a nation that eradicated all forms of inequality and would use armed struggle to achieve total freedom from colonial rule. (Smith 2004)

Over the next few years the Polisario Front organized several successful attacks on Spanish targets with growing support of the broader Sahrawi population. By 1975 when the International Court of Justice was called in to give the opinion that revoked *terra nullius* in the Western Sahara, Spain was drawing great wealth as the world's sixth major exporter of phosphates from the Saharan deposits. Spain made a secret deal with Morocco and Mauritania allowing them to divide the Western Sahara between them, excluding the Sahrawi and leaving Spain with a 35 percent share of the phosphate wealth.

Today's Sahrawi youth would know these historical events from their parents as well. They would know that in 1976, Moroccan planes bombed Sahrawi civilian camps in the interior of Western Sahara with banned napalm and cluster bombs, and that the Polisario would be forced to move the Sahrawi population to the south-western desert region near the Algerian city of Tindouf. Present day Sahrawi identity would be formed by these stories as sure as it is formed by the Tindouf refugee camps where they were born decades later and where the largest group of Sahrawi has now been living since 1976. Even though they still have ancestors, some ten to thirty thousand Sahrawi, who continue to practice a nomadic pastoral life in the "liberated zone," they all know about the one to two million landmines that lay hidden in the blowing sands of that "liberated" region (Smith 2004).

The genealogical memory of today's Sahrawi generation is formed within the flexible, bio-figural, legitimation discourse that gives the tribe room to reinterpret its history with each generation. All these Sahrawi and all this history would need to be voiced in the census and referendum, if it ever comes.

Conclusion

In this case of the revocation of *terra nullius*, the state (occupying the interstate space of the United Nations) is asked to decolonize Northern Africa by providing the Sahrawi peoples, until relatively recently nomadic tribes, the structures within which they might assert self-determination. The statist structures of the census and referendum fail on two pivotal accounts. First, they fail in not providing the means for the Sahrawi as a stateless people to represent themselves in the International Court of Justice. Secondly, they fail to provide a structure in which the Sahrawi can move to access statehood. The census and the subsequent referendum are the only form(forum) within which the Sahrawi can voice (vote) the self that will determine their future. The mechanism of the census, caught in the military power of the Moroccan state and the commercial interests of phosphate mining for a globally industrialized agriculture, proved inadequate to the resolution of the Sahrawi case. The census is a state form of identification, a system of legitimation in which the Sahrawi's genealogical tribal identity and the international community's justice process was skewed. This case foregrounds the failure of the state to provide the categories within which Sahrawi can assert themselves in state space and accede to the power of statehood.

Chapter 7

Negotiations and the *Mabo* Case: Comparative Epistemic Imaginaries

Introduction

On June 3, 1992 the High Court of Australia overturned the orthodox legal view of the British settlement of Australia. In *Mabo v. Queensland* the court found that in 1788, contrary to established history, Australia never was *terra nullius*, land-belonging-to-no-one.[1] Once overturned, the path was clear for the passage of the Native Title Act and the beginning of a new type of negotiation between Aboriginal and settler Australians over how Indigenous peoples' values in the land could be asserted over nearly half the territory of Australia. If the epistemic imaginary of Western sovereignty and property law mediates our relation to land through empty space, the Aboriginal repertoire of ancestral stories and images foreground the work of the imaginary in our relation to land. Native title emerges from the dismissal of *terra nullius* and the refusal to let empty space remain the common ground of negotiations about what counts as valuable. In post-*terra nullius* Australia ranchers, multinational mining corporations, and municipalities meet with Aboriginal Australians without the legal imposition of a common epistemic ground to negotiate common space. In this chapter I examine how this works and what these new limits on Western sovereignty mean for how land is shared.[2]

---

1 The *terra nullius* doctrine of land acquisition has been controversial since its inception. It is only recently that its legitimacy has been rejected in the highest courts of law. With respect to English law, Blackstone himself said of the doctrine of *terra nullius*: "so long as it was confined to the stocking and cultivation of desert uninhabited countries, it kept strictly within the limits of the law of nature. But how far the seizing on countries already peopled, and driving out or massacring the innocent and defenseless natives, merely because they differed from their invaders in language, in religion, in customs, in government or in color; how far such a conduct was consonant to nature, to reason, or to Christianity, deserved well to be considered by those who have rendered their names immortal by thus civilizing mankind." In Blackstone, *Commentaries on the Laws of England*, 17th edn. (1830), Bk II, Ch. 1, p. 7, cited in Mark Gregory, "Rewriting History I: Mabo v Queenland: The Decision," *Alternative Law Review* 17, no. 4 (August 1992): 157.

2 Framing the genocide of Aboriginal peoples in Australia as an issue of clashing legal doctrines is of course reductive. Native Title is one important achievement in a long historical struggle of Australia's Indigenous peoples against colonialism.

Mabo v. Queensland, 1992: A History of the Legal Decisions

Although the *terra nullius* doctrine was not applied in all British colonies—in particular those it claimed to acquire through conquest or cession—it was used in the possession of the Murray Islands, the easternmost of Torres Strait Islands. Eddie Mabo is the Murray islander who brought the case against the Queensland government. Indigenous inhabitants of the Murray Islands (also called Meriam peoples) are Melanesians who probably came to the islands from Papua New Guinea. According to court testimony the Meriam cultivated the soil on the islands from time immemorial.[3] Over the years their population fluctuated from around four hundred to one thousand inhabitants. Since the early days of colonial contact in the 1830s, European influence on the customary society of the Meriam peoples has been minimal. Few foreigners have lived among them and they have maintained distinctive subsistence land-use practices.[4]

Before the islands were annexed to Queensland in 1879, little contact had occurred. The London Missionary Society had been active there since 1871 and in 1882 had acquired a lease of two acres from the Queensland government. Also in 1882, the government declared that the rest of the islands were reserved for the islanders, thereby restricting further land acquisition by outsiders. In 1931 leases were granted on two of the smaller islands for the construction of a sardine factory. These leases were forfeited in 1938 to allow the Islanders unrestricted access. The following year the reserved lands of the Islands were put under a trust arrangement that continued under the Land Act of 1962 which dealt with Crown land and Indigenous reserves.

Some Islanders first appealed to a single High Court judge in 1982, seeking a decision that would assure that their "garden plots" remained their own property despite the history of annexation, subsequent leasing and the reservation and trust status effected by the Queensland government. In effect they were arguing for Native Title, a form of sovereignty that not only could survive institutions of colonial government, but could be respected in terms of colonial law. Native title was a concept that had heretofore not been recognized by English law. While

3 Background information to this case comes from a number of sources: Gordon Brysland, "Rewriting History 2: The Wider Significance of Mabo v Queenland," *Alternative Law Review* 17, no. 4 (August 1992): 162–165; Mark Gregory, "Rewriting History I: Mabo v Queenland: The Decision," *Alternative Law Review* 17, no. 4 (August 1992): 157–161; Henry Reynolds, "Mabo and Pastoral Leases," *Aboriginal Law Bulletin* 2, no. 59 (December 1992): 8–10; Brian Keon-Cohen, "Case Notes: Eddie Mabo and Ors v The State of Qyeensland," *Aboriginal Law Bulletin* 2, no. 52 (June 1992): 22–23; Justin Malbon, "The Implications of Mabo v Queensland," *Aboriginal Law Bulletin* 2, no. 57 (August 1992); Michael Hunt, "Opposition to Mining Projects by Indigenous Peoples and Special Interest Groups," *Murdoch University Electronic Journal of Law* 4, no. 2 (June 1997).

4 According to court documents, the Meriam's system of land tenure was comprised of garden systems with plots held by individuals or family groups.

the decision was still pending, the Queensland government tried to suppress the Islanders' claims by declaring, in the *Queensland Coast Islands Declaratory Act* of 1985, that any Native land rights which may have survived annexation in 1879 were thereby extinguished. The attempt to retroactively extinguish Native title was one of the first issues addressed by the High Court in its decision on the *Mabo* case. The High Court found the 1985 Act to be unconstitutional because it was not consistent with the *Racial Discrimination Act* 1975, a provision enacted to fulfill Australia's obligations under the *United Nations Convention on the Elimination of All Forms of Racial Discrimination* (United Nations 2008). This initial finding was simply the official rhetoric for saying that the 1985 Act was racist.

Before deciding whether the Islanders' customary land system had in fact survived the state's annexation and subsequent leasing arrangements, the Court had to rule on whether the Meriam peoples' Indigenous form of land tenure could be protected under Australian common law. This involved the Court's figuring out how to assert Native Title without having it be a challenge to the Crown's sovereignty. The judges did this by deciding, by the narrowest of majorities, that the claim that these lands were *terra nullius* because the Meriam peoples were not a self-governing society at the time the British first landed on their islands was inherently racist. Writing for the majority, Justice Brennan stated:

> … it is imperative in today's world that the common law should neither be nor be seen to be frozen in an age of racial discrimination … The fiction by which the rights and interests of Indigenous inhabitants in land were treated as non-existent was justified by a policy (*Terra Nullius*) which has no place in the contemporary law of this country. (High Court of Australia 1992: 42)

While dismissing the legality of the doctrine of *terra nullius*, Justice Brennan also noted the following contradiction: "this Court is not free to adopt rules that accord with contemporary notions of justice and human rights if their adoption would fracture the skeleton of principle which gives the body of our law its shape and internal consistency" (cited in Brysland 1992: 163). Thus a challenge to the legitimacy of *terra nullius*, the very fundamentals of colonial legal theory, raised the issue of how to modify the law in accordance with modern notions of justice and human rights without causing the collapse of the legal system itself. And since all the judges agreed that "the acquisition of new land by a sovereign state is an act of state which cannot be challenged in the courts," the solution lay in arguing for a notion of communal Native Title that could also survive a proclamation of sovereignty by the Crown (Gregory 1992: 158).

The seeming contradiction was resolved by the Court's making a distinction between an acquisition of sovereignty and an acquisition of territory or title. The Crown, the Court found, had indeed acquired sovereignty in eastern Australia by an act of state in 1788. According to the common law principles of the time—feudally-based doctrines of tenure which remain fundamental structures of the contemporary system of English land law—all private land, even a fee simple or freehold title, could not theoretically be considered full ownership because the Crown held ultimate title, or what is called radical title.[5] In a logical attempt to halt infinite regression in property law, English common law calls radical title the ultimate title on which all other titles are based, a rhetorical move that might also be called a founding (and variously persistent) myth of sovereignty and property. With the concept of radical title, the Court could find that the Crown's radical title to all land over which it has acquired sovereignty is not the same as an acquisition of full ownership of territory. If sovereignty (radical title) basically means exercising jurisdiction with respect to international and constitutional law over an area, then ownership of territory means having proprietary rights that are something like municipal laws of property. Spatially speaking, one jurisdiction is extensive—involving a state or international order—the other is local, or municipal. Heretofore, the orthodox assumption in Australia had been that both forms of title—radical title and full ownership of territory—had been acquired by the Crown when it acquired sovereignty. By making the distinction, the court could decide that a change in sovereignty did not necessarily extinguish ownership right of Native title to the land. The Murray Islanders could have retained their Native title; they could "own" the territory, despite the Crown's ultimate radical title over their land.

The *Mabo* judgment, then, meant that Native title—the nature and content of which, in this case, comes from Meriam law and custom—is at once protected under as well as subject to Australian law. Furthermore, given the thrust of the decision—namely, that an acquisition or extension of sovereignty to an inhabited, settled colony does not, in and of itself, extinguish Native title—the case had important consequences for the rest of Australia nearly half of which is now (in various ways) subject to Aboriginal claims.

After *Mabo*: Native Title Act (1993) and Subsequent Legislation

The direct legislative response to *Mabo* was the Native Title Act passed by the Federal Government in 1993. While *Mabo* stated that the source of Native title would be in common law, more specifically in the traditional Aboriginal laws and customs of the land in question, it also stated that Native title could be extinguished by an Act of the Crown. The Crown can extinguish Native title either by appropriating land to itself or by granting land to a third party which is inconsistent with a continuing right to enjoy Native title. Thus, when Parliament was debating the Native Title Bill—a Bill to create a procedure for the assertion of Native title—many thought that the third party pastoral lease grants which cover

5 In England the Queen holds ultimate title to the seashore, whereas in Civil Law traditions, the shoreline is subject to the Roman doctrine of *res communis* and the state holds the title to the seashore as public property.

nearly half the land mass of Australia would render that land exempt from claims of Native title (Ladbury and Chin 1994). With pastoral lease land out of the picture, Indigenous claims seemed manageable to Australian ranchers.

As it turned out, in December of 1996 in the *Wik* case, the High Court found that Native title was not necessarily extinguished by the grant of a pastoral lease. The Native Title Act did exempt all titles for land, mineral exploration, and mining (including production titles under the onshore and offshore petroleum laws) granted before January 1, 1994. In these cases of exemptions, the state would monetarily compensate Aboriginal claimants if Native title was found to have existed over the land or waters in question. After 1994, however, Native title was in effect. Just to give an example of the extent of the challenge to business as usual when the *Wik* decision came out, there had been 3,500 mining titles issued in the pastoral lease land of Western Australia since 1994. All of these were potentially invalidated by the 1996 *Wik* decision. With pastoral lease land covering almost half of the continent of Australia, the stakes of the decision for ranching and mining interests were enormous (Hunt 1997: 16).

The *Wik* decision put in place a Native Title Act procedure that would affect all mineral, petroleum, and land title projects granted since 1994. The procedure required that when the state intends to grant a land, petroleum, or mineral title to a particular company, notification of this intent must be made to the Aboriginal community (including the National Native Title Tribunal established by the Native Title Act), to the press, and to any other Native title claimants. Native title claimants would have two months to contest the government's grant. If no relevant objection were made, the grant would be executed. If an objection were upheld, a "right to negotiate procedure" would be followed. In this case, the state, Native title claimant, and petroleum or mining company would need to negotiate an agreement. If no agreement could be reached through negotiation, the grant application would be referred to the National Native Title Tribunal which would have the power to decide whether or not the grant could be made. The decision of the Tribunal could be vetoed by the Federal Minister for Aboriginal Affairs.

An expedited procedure was also provided by the law allowing private parties to negotiate directly with sovereign Indigenous communities about the use and management of disputed land and waters. The stated aim of such negotiation was to find a practical and flexible arrangement without using the court system. Companies were encouraged to use this process if they felt their operations would not interfere with an Aboriginal community. According to the law, it is the Indigenous peoples who decide whether the project is offensive and they are allowed to use physical as well as spiritual criteria in making their decision.

Since the *Wik* decision, various legal developments have both weakened and strengthened Native title in Australia. A right wing political party, "One Nation," was formed with the central aim of abolishing Native title (Farnsworth 1997). In the context of this backlash, the federal government passed an amendment to the Native Title Act in 1998 allowing the state to buy out Native Title claims when negotiations with pastoralists fail. The court-determined standard for failure was lack of "reasonable" endeavor within a given time frame. These amendments further secured the tenure of non-Indigenous pastoral and other land lease holders. On the side of Indigenous empowerment, in 2006 the Federal Court came out with a judgment in favor of Native title holders by finding that *Noongar* Native Title existed over the Perth metropolitan area. Relying on an extensive archive of historical material showing shared language use and interactions with other communities, the federal judge found that the *Noongar* community had continued to exist despite the disruptions of mixed marriages and people forced off the land through white settlement and government policies. In 2008 parts of the decision survived the appeal process with other appeals still pending as of this writing. The *Noongar* decision has far reaching potential for extending Native title into urban areas.

According to the government website of the National Native Title Tribunal, 580 Native title claims have been registered but not yet determined. As of 2008, the Tribunal had also registered more than 340 Indigenous land use agreements. These agreements are binding documents and can be negotiated over areas where Native title has, or has not yet, been determined to exist (Federal Government of Australia 2009).

Native title opened an arena for renegotiating national sovereignty in the modern era. Suddenly, huge tracts of Australia that had been enclosed by state and commercial interests potentially reopened to peoples who would bring to a Western legal framework non-Western concepts of land tenure and land values. In this new arena, the sovereignty of all parties (nation-state, Aboriginal community, and private industries) would theoretically be limited, even as Indigenous sovereignty would theoretically be expanded. At the cultural level, the dismissal of *terra nullius* in Australia has removed the legal fiction of an original empty space. In its place a terrain of negotiation has opened up. Without pretending that the power differential among Indigenous peoples, the state, private mining corporations, and ranching industries has disappeared along with *terra nullius*, for indeed it has not, the differently-empowered negotiations taking place among these entities thanks to the Native Title Act can be examined for lessons on the capacity of Western legal thought to negotiate without common ground.

Songlines and Dreamings: Preliminary Representations of Aboriginal Land Tenure Systems in European Thought

Before examining a case of negotiated Aboriginal tenure under the Native Title Act, it is important to consider the cultural differences between Indigenous and state sanctioned land tenure systems. Euro-Americans may be familiar with the Werner Herzog film shot of Aboriginal clan members convening cross-legged in the aisle of a supermarket, the spot where a sacred tree once stood, their ancestral homelands viewed through a pan shot of the desert scarred by holes and dirt mounds from uranium, copper and zinc excavations with a scatter of rusted shacks housing those who refused to leave (Herzog 1984). Like the Herzog film, the following examples do not portray the Indigenous systems' response to the devastation of Aboriginal lands and lifeways, or the violence and corruption of the state's land tenure system that permitted commercial mining leases on and mass removal from ancestral lands. The representational schemes that follow are abstractions, frozen (albeit poetic) attempts to capture the cultural logic of a non-Western worldview. They are used here to present something of the difficulty of representing Aboriginal land tenure in Western frameworks.

A basic concept of the Indigenous tenure system is something referred to in English as "songlines." In their book *Singing the Land, Signing the Land*, Watson and Chambers use the following excerpt to show how "one can both get it (the idea of the songlines) wrong and still convey it's intricacy, coherence and relevance to European thought" (1993: 16). They offer the following passage from a well received English documentary novel by Bruce Chatwin called *The Songlines* (Chatwin 1988). As a student of literature, my first contact with the representation of Aboriginal land tenure came in this novel. Here is a long passage where the author/narrator explains his interest in the songlines:

> My reason for coming to Australia was to try to learn for myself, and not from others, what a songline was—and how it worked. Obviously, I was not going to get to the heart of the matter, nor would I want to. I had asked a friend in Adelaide if she knew of an expert …
>
> (the 'expert', located in central Australia, began by explaining the importance of the Ancestors and how each) while traveling through the country, was thought to have scattered a trail of words and *musical notes* along the line of his footprints, and how these Dreaming-tracks lay over the land …
>
> In theory, at least, the whole of Australia could be read as a *musical score*. There was hardly a rock or creek in the country that could not or had not been sung. One should perhaps visualize the Songlines as a spaghetti of *Illiads and Odysseys*, writhing this way and that, in which every 'episode' was readable in terms of geology.
>
> 'By episode', I asked, 'do you mean "sacred site"?'
>
> 'I do.' …
>
> 'And the distance between two such sites can be measured as a stretch of song? …'
>
> By singing the world into existence, he said, the Ancestors had been poets in the original sense of *poesis*, meaning 'creation.' No Aboriginal could conceive that

> the created world was in any way imperfect. His religious life had a single aim: to keep the land the way it was and should be. The man who went 'Walkabout' was making a ritual journey. He trod in the footprints of his Ancestor. He sang the Ancestor's stanzas without changing a word or note—and so recreated the Creation.
>
> 'Sometimes … we'll come across a ridge of sandhills, and suddenly they'll all start singing. "What are you mob singing?" I'll ask, and they'll say, "Singing up the country, boss. Makes the country come up quicker".' … just as, in the Dreamtime, the country had not existed until the Ancestors sang it.
>
> 'So the land', I said, '*must first exist as a concept in the mind*? Then it must be sung? Only then can it be said *to exist?*'
>
> 'True.'
>
> 'In other words, "to exist" is "*to be perceived*"?'
>
> 'Yes.'
>
> 'Sounds suspiciously like Bishop Berkeley's Refutation of Matter.'
>
> 'Or Pure Mind Buddhism … which also sees the world as an *illusion.*' (Chatwin 1988: 14–16, my emphasis)

To render Aboriginal land tenure understandable to his English-speaking audience, Chatwin/the narrator explains Indigenous oral traditions in terms of Western written traditions—musical scores and notes; the Iliad and Odyssey. Also, the author/narrator invites the reader to consider a narrated figure of Indigenous land as "a concept in the mind." In this comparison, Chatwin maintains a heuristic distinction between illusion and reality which is well entrenched in Western philosophy but not in the Aboriginal worldview. These interpretive tropes in Chatwin's work are important to consider, not so much to show that the novel "gets it wrong," but rather to foreground that the act of understanding cultural difference is always a translation into familiar terms which are themselves, as the Sapir-Whorf hypothesis would have it, constrained by "linguistic and associative processes of which we are only dimly aware" (Tyler 1986: 34). Songlines are a fundamental element of Aboriginal land tenure and the Native Title Act makes the songlines legitimate and reasonable bases for property claims in Australia.

A second example of a Western representation of Aboriginal land tenure follows a diagram by Richard Barwick, showing "how *gurrutu* (an abstract recursion) and narrative tracks (metaphors) are worked together in *Yolngu* life to create a working system of land tenure in much the same way that Westerners use numbers (an abstract recursion) and qualities (metaphors) in constituting a working system of land tenure" (Watson and Chambers 1993: 37).[6] Thus the anthropologists invite us to think of the *Yolngu* land tenure system through an analogy from Western science: "if one doesn't apply the model too literally, it might be useful to think of the *gurrutu* as approximated by a double helix. The two chains symbolize the two moieties (two kinship groups that make up a tribe's kinship system), and the base pairs symbolize the kinship linkages that occur throughout the social and natural world. The lines crossing over each other may be taken as symbolizing the generations" (38). Ancestral tracks encode multigenerational clan and family relationships just as DNA does in Western science. In the Aboriginal system, the tracks code the ancestral relations to the land. With the introduction of the Native title, Australian courts, civil society, and commercial groups struggle to find comparative figures to better understand the newly legitimate evidence of Aboriginal rights to land in Australia.

A third example of a Western framework in which to present renderings of Aboriginal land tenure comes from an exhibit on Aboriginal paintings that toured the United States in 1989. Curators suggested that certain Aboriginal images might be the equivalent of a Western deed for title in their authority to explain the belonging status of a specific tract of land. The catalogue of the exhibit is careful to explain that when senior members of the *Yirrkala* community were interviewed about the inclusion of certain paintings in the exhibition book, they warned of "the harm that would come from the misappropriation of other people's designs. Even to 'speak for' another group's clan design was to invite serious trouble, especially from 'the old peoples' (the traditional-oriented Aborigines)" (Sutton 1988: 20). With that warning in mind, and insufficient time to procure correct permissions, I am not including any of the paintings used to represent Aboriginal "deed" to land. The text of the exhibit, however, offers this explanation of the land tenure system represented in the paintings:

> In North East Arnhem, clan designs fall into two main groups associated with the two intermarrying moieties (halves) of society … Clans, which are the primary landowning units and generally small groups of people linked by descent in the male line, belong to one moiety or the other. Each of the clans has its own distinctive designs. These designs … consist of repeated sequences of geometric

6 Some explanations of the songlines note that the land (and corresponding ancestral footprint) where a mother feels the first stirring of life in her womb becomes the site of a songline that "belongs" to the child/tribe. Since the ancestral footprint is connected to the Ancestor's Dreaming, that story about the land will be carried in the songline assigned to that child. Thus the tribe builds kinship relationships between the Ancestors, their footprints or "tracks" along the land, and their stories about the land. As noted in Chapter 6 regarding the Sahrawi kinship system that became part of the Western legal consideration of who could and could not be part of the census, anthropological accounts of Indigenous kinship systems may or may not have any "psychological reality" to "the native."

> elements elaborately infilled with cross-hatching. The designs vary according to which Ancestral Beings the design is associated with and which clan it belongs to. (Morphy in Sutton 1988: 20)

Commenting on the anthropologist's study of the artistic system of North East Arnhem Land, the editor of the exhibit catalogue notes, "there is no simple relationship between the painters as members of clans, the Dreaming sites of clan estates (owned lands), and the clan designs. The artistic system of this region encodes relations between people and land, but not in exactly the same form as other systems in the culture" (Sutton 1988: 21). While the paintings function as assertions of clan land ownership for the Indigenous group, different individuals tend mainly to paint only certain parts of their clan lands. A smaller painting will tend to show fewer episodes of myths than a larger one. "Particular ancestral designs used in a painting emphasize some parts of a clan's lands rather than others by calling attention to sites where the ancestors traveled. The paintings are thus not simply topographical maps but actually map relationships between certain mythologically significant features in the landscape." There are further idiosyncrasies (or singularities) in the representations: some clans have made formerly secret designs available for public screening while others have made only certain levels of meaning available to viewers. Also, "the use of figurative elements appears to have increased considerably after the 1940s and 1950s" (22). If these representations were the functional equivalent of a deed for title, consider the enormous variability in the Aboriginal representational process.

The exhibit details the complexity of representing the social system of belonging between land and humans in Aboriginal culture. One criticism made of the exhibit was that it left out the tradition of women's paintings (designs often done for ceremonial dances on women's bodies where the paint would eventually run together with the flow of sweat). Critics wondered whether the sex of the curator or anthropologist gathering information mattered. Were Aboriginal men empowered differently than Aboriginal women to speak about and hand over their clan paintings? Feminist reflection on the anthropological record has observed that asking peoples who held restricted knowledge—secret designs depicting certain heavily guarded relations to the land, or designs not meant to last for more than one ceremonial dance—for knowledge that could be translated into Western forms circulating without restrictions (as they now circulating in this book, I might add) means being aware of gender restrictions.[7]

---

7 For a discussion of how Aboriginal women's ceremonies and works express rules and laws related to land tenure see Diane Bell and Pam Ditton, *Law: The Old and the New* (Canberra: Aboriginal History, 1980). See K. Benterrak, P. Roe and S. Muecke, *Reading the Country* (Fremantle: Fremantle Arts Centre Press, 1984: 187) for a discussion of how the European vision of Aboriginal culture may be subject to the Jungian illusion that projects the lost anima of the West on to "the other" perceiving it as "the unconscious counterpart to modern western man's consciousness of himself as a laboring, investigating, suffering

The above focus on representations is meant to illustrate the complexity of Aboriginal land tenure systems and the difficulty that Aborigines, anthropologists and others have had in communicating that complexity to a Western audience. These same complexities arise in the courtroom, in corridors of negotiation, and in the press as Aboriginal communities, the state, private interests, and public opinion struggle to create new land-sharing arrangements under the Native Title Act. Just as Western concepts of property and sovereignty are connected to broader cultural representational schemata involving empty space, the one point perspective system, Enlightenment concepts of reason, and historically embedded power relations as we have seen throughout this volume, Aboriginal notions of belonging in relation to land partake in the sort of wider cultural representational patterns noted above. There is no simple way to explain Aboriginal land tenure systems inside or outside the post-*terra nullius* framework. But the most basic thing we might say is that Aboriginal tenure systems are not based in an epistemic imaginary of empty space.

The New Reasonable Standard in Negotiating: Aboriginal Claimants and Multinational Mining Corporation CRT-RTZ (Rio Tinto) at the Century Zinc Mine Site

How do the radically different land tenure systems of Euro-Australian and international law and Aboriginals co-exist and communicate with each other since the *Mabo* decision? The process is so arduous that the Native Title Act recommends that Aboriginal groups and commercial entities avoid the common ground of the courtroom despite its new capacity to recognize songlines and ancestral Dreamings as legitimate forms of title. In place of the courtroom with its lengthy and expensive process, the law encourages parties to negotiate binding agreements directly with each other. The 1998 amendments to the Native Title Act added their own common ground to quicken the process of negotiation: the "reasonable" standard requirement. While the reasonable standard is a vague and undefined concept, it is in fact a powerful rhetorical operator. It is well known to favor non-Indigenous claimants but how it favors them is obfuscated by what makes it appear so deceptively simple: its epistemic imaginary of empty space as the common ground. Furthermore, if a claimant takes too long meeting the reasonable standard, they lose the right to negotiate the case.

---

being—one who has lost 'nature' and innocence with the rise of industrialization." This observation is used as cautionary remark to the binary system with which Veronica Strang concludes her fascinating ethnography of pastorialists and Aboriginal inhabitants of the Cape York region of Australia. Veronica Strang, *Uncommon Ground: Cultural Landscapes and Environmental Values* (Oxford/New York: Berg, 1997: 285).

The following analysis examines how the new common sense of the reasonable standard works in practice. The case I examine is that of a temporarily failed negotiation between Aboriginal claimants and a multinational corporation which owned the lease on the world's second largest zinc deposit at the Century Zinc mine in Eastern Australia. Century Zinc's owner is CRA-RTZ—a forgettable acronym for a company that would rightly wish invisible its reputation for untold worldwide devastation to peoples and environments unfortunate enough to reside atop globally traded mineral deposits.[8] CRA-RTZ owned the Century Zinc mine on federally leased land and was planning a one billion dollar expansion but, under the Native Title Act, needed permission from Aboriginal clans who also had legitimate claims to the site and would be more than familiar with the

8 It is difficult to know where to begin a brief history of this corporation with regard to the land rights of Aborigines. At the time of the Century Zinc mine case, the owner, CRA-RTZ was among the world's top six mining corporations and infamous in Australia for its plunder and destruction of Aboriginal lands. Through a history of name changes and share sales, CRA has been associated, during the 1950s (through its predecessor company Conzinc and its subsidiary Colmaco) with the government-sanctioned theft of 2,270 square miles of Aboriginal reserve land on the west coast of Cape York, and nearly 2,000 square miles (1982) on the east coast in the vicinity of the Century Zinc mine. This was traditional Aboriginal land, though not classified as a reserve. According to Roger Moody's well-documented history of this company, Colmaco was given all timber, cattle-grazing, water, and farming rights in the lease area; $8.5 million in government aid for infrastructure; and exemption from the Clean Water Act. The company was involved in the evictions of Aborigines from Mapoon and Weipa in Cape York province, Queensland, site of the world's largest open-cast bauxite mine. According to Moody,

> These two places have become synonymous with the devastation and social breakdown caused by mining … In a lengthy report, in 1976, Melbourne Age reporter David Broadbent delivered one of the most powerful attacks on the human effects of mining ever made, after a visit to Cape York. 'If men ever establish a base on the barren surface of Mars,' he wrote, 'it will look like Weipa'. By then Comalco had been mining at Weipa for a decade—the result, declared Broadbent, was 'acres of dead craters unrelieved by a single growing thing.' The conditions at South Weipa—site of the main Aboriginal relocation—were such that 'traditions have disappeared and alcohol has wreaked havoc … the Weipa operations have caused alarm in every Aboriginal community throughout the north of Australia.' (G5)

Moody refers to the study by sociologist Paul Wilson, who found that the rate of imprisonment among Aboriginal people at Weipa was the highest in Australia; the rate of violent crime and self-inflicted violence (a convincing indication of deep psychological malaise) was profoundly disturbing. A film by well-known Australian film-maker David Bradbury (1989), *State of Shock*, graphically describes the situation in this region, one which had not improved over the ten years since reporters first brought the situation to wide public. (Roger Moody, *The Gulliver File – Mines, People and Land: A Global Battleground* (London: Minewatch, 1992) in particular the section on CRA violent history of the company in the region. The Century Zinc negotiations failed as the federal government was still debating the 1998 amendments. As the amendments were finalized, CRA-RTZ reached a settlement with the Aboriginals who had previously refused to negotiate. According to a lawyer representing the mining industry, "Century will be the new benchmark, setting not only the level and type of compensation for approval of projects on land covered by native title claims (which is just about all of them) but also the way the offers are made and negotiated and the money distributed" (Hunt 1997: 90). Since our interest in this case concerns the standard of "reasonable" negotiation, we need to ask: what was considered reasonable and unreasonable in the Century case?

The mining corporation's frustration over the initial failure of clans to reasonably negotiate was expressed in a law review article entitled "Opposition to Mining Projects by Indigenous Peoples and Special Interest Groups" written by Michael Hunt, a lawyer representing the mining industry (Hunt 1997). Hunt's frustration with the situation—it will cause "huge setback for both the mining and the native title industry (sic)"—is best understood in the following paragraph from his article:

> For the National Native Title Tribunal and the Aboriginal and Torres Strait Islanders Commission, Century is a disaster. The whole system of native title is, to a large extent, built on the presumption that *regional* Aboriginal groups are prepared and able to negotiate *reasonable* outcomes with landowners and leaseholders. Three times now CRA (Century Zinc's vendor) has got close to a deal on Century and each time it has hit a brick wall of *native title claimants who simply 'will not negotiate.'* The system is flawed in that it is too easy to lodge a native title claim (there is no real acceptance test) and the fact of *simply lodging a claim is sufficient to give standing in the 'right to negotiate' process.* At Century, CRA needed signatures of all twelve claimants which means that each of them has a veto. I understand that six claimants agreed but six would not accept CRA's offer. Those in favor represented about 700 people; those against represented about 60 and *many of them lived a long way from the mine site.* The offer totaled $60 million over the life of the mine and was to be paid in a number of ways: the transfer of four pastoral properties to the local communities, an employment and training package, an environmental monitoring program, a business opportunities program using a trust fund for

---

and Aborigines.) This then is the tip of the iceberg for what Aboriginal clans knew about CRA when the company came to them in the late 1990s for permission to expand operations at the Century Zinc mine. At the time, CRA was showing exceptionally high profits with its partner RTZ (see Business Wire-London, "The RTZ Corporation," March 7, 1996, http://www.encyclopedia.com/doc/1G1-18061968.html (accessed December 1,

> venture capital to be provided to the locals, a community development trust, an Aboriginal heritage preservation program and retrospective compensation for the bulk sample that has already been mined from Century. (93, my emphasis)

The details of agreements negotiated with private companies and Aboriginal groups are generally not made known to the public, so the author's inside information is useful for our analysis of what the mining companies might think is a "reasonable" offer of negotiation.[9] I do not know why the Aboriginal groups who refused the package did so. Inexplicably, the author does not give their reasons. Rather there is a tone in this paragraph suggesting that any reasonable person would have agreed with CRA's offer.

Examining rhetorical features of the paragraph reveals certain assumptions about what the mining company thought was reasonable. First, there is an incredulity that so many diverse Aboriginal groups had a say in the negotiations over the Century mine, as if it were unreasonable to have so many claimants some of whom were from outside the "region." "The whole system of native title" writes Hunt, "is, to a large extent, built on the presumption that *regional* Aboriginal groups are prepared and able to negotiate *reasonable* outcomes." Of course it is obvious why several Aboriginal claimants were involved in the case if one understands the nomadic character of the clans and their relation to the land. Aboriginal land tenure involves various clans of differing cultural and political formations moving through the land now called Australia. They move in trajectories (recorded in songlines) that could extend a thousand miles, passing through common water and food sites that produced common nodal points in the clans' songlines. One such common node was CRA-RTZ's Century Zinc mining site. An understanding of the nomadic character of the Indigenous tenure system would make it reasonable to expect clans from distant areas to have a tenure stake in the site. But Hunt appeals to a kind of *terra nullius* Western common sense expectation of a linear, static "region" with regard to the mine.

2009). In the Century Zinc mine negotiations, the Native Title Act was testing its newest amendments that gave an advantage to mining interests. Aboriginal clans who refused to negotiate and disagreed with the expansion of the mine were facing a company with long experience in the field, RTZ-CRA, also known then as the multinational giant Rio Tinto with a worldwide reputation for mining disasters, environmental tragedies and human rights abuses. (Reuters, "Rio Tinto PLC/Ltd—The Merger of CRA & RTZ," http://www.sea-us.org.au/corpfilez/riverofblood.html, accessed December 1, 2009).

9 I interviewed the author about negotiations he has worked on under the Native Title Act between mining companies and Aboriginal groups. He told me that he couldn't reveal any information as these terms were generally not made public and him doing so would violate attorney client privilege.

Secondly, the journalist implies that the process of making an Aboriginal claim is too easy. How can companies know that these Aboriginal claimants have legitimate claims before they start negotiating with them? How do they verify that these Indigenous groups have standing in law? The new amendments (1998) indeed have asked the state to come up with a way of deciding whether Aboriginal groups are qualified to make a claim. Not only is this asking the state to codify Aboriginal identity, it also places the burden of proof (of identity) on the Aborigines and becomes an efficient way of eliminating Indigenous groups which do not have the means to hire legitimation experts (lawyers and anthropologists) to speak for them.[10]

Finally, the article implies that those who live far from the mine site should have less authority to speak in the negotiations. Nowhere is it suggested that Aboriginal claimants, whose nomadic trajectories through the land can easily cover one thousand miles in a three year period, might have legitimated sacred sites scattered far and wide across the countryside. This spatial proximity is apparently only a requirement of the Aborigines since the proximity of the multinational corporate authorities to their mine sites is never at issue (CRA-RTZ is headquartered in London). Thus we have a negotiation where the Aborigines are, on the one hand, expected to be just like the mining corporation (rational and legally identified by the state) and, on the other hand, not like the mining industry (that is to say, not living in the structure of contemporary political economy that scatters people from their ancestral origins).

There are a number of other observations by the mining industry lawyer Michael Hunt that show how culturally and politically hegemonic demands can easily be placed on Indigenous claimants thanks to the 1998 amendments to the Native Title Act. For example, Hunt asserts that "Aboriginals now commonly claim that entry on the land by an explorationist offends their community's spiritual life, even if the community is located a long way from the land. It might even be argued that aerial geophysical survey can interfere with spiritual beliefs" (44).[11] The incredulous tone of this statement is dismissive of the true conflict between Aboriginal and

10 This was done to Indigenous peoples in the United States by establishing federal criteria for the official recognition of Indian tribes. This involves racist notions of blood quantum and it has left many tribes with the status of "federally unrecognized," thus restricting their access to federal funds and programs.

11 This argument was also made in the study I have worked on with Pemina Yellow Bird from the Three Affiliated Tribes on the Fort Berthold Reservation in North Dakota. There, the Intertribal Reinterrment Committee, when setting up provisions that would protect their ancestors' graves from the inquisitive techniques of archeologists, made sure that infrared aerial photography not be done over land suspected of containing Indian graves. This was seen as an interference with the spiritual journey of the ancestors. It also made maps available to all manner of people who would dig in Indian graves for various and sundry reasons: those who collected Indian skulls for coffee table ashtrays or those who sold Indian remains and sacred grave goods on the antiquities market. It is important to note that many native peoples do not see much of a different between the professional

Western scientific ways of knowing and rendering visible the land. And later, more cynically Hunt adds, "Aboriginals are now realizing the potency of the 'future act' 'right to negotiate' weapon they have been given. Some Aboriginals are indulging in blatant opportunism, seeking to be 'bought off'" (49). Although the author does not discuss mining or petroleum industries as themselves engaging in "blatant opportunism" he states that "(c)ynics view this exercise (of Native title assertion) as one of cash generation for the Aboriginal interests" (82). Again, making money and living far from one's relatives, normal behavior in the dominant Australian political economy, is considered suspicious and unreasonable in Aboriginals staking Native title claims.

The frustrated negotiations between Aboriginal groups and CRT-RTZ/Century Zinc to predistribute profits from a mining operation on land susceptible to Native title reveals another element in the withdrawal of *terra nullius*. To borrow the theoretical terminology of Deleuze and Guattari, Aboriginals who are newly empowered by a pre-state (yet state recognized) title to the land and encouraged to negotiate a settlement outside the state court system join mining companies in a "smooth," nonstate space. Multinational mining operations have long been functioning as worldwide machines in "smooth" space, getting states to sponsor their activities which overlap with state and Indigenous lands. Aboriginal groups too have been increasingly using nonstate space to their advantage. In the late 1990s Indigenous groups used worldwide sports and mass media networks to communicate their aim to boycott the 2000 Sydney Olympics as a way to bring attention to how Native title was being undercut by the 1998 amendments (Lenskyj 2002).[12]

The cultural expectations of the reasonable standard skew to the status quo rather than to equity as required by the Native Title Act. If Hunt's article is any indication of what would pass for reasonable in Native title land claim negotiations, the standard of reasonable is not yet part of a post-*terra nullius* world.

---

archeological use of their ancestor's remains and grave goods and the amateur uses to which pot hunters put these sacred objects.

12 There is a long tradition of using the Olympic Games as a global platform for protest. The Calgary Winter Olympics in 1988 were boycotted by the Lubicon Cree, and Canada's First Nations are organizing to do the same at the 2010 Vancouver Winter Games: "The Olympics are not about the human spirit & have little to do with athletic excellence; they are a multi-billion dollar industry backed by powerful elites, real estate, construction, hotel, tourism and television corporations, working hand in hand with their partners in crime: government officials & members of the International Olympic Committee (IOC)." See No 2010 Olympics on Stolen Native Land, *Why We Resist: The 2010 Winter Olympics*, January 1, 2010, http://no2010.com/node/18 (accessed January 1, 2010).

Post-*Terra Nullius* Mediations I: A Philosophical Look at the Role of the Imagination and its Relation to Property as Exclusion

The Australian philosopher Helen Watson-Verran wrote about the communication failures she observed in the early days of the Native Title Act. Everyone understood, she notes, that because the Native Title Act recognizes Aboriginal land tenure, it must also recognize Aboriginal systems of knowledge. But that was not what was happening. Australians could read on the front page of their newspapers that "Cape York pastoralists and Aborigines (had) jointly called for state and federal governments to legislate ... a form of statutory co-existence of title on pastoral leases," but it was well known that these negotiations were generally failing (Watson-Verran 1994). For Watson-Verran, the cause of the failure was that pastoralists did not recognize the rationality of the knowledge systems of Indigenous Australians. They knew about the storied, mythic part of the Aboriginal land tenure system, but they did not see that it corresponded to a systematic kind of knowledge about the land. In order for them to recognize this, pastoralists would first have to understand how their own systems of rationality are, like their Indigenous counterpart, inseparable from an "epistemic imaginary," that is to say, inseparable from a repertoire of pictures and stories that are inherent to the operation of Western systems of knowledge. If they could understand that both rational systems of land tenure—the Aboriginals' genealogical one which is embedded in what in English has come to be known as "the dreaming" and the Western exclusionary one (which, as we have noted in this book, is embedded in empty, homogeneous space)—involve the work of cultural imagination, then the negotiations would have a better chance of succeeding.

From a philosophical perspective, asking pastoralists to look at the imaginary that enables their own epistemic knowledge, is asking them to recognize that "*middle* between the sensible and the intelligible that has been identified as the function of image, the schemata, the phantasm—all of those figuring figurations that are simultaneously both particular and universal, both sensible and intelligible, both *de jure* and *de facto*" (Tyler 1998: 36).[13] In modernity, the figure of empty space has mediated communication between a Western consciousness full of stories of historical horrors and Utopian aspirations, on the one hand, and categories of law, order, measurement, in short what we call reason, on the other. In modernity empty space shuts down communication between these two domains of human being. One domain is that of experience and the other the domain of knowledge. Modern Western knowledge is more intent on banishing the storied imagination to an inferior position. The imagination, modern

13 "A-categorical thought," Tyler explains, "is before identity. All identity is a sham—always an other posing as the same. It cannot be thematized, cannot consist of recurrent *sames*. Consequently, there can be no *principle of difference*, for the function of *principle* is to thematize, to make an identity of difference. We cannot construct the unity of difference, a unity within difference, or an identity within difference" (36).

knowledge thinks, is mere psychological construct or mere fiction. Law, science, reason, and other forms of categorical thought have authority in modernity while the imagination is closer to a form of pathology. The revocation of *terra nullius* in Australia was supposed to represent a break from this dialectic of modernity where empty space continues to denigrate and block communication between the imagination and reason. With the implementation of the Native Title Act, pastoralists, Watson-Verran thought, had a historic opportunity to re-examine the role of the imagination in their knowledge systems.[14]

As an example of how the imaginary is at work in the logic of Western property in Australian land rights, Watson-Verran considers a 1970 land rights case that was an important precursor to the 1992 decision on Native title. The case involved *Milpirrum* and other *Yolngu* men who challenged the federal government's plan to develop an immense bauxite mine and mining town on land which they, the *Yolngu*, claimed to own. The judge found that indeed the *Yolngu* claimants were able to establish the existence of "a subtle and powerful knowledge system recognizable as law. Through this (system) particular clans were linked via identifiable sites, both to sections of land and to each other." Nevertheless, the judge found that this knowledge system "did not provide for any proprietary interest in the clans in any part of the areas claimed." Rather, " … it seems easier on the evidence to say that the clan belongs to the land than that the land belongs to the clan" (Federal Government of Australia 1971, cited in Watson-Verran 1994: 3). The judge was correct in identifying that quite different notions of agency are involved in Aboriginal knowledge systems, Watson-Verran observes. But his conclusion that the clans thus had no proprietary interest was

14 Economic calculations partake of the dialectical authority of empty space when economic reason produces a cost-benefit analysis that does not take into account a society's empirically informed sense that historical violence will repeat itself if certain conditions continue. Perhaps this was the reason that certain Indigenous clans refused to negotiate with CRA-RTZ's project to expand the Century Zinc mine. They would have had every reason to resist further mining on their ancestral lands given the historical relationships and events they have experienced at the hands of mining corporations. How unreasonable was it to refuse the company's offer of profit-sharing, a cultural center, a venture capital fund and more? All of these negotiated forms of reparation are milestones in the history of the mining industry's relations with Aboriginal peoples. But a cost-benefit analysis that would find this reasonable is one that would also view and treat land as space emptied of social relations. Certainly, based on this history, it makes sense, it is reasonable that Indigenous peoples would also resist. The Native Title Act is a law that incorporates the history of colonial violence along with the need for reparations into legal consciousness; therefore Australians should be able to assume that in some cases it is reasonable for mining projects to be denied. It is a historical irony that today the Century Zinc mine has been bought out by a Chinese company after running in the red—in November of 2008 zinc was "fetch((ing)) $0.54 a pound on the London Metal Exchange but it costs $0.69 a pound to mine at Century, though Citigroup said a lower fuel bill could cut Century's

another matter. What evidence, Watson-Verran asks, did the judge find for determining that the land was not the property of the clan? "The crux of it was the limited rights of exclusion that clans had." She quotes from the decision:

> The clan's right to exclude others is not apparent … the greatest extent to which this right can be said to exist is in the realm of ritual. But it was never suggested that rituals ever excluded members of the other clans completely from clan territory; the exclusion was only from sites. (Federal Government of Australia 1971: 272; cited in Watson-Verran 1994: 4)

Watson-Verran finds that the judge's "reification of exclusion" as the defining characteristic of ownership of land is at the bottom of the continually failed negotiations between pastoralists and Aboriginal groups. This is another way of saying that the court did not know how to work with Aboriginal forms of limited sovereignty within Western categories of full property and ownership. In the land negotiations over the assertion of Native title exclusionary principles are a hindrance (and a loss to Aboriginals). In sum, pastoralists (and courts) should critique their legally-sanctioned exclusionary practices and forms of knowing with respect to the land. Once the fuller cultural sense of Aboriginal belonging to the land is known, the introduction of nonexclusionary laws like those allowed through the Native Title Act would be mediated by an expanded cultural imaginary and that 40 percent of Australia that had incorporated the limited property status of the songlines would become a sort of commons filled with heterogeneous ways of belonging on the land.

Would further self-knowledge help pastoralists negotiate with Aboriginals? According to Watson-Verran, pastoralists "hav(e) trouble with Aborigines as knowers: they hope (in vain) that they are negotiating over whether *Wik* people can come onto the land to collect water lily bulbs or shoot a few kangaroo." Furthermore, pastoralists don't know how to think of the consequences of their practices on the land. They cannot imagine what Aborigines might mean "when they talk of the land as crying at present, as needing to be 'quietened'" They cannot think of their "corporations as being responsible to the places where their cattle roam, pulverizing the soil with their hard cutting hooves." How then, Watson asks, "can they think of their companies as being owned by the land? Like Justice Blackburn, the pastoralists are having trouble with agency." Given this situation, the pastoralists don't know how to begin to institutionally recognize a different system of knowing and thus owning land. In Watson's words, "they are suffering

costs, trimming losses" (Reuters, "Century zinc mine may not close," *Reuters Online*, November 21, 2008). So those Aboriginal clans who refused to be compensated for the use of their ancestral lands through profit sharing with Century Zinc had made a good decision in retrospect.

from a case of 'hardening of the categories'" and would be greatly helped in this by investigating the imaginary stakes of the categories they use (4).[15]

15 The problem of agency here needs more development. In this light I offer the following experiment by Watson/Chambers of some categorical differences between English and Yolngu (Aboriginal) speakers in Australia. Two girls, an English speaker and Yolngu speaker, are asked to describe the photograph in Figure 7, p. 14, boats on the shore. The English speaker says: "Canoes are lying on the beach." The Yolngu *matha* speaker says: "Rangi-ngura nykel lipalipa," which roughly translates as "Beach-on staying canoe." The anthropological linguists go on to analyze these different descriptions in terms of the English language's preference for subject/predicate relations. The Yolngu *matha* description, on the other hand, begins with a suffixed term (beach-on) which emphasizes a spatial relation between elements of the world. "In Yolngu *matha*," Watson/Chambers note, "the subject of each sentence both names the thing and points to its relatedness. That is to say, the Yolngu start with the view that the world is a related whole, and when constructing sentences they focus on particular relations ... (as opposed to the English tendency to foreground) separate things in nature which may often have a separate focus as subjects of sentences" (15). This difference is offered the following gloss from Whorf:

> The Indo-European languages and many others give great prominence to a type of sentence having two parts, each built around a class of word-substantives and verbs—which those languages treat differently in grammar ... the contrast has been stated in logic in many ways: subject and predicate, actor and action, things and relations between things ... By these more or less distinct terms, we ascribe a semifictious isolation to parts of experience. English terms like 'sky, hill, swamp,' persuade us to regard some elusive aspect of nature's endless variety as a distinct *thing*, almost like a table or chair. Thus, English and similar tongues lead us to think of the universe as a collection of rather distinct objects and events corresponding to words ... The real question is: What do different languages do, not with these artificially isolated objects but with the flowing face of nature in its motion, color, and changing form; with clouds, beaches, and yonder flight of birds? For, as goes our segmentation of the face of nature, so goes our physics of the Cosmos. (Whorf, Benjamin, "Languages and Logic." In *Language, Thought and Reality*. J.B. Carroll. Cambridge, MA, MIT Press, 1956, 233-45)

These observations on relatedness are important for several reasons. First, because we are framing negotiations between (newly instituted but of ancient durée) Indigenous tenure systems and (dominant) capitalist property relations as a problem between a (Western) subject encountering a (non-Western) other, we should keep in mind that the formulation of the problem in these terms is consonant with a particular structure of language as well as a particular philosophical tradition. Formulating the problem of this encounter with radical difference may well deserve to be treated without the grammatical structures of subject and object which lend an easy "thematization" to the problem of "thinking

Post-*Terra Nullius* Mediations II: An Anthropological Perspective on Comparative Epistemic Imaginaries

Anthropologists who have looked comparatively at the epistemic imaginaries supporting Aboriginal and Western land tenure systems have made further suggestions to mediate understanding between these groups.[16] Westerners, they point out, own land though the mediation of number. They use number to translate qualities said to inhere in the land, qualities such as area and length. These qualities can be quantified, that is to say they can be rendered in a recursive pattern (number is a recursive pattern based on the fingers of the hand; these digits become units of ten that recur). The Aboriginal system of owning the land is mediated by another way of knowing. For Aboriginal Australians, land exists as a set of sites whose foci inhere in the land. These sites are connected in particular ways that make the land meaningful. The logic that connects these focal sites is the material pattern of kinship relations. Thus, just as number translates the qualities that inhere in the land for Western system of ownership, genealogical patterns translate the inherent meaning of the land for Aboriginal system of land tenure.

According to this view, one of the main differences in the two systems is the value accorded to the key terms. For the Aboriginal Australian, the mystery of the origins of the sets of focal land sites is celebrated. The stories that explain how these sites came into being are prolific in the culture and their rich metaphors are a centrally discussed topic. In Western property systems, on the other hand, the mystery of the origin of "qualities" is considered unknowable by reason and is therefore called "a priori." Any further investigation of this is excluded from the system of numerical knowing that renders land valuable. In the Western system, telling how you know about the inherent land value (epistemology) is generally denied. And the role of the imagination in this knowing is theoretically absent. For Indigenous Australians, the role of the imagination, the pictures and storytelling, are publicly expressed features of knowing the land and of thus articulating the Aboriginal structure of land ownership.

Within the Western knowledge system, denial of the role of the imagination only helps the system run more efficiently. When this system is forced to co-exist and thus negotiate with one so different, the denial of the imaginary becomes more obvious and its restrictive nature more apparent. With regard to Native title claims on lands leased to western ranchers, if pastoralists understand that their system of knowledge-making relies on both image and logic, they will see that their negotiations with Aborigines are about knowledge-making and not just corrupt politics. They have enjoyed living in a world where true knowledge had

---

difference as difference" (135). Perhaps something more akin to the sort of relatedness in the Yolngu sentence would be appropriate. This problem of a too easy thematization is of course a problem of categories, how and where their striations are drawn in the world.

16 This section relies on the work of Helen Watson and David Wade Chambers, *Singing The Land, Signing the Land* (Geelong, Victoria: Deakin University Press, 1993).

no relation to the imaginary. Indeed, what is characteristic of modernity is that the imagination is banished to the category of the aesthetic and excluded from the epistemic. Seeing the need for an epistemic imaginary, for looking at the stories and pictures inherent in the Western knowledge system, would make them better negotiators.

The position of comparative anthropology argues that "(pastoralists) need a picture of the ways the things we take for granted have been made. They need a story of the construction of the basic categories though which land is known in a public sense" (Watson and Chambers 1993: 7). This revelation has the potential to create new categories of knowers, new kinds of agents who can be seated at the negotiating table. At this moment in our life on the earth, these anthropologists argue, we most desperately need to hear from the land and, more generally, from the non-human world. For the Aboriginal these non-human agents have much to teach us, not as objects of our knowledge (not as "Nature") but rather as subjects in their own right.

In post-*terra nullius* Australia, the anthropological position of Watson and Chambers reanimates a Western legal imaginary (stunted, I would say, by the dominance of empty space). It views Indigenous Australians as agents who, with their own radical form of land title, bring to the negotiating table epistemic resources that can acknowledge and mediate disparate ways of knowing the land. It revalues the genealogical system that has allowed Aboriginals to live on their land over a geological time frame, suggesting its usefulness for contemporary problem solving with regard to long term environmental problems like nuclear waste storage and global warming, problems whose solutions demand a political imagination that exceeds the temporal and spatial form of the nation-state.

"Owners" of genealogically known land, the theory explains, understand "owning" as a public articulation of stories through which land was sung into being by Ancestors. Aboriginal Australians have a vast repertoire by which the world can be re-imagined, a repertoire known in English as 'the dreaming'. This conceptual resource, the "epistemic imaginary," comprises stories and images that enable "the reconciliation of the many local knowledges that constitute Aboriginal knowledge systems." Because Western legal systems are so alienated from their own "imaginary," Watson and Chambers conclude, Aboriginals well versed in the songs of their land tenure systems would make better negotiators than English jurists or even self-reflective pastoralists when it comes to implementing the spirit of Native title over pastoral lease land.

I have one reservation about the comparative model Watson and Chambers employ. The authors imply that genealogical patterns can be compared to the recursive patterns we find in Western systems of counting and quantifying. But is this really so? Are genealogies recursive systems? The issues we raised in our study of the Sahrawi census suggest that genealogies of nomadic peoples, their "bio-figures" as the anthropologist Marilyn Strathern would say, are also characterized by a certain openness that allows each generation to narrate the historical differences they experience and to create new kinship alliances based on contingencies of life. Such flexibility in the form suggests something other than the recursive focus of Watson and Chambers' model. (Perhaps even Western thinking about DNA needs a more open schema to account for the ability of genetic material to interact and recode based on environmental factors.) The method of finding a similar category—the recursive in this case—as a basis for comparison lends a common categorical ground to the Aboriginal and Western cultural systems. We can see how this kind of categorical thinking would favor Western cultural figures and perhaps further block our understanding and appreciation of the creative usefulness of the difference of Aboriginal figures of thought. Can the Aboriginal and Western systems of land tenure communicate without finding a common epistemological ground? Perhaps there is an analogy in the way that languages work, through translation. Recursive systems are to genealogical memory what grammar is to language. Grammar is an invention of sixteenth-century Europe. Grammar is not translation nor does it account for the creative role languages play in the worldmaking ways of cultures. But grammar does resemble law. Grammar, like law, is a set of rules that relate to language use. It is like the civil code that organizes legal thinking around categories. But compare this to the common law tradition that organizes legal thinking around precedent. Before written law, precedent was a lot more like genealogical memory. It was what stayed in the cultural memory of the oral traditions of a group. Aboriginal songlines are thought to relate stories about the land that go back some forty thousand years. The ways in which cultures combine poetic figures with biology in genealogical memory is an amazing art and suggests a model of comparative epistemology different than the recursive model offered by Watson and Chambers.

Conclusion

English colonial sovereignty ignored long-established ways of social, spiritual and political being-with-the-land held by Australia's first peoples. They did not appreciate the Aboriginal's legal ways, what Watson-Verran calls "the abstract knowledge, the practical and conceptual skills, the structures of authority, the belief system or the social mechanisms through which control was exerted" (44). Instead, English colonists declared the land *terra nullius*, and went on to make it their own by institutionalizing a set of boundaries that generally speaking had nothing to do with the land itself. The names they gave to the areas they declared Crown lands, names like "Disappointment Peak," reveal the often frustrating and arduous nature of their project to make the land reflect the world from which they had come (Carter 1987). Based on principles of quantification, the English divided the land into bounded plots that could be given to people with no prior claim to the land and administered from great distances. This European knowledge-power network which they distributed over the land was inscribed in pieces of paper that were put away for safe keeping in title offices and banks (Watson and Chambers 1993). The *Mabo* decision in 1992 severely weakened the security systems of these institutions. Native Title, as a new form in Australian law, limits the sovereignty of European knowledge-power networks as it limits the sovereignty of the state. Compared to Western forms of property, the Aboriginal songlines are not based on exclusion but on managing multiple users. Their formal appearance in Western law in the form of the Native Title Act creates new legal solutions for land sharing and reparations. Importantly, as a result of the revocation of *terra nullius*, Native Title in Australia gives the earth a newly empowered voice to negotiate with some of its most rapacious modern opponents.

Conclusion on the *Mabo* and *Western Sahara* Cases

At the outset of this section I suggested that the form of decolonization that arises with the revocation of *terra nullius* is different than that which took place during the 1960s. Post-*terra nullius* decolonization is linked to reparations and to limitations on the sovereignty of the state. At the same time, it accompanies an increase in the nonstatist sovereignty status of Indigenous peoples, suggesting the transformation of the colonial-based concept of sovereignty in international law.[17] At a broader level that includes the global commons, these changes are indicative of a shifting spatial imaginary in international law that can bring greater limitations to the full sovereignty of states and create new categories for limited user rights of and collective responsibility for shared domains of the global commons.

Although the doctrine of *terra nullius* was deployed most pervasively by European powers in the late nineteenth and early twentieth centuries, its revocation in the Western Sahara Case is a sign of a further step from decolonization to self-determination. Decolonization and self-determination are terms that were interchangeable until the 1960s when most former colonies had acquired independence. Policies of decolonization have traditionally supported frameworks of self-government grounded in European-based legal practices. Self-determination, on the other hand, has the potential to be a concept of government based on Indigenous processes that demonstrate how contemporary Indigenous peoples interpret their traditions (Deloria and Lytle 1984: 244–264). The assertion of Native title in Australia seeks to do precisely this. Both the Aboriginal and the Sahrawi cases foretell both the importance and the dangers of using statist legal forms to channel and empower Indigenous self-determination. Importantly, they show the urgency of foregrounding the epistemic imaginary of empty space in the legitimation discourses of modern land tenure and of understanding how other

17 Thus in the last 40 years Indigenous peoples have achieved legislative gains for the protection of sacred sites, repatriation of cultural patrimony, tribal and clan sovereignty, pan Indigenous representation and United Nations representation.

bio-figures like genealogical memory communicate their legitimate ways of being on and organizing the land.[18]

18 It is important to note that although I have sometimes used Deleuze and Guattari's concepts of smooth and striated space to understand abstract relationships of sovereignty (nomadic or statist) in the West, these chapters on Indigenous sovereignty assertions of formerly nomadic Sahrawi and Aboriginal peoples in modern nation-states require a note of clarification. First, it should be clear that the philosophical concept of "nomadic *nomos*" is not the same as the descriptions of nomadic culture I have outlined for Aboriginal inhabitants of Australia and the Sahrawi peoples of the Western Sahara. "Nomadic *nomos*" is merely a philosophical concept; its historical and cultural reference to actual nomadic peoples is oblique at best.

Secondly, the authors of *A Thousand Plateaus* repeatedly warn that smooth space is not going to save us. In terms of these last chapters, this means that while nonstatist smooth space does appear essential to the project of self-determination: Indigenous peoples are now availing themselves of international and global arenas like the United Nations, NGOs, the Internet, and the global sports and entertainment industries, in short, inter- and nonstate spaces where local native peoples may appeal and gain more clout than in their national domains (Deloria and Lytle 1984). However, the increased sovereignty which results for some Indigenous groups may also invite a newly parasitic relationship with states. This is happening in the United States where Indian reservations, thanks to their special status as dependent sovereign nations standing outside of many local state and national federal laws, are now being targeted by federal agencies and private waste disposal companies as sites for nuclear waste storage. (Randel Hanson, "From Bads to Goods: Marketing Nuclear Waste to American Indian Tribes "Minneapolis: PhD Dissertation; University of Minnesota, 1998). Although they may not have been able to predict this in the 1950s during the termination period, states need these reservations as their own nonstatist space, a space they create outside of the federal and state laws which govern the acceptable levels of toxicity in the soil and radioactivity risk in the air. So, my interest in these chapters was not to romanticize Indigenous people's newfound leverage among states (smooth space is not going to save us). Rather it was to connect some insights from their experience of the revocation of empty space/*terra nullius* to the experience of empty space/*res nullius* in the global commons.

Conclusion: Beyond Empty Space—Expanding the Epistemological Repertoire of the Global Commons through Biofigural and Technological Imaginaries

> The deep imperative (of contemporary ethnography) is to expand our epistemological repertoire. We need perhaps today a more informatics and biological imagination. Both biology and information are lively, ever escaping their temporary restraints and regulators, creating anew. Ethnography today is thus held to a higher standard than ever: it is a matter of opening the simplified accounts, making accountability possible at different granularities, signposting the labyrinths of possible inquiries for their relevance, their points of no return, their conceptual reruns, of reinvigorating civil society and its recursive public spheres. (Fischer 2009: 18)

Who owns the oceans, outer space, the radio frequency spectrum, the Internet, the earth's atmosphere and biodiversity? The answer "everyone and no-one" is the recurring paradox of the global commons today. It is the sign that we are caught in a dead-end but dominant cultural logic, one that has been sustained in modernity by the rhetorical figure of empty space. Empty space is the figure of thought that has anchored international law of the global commons in the modern era. Conceptualized at first as the ungovernable outside of the international legal order in the law of the seas, the global commons arose as a default zone in international law. From the law of the seas to the law of the seed, *The Political Uncommons* examined the epistemological repertoire of the modern global commons and found it dominated by the metaphorics of empty space, complicit with the doctrines of *res nullius* and *terra nullius*, and implicated in the failure of international law to create effective and equitable regimes to sustainably manage and to share the benefits of commons at the global level.

I began this inquiry into the epistemological imaginary of the global commons with an example of how the Inuit's Indigenous tenure system, with its strong geographical and biographical relations to the earth, might provide a platform from which to challenge long entrenched, ineffective traditions of global commons management by side-stepping the rule of property and invoking the rule of liability in international law. Rather than ask who owns the atmospheric commons, the Inuit case frames global commons in terms of the reciprocal relations that users have a duty to uphold. Without invoking the epistemic imaginary of an inside/outside status of global commons with respect to the full sovereignty of states, the Inuit claim appealed to the global commons as an interconnected legal whole, a nonstate domain that was not defined as the outside of the nation state. Avoiding the paradoxes of empty space, the Inuit could bypass the seemingly boundless authority of the territorial state—what the nineteenth century philosopher Soren Kierkegaard calls "bad infinity"—and appeal to the limited sovereignty of states as global citizens.

In the final chapters I returned to the issue of how Indigenous tenure systems persisted as a challenge to the European concepts that dominate juridical thinking about shared domains at the global scale. The last two chapters thus focused on genealogical memory, a biofigural schema that the Sahrawi and Aboriginal inhabitants of Australia use to create recursive cultural infrastructure allowing them to express reciprocal relationships that connect humans to each other and to the land. Viewing the Indigenous, nomadic forms of land sharing as persistent forms within and in spite of the colonial (*res* and *terra nullius*) history of the modern global commons brought a comparative cultural analysis to the modern global commons. This conclusion can now reflect on the results of that cross-cultural comparison and use them to expand the epistemological repertoire of international law with regard to the global commons.

The persistent viability of nonEuropean tenure systems despite the dominant authority of Euro-centric international law has always offered epistemological variety to human forms of relation to the earth. But the legal recognition of Indigenous tenure systems by international law is something different. It is an occasion to expand the epistemological repertoire of the international legal imaginary, a chance to invent juridical forms that can be used by and empower nonstate social actors.

With regard to the global commons, this book has focused on how such recognition included a renunciation of the rhetorical power of empty space by revoking the doctrine of *terra nullius*. The Sahrawi and Aboriginal Australian cases illustrated how an expanded epistemic imaginary may or may not arise when the logical precondition of *terra nullius*/empty space is unavailable to the authoritative arguments of the state. In the case of the Western Sahara, the democratic political institutions of the census and referendum were ineffective vehicles to voice Sahrawi land tenure after the revocation of *terra nullius*, and no effective alternative political imaginaries gained significant authority in their place. No new international legal institutions arose to hold the genealogical, biofigural authority of ancestral belonging to the land. And thus the Western Sahara remains a case of two recognized but economically unequal states warring with each other. As a modern state, the Western Sahara may as well be an island in the middle of the *res nullius* Atlantic instead of a land of deep ancestral ties to the precolonial Sahrawi nomads of Africa. Without dismissing the military power of Morocco and the greed of transnational mining corporations, we must lament the lack of political imagination in international law that held out state sovereignty as the only form of political organization for the Sahrawi community to hold onto their ancestral lands.

In the wake of the dismissal of *terra nullius*, Aboriginal Australia, on the other hand, became co-creators of a new political form, Native Title, through which to exercise their biofigural understanding of land tenure. Without losing site of the pitfalls of this model, we can appreciate how Native Title expanded the epistemological repertoire of civil society in Australia. Furthermore, the newly empowered songlines create a new kind of recursive public sphere across the land. In the recurring negotiations that reorganize land use subject to Native title, Indigenous peoples speak through the authority of ancestral stories that spell out their belonging to the land while ranchers and mining corporations respond through the authority of the state licenses through which they hold their private property. The disparate forms of authority and differing modes of representing human relations to the land form a disjunctive common sphere with no aim to invent a common denominator. The political form of Native title then demands that time-consuming negotiation (and not war) will establish the rules of the game in this emergent public sphere. With full awareness that Indigenous peoples are not equally empowered players and that the dominant appeal to a "reasonable standard" of negotiation is set to work against them, we can still note how songlines expand the epistemological repertoire through which land use is legitimized in Australia. Without an *a priori* legal appeal to a *terra nullius* derived ground zero, both systems of land tenure—the genealogical one where belonging is embedded in the dreamings and the Western exclusionary one where property is embedded in empty homogenous space—foreground the repertoire of pictures and stories that are inherent to the operations of their respective knowledge systems. The cross-cultural negotiations engage these various knowledge systems and create a public sphere where incommensurable cultural imaginaries speak to each other.

What do the warring and negotiating public spheres that emerge from the revocation of *terra nullius*/empty space tell us about global commons? If we are convinced that we need to reimagine global commons beyond the cultural logic of *res nullius*/empty space, we can learn how to do this by studying the persistent residual (Indigenous) and the emergent (technological and biological) forms of civil society created by nonstate entities. The Internet that operates in the government regulated electromagnetic field and the migratory whales that thrive across the moratorium-governed seas are both examples of emergent forms of nonstate political organization. They are emergent global commons regimes. They share a key dimension with the struggles of the Sahrawi and the Aboriginal Australians in that they struggle to legitimize their respective knowledge systems—biofigural and technological—by expanding the epistemological repertoire of legal concepts we use to engage the Western, exclusionary knowledge system of property. And, it is no coincidence that these nonstate entities share a common spatial characteristic: their spatial imaginary involves movement and intensity rather than stasis and extension. Like the expansive liability coverage (described in Chapter 5) that outer space law brought to radiological contamination of the earth because it was written to cover objects in space that moves, the legal regimes we create to cover the variety of domains not yet (or not legitimately) propertized by state or private entities—the domains we call the global commons—must be thought within this expansive spatial imaginary that is not restricted by the repertoire of pictures and stories embedded in the cultural logic of empty space.

The Political Uncommons has pointed to the limits of the epistemic imaginary that currently informs the international law of the global commons. Historically and culturally, commons are a project of human solidarity different than that of the modern nation state. But the current law of the global commons frames commons in terms of interstate and nonstate space, the in-between space of states or the outside space of states. While, on the one hand, the ambiguous nonstate jurisdiction of the global commons gives rights of passage and use not only to states but to a heterogeneous array of social agents—from individuals of all geographic provenance to environmental action groups, multinational mining corporations, and nuclear testing states, it does so within the category of Grotius' *mare liberum*, the freedom of the seas. This freedom, which is extended to all modern global commons, is an inclusive freedom but one without clear reciprocal duties. It is a freedom that mirrors unregulated, neoliberal free markets. In this regard it has no resemblance to the commons of small scale societies where reciprocal relationships, not individual freedom, defines its commons character. Thus, despite this openness to nonstate entities, international law imagines global commons within an epistemological repertoire dominated by the experience and needs of the territorial state. As I have discussed throughout this volume, the restrictive nature of these categories operates as a powerful "political uncommons" to our global commons domains. The categories of interstate and nonstate space are in fact a cultural machine that undermines the most basic principles of commons. Where commons should be based on relations of reciprocity, international law offers relations of exchange; where commons would emphasize duties and obligations of commons users, international law would protect their individual freedom; where commons would spell out the limited sovereignty of states, international law has more often provided rules for the full exercise of state sovereignty in global commons. At the least, global commons should make of states something closer to what the United States made of Native American tribes—domestic, dependent nations within a larger global imperative.

Compared to the picture of commons that international law inherited from its Roman predecessors, the contemporary global commons is insufficient. Unlike *res communis*, a Roman category of common property that included areas like the shoreline understood as a necessary part of human's subsistence right to fish, the law of the modern global commons draws a blank with regard to subsistence rights in common. As discussed throughout this book, when international law has considered what subsistence needs the global commons should meet (the needs of whales to their global migratory routes; the needs of farmers to the genetic diversity of seeds; the needs of all life forms to the global climate system) and when global commons regimes have sought to establish the legal and economic infrastructure to meet these needs (by declaring a moratorium on whale killing; by invoking the Common Heritage Principle to create a seed bank; by proposing a global tax on financial markets of the global North to pay for the sustainable management of the rainforests of the global South) in each case rules of private property interfere with the proposed common property solution. There is no effective idea of common property in modern global commons because at bottom there is no solid idea of what cannot be propertized, what cannot be commodified. Things and practices that are needed for subsistence should not fall under a rule of property exchange. Rather they should benefit from reinvigorated rules of reciprocity and liability, economies of gifting and paying forward one's debt to the common good.[1]

There are deep cultural roots to the difficulty of thinking and creating noncommodifiable domains with the tools offered by the international law of the global commons. Unlike the Roman property system, the secular framework of modern global commons had no place for the category of *res divini juris*, things which, in the Justinian code, belonged to the Roman gods and were therefore protected from state or private ownership (see Chapter 4). As we have seen in multiple cases throughout this volume, the secular contours of the modern global commons helped to create a class of things belonging to everyone, *res communis*, that was indistinguishable from the class of things belonging to no one, *res nullius*, that proto-form of exclusive property. And thus, as we have seen time and again in the lament of international relations scholars, "the state of the global commons today is *res nullius*." The paradoxical logic of things belonging to both everybody and nobody is a logic embedded in the cultural imaginary of empty space. It is complicit with the legal circumscription of global commons that are both excluded

1 In the US context, my own work to reclaim urban right-of-way for a commons-sector, community trust-owned solar energy system is an example of "reinvigorating" legal rules that fortify and expand our recursive public spheres. "Right-of-way," I argue, is a remnant of the ancient, pre-state commons. Like the Songlines that persist in Native Title in Australia or the concept of *estovers*—wood gleanings—that are protected by the Forest Charter of the Magna Carta (Linebaugh 2008), the category of a "right" of way outlines the persistence of a rule in commons, one that predates the rule of property protected by the modern state. "Right-of-way" is a legal tool created at the end of feudal era to solve a problem caused by the enclosure of the English commons (Polanyi 2001). Peasants needed legal access across their formerly common agricultural fields and pastures. In the Common Law tradition, right-of-way is thus a vestige of a pre-modern commons tradition. By exercising usufruct in right of way, a community trust, I demonstrate, can "own" a solar energy production system and use the income generated from energy sales to support subsistence needs in low-income housing. See Kathryn Milun, *The Solar Commons Demonstration Project* at http://solarcommons.org (accessed December 2009). The Solar Commons project is a hybrid form that resembles in interesting ways other non-statist commons persisting in today's statist era—US Indian reservations, the oceans, the Internet, and other global commons domains. All these entities engage pre-modern (or post-modern) notions of rightful belonging even as they operate within and alongside modern categories of state ownership.

(as an open-access, empty juridical outside of the state) and—ineffectively thus tragically—included (in the law of nation-states). Thus international law both regulates global commons (albeit poorly) by describing them as a form of interstate space and deregulates global commons by describing them as the lawless arena of nonstate space.

By focusing on the epistemic imaginary of the global commons, this volume was able to connect diverse realms within a common political problematic: neither states nor markets have provided the terms to sufficiently move civil society towards a sustainable mode of living on the earth. Connecting emergent global commons domains such as the Internet, outer space, and biodiversity with the residual sovereignty of Indigenous land tenure systems allows us to expand our epistemological repertoire in order to move beyond the paradox of modern property that would have global commons belong to everyone and no-one.

Bibliography

Agamben, Giorgio. *Homo Sacer: Sovereign Power and Bare Life.* Stanford, CA: Stanford University Press, 1998.

——. *The State of Exception.* Chicago: University of Chicago Press, 2005.

——. *Infancy and History: On the Destruction of Experience (Radical Thinkers).* London: Verso, 2007.

Alverson, Keith, Raymond Bradley and Thomas Pedersen. "Environmental Variability and Climate Changes." International Geosphere-Biosphere Program Series, 2001.

Anderson, Benedict. *Imagined Communities: Reflections on the Origin and Spread of Nationalism.* London: Verso, 1991.

Arctic Council. *Arctic Climate Impact Assessment.* November 24, 2004. http.//www.acia.uaf.edu/ (accessed July 22, 2010).

Arend, Anthony Clark. *A New Outer Space Treaty?* July 19, 2009. http://anthonyclarkarend.com/internationallaw/a-new-outer-space-treaty/ (accessed December 1, 2009).

Augé, Marc. *An Anthropology for Contemporaneous Worlds.* Translated by Amy Jacobs. Stanford, CA: Stanford University Press, 1995.

Bainbridge, Stephen. *Revising the Outer Space Treaty.* July 20, 2009. http://www.professorbainbridge.com/professorbainbridgecom/2009/07/revising-the-outer-space-treaty.html (accessed December 1, 2009).

Ball, Jane. "The Boundaries of Property Rights in English Law: Report to the XVIIth International Congress of Comparative Law." *Electronc Journal of Comparative Law.* December 2006: 1–33.

Barlett, Donald and James B. Steele. "Monsanto's Harvest of Fear." *Vanity Fair.* May 2008. http://www.vanityfair.com/politics/features/2008/05/monsanto200805 (accessed August 11, 2009).

Barnes, Peter. *Capitalism 3.0; A Guide to Reclaiming the Commons.* San Francisco, CA: Berrett-Koehler Publishers, 2006.

Barstow, Robbins. "The Moral Imperative for Whale Protection." *Cetacean Society International, Inc.* July 2001. http://csiwhalesalive.org/csi01301.html (accessed December 19, 2009).

Barthes, Roland. *Writing Degree Zero.* Translated by Annette Lavers and Collin Smith. New York: Hill and Wang, 1968.

Baslar, Kemal. *The Concept of the Common Heritage of Mankind in International Law.* The Hague: Kluwer Law International, 1998.

Bauman, Zygmunt. *Globalization: The Human Consequences.* New York: Columbia University Press, 1998.

Beaujouan, L. "Science livresque et nautique au XVe siecle." Edited by Paul Adam Michel Mollat. *Ve Colloque International D'historie Maritime.* Paris: SEVPEN, 1960: 61–90.

Beder, Sharon. *Global Spin: The Corporate Assault on Environmentalism.* Chelsea: Green Publishing Company, 2002

Beebe, Barton. "Law's Empire and the Final Frontier: Legalizing the Future in the Early Corpus Juris Spatialis." *Yale Law Journal* 108, no. 7 (May 1999): 1737–73.

Bell, Diane and Pam Ditton. *Law: The Old and the New.* Canberra: Aboriginal History, 1980.

Benkler, Yochai. "Overcoming Agoraphobia: Building the Commons of the Digitally Networked Environment." *Harvard Journal of Law and Technology* 11, no. 2 (1998): 287–400.

——. *The Wealth of Networks: How Social Production Transforms Markets and Freedom.* New Haven, CT: Yale University Press, 2006.

Benterrak, K., P. Roe and S. Muecke. *Reading the Country.* Fremantle: Fremantle Arts Centre Press, 1984.

Berry, David M. and Giles Moss. "The Politics of the Libre Commons." Vol. 11, *First Monday.* September 4, 2006. http://firstmonday.org/issues/issue11_9/berry/index.html.

Birnie, Patricia and Alan Boyle. *International Law and the Environment.* New York: Oxford University Press, 1992.

Blackstone, William. *Commentaries on the Laws of England*, 17, 1830.

Bollier, David. *Viral Spiral: How the Commoners Created their Own Digital Republic.* New York: The New Press, 2008.

Bovenberg, Jasper A. "Mining the Common Heritage of our DNA: Lessons Learned from Grotius and Pardo." *Duke Law and Technology Review* 3, 8, 2006: 1–19.

Boyle, James. *Shamans, Software and Spleens: Law and the Construction of the Information Society.* Cambridge, MA: Harvard University Press, 1996.

Broder, John M. "5 Nations Forge Pact on Climate; Goals Go Unmet." *New York Times*, December 19, 2009: A1.

Brysland, Gordon. "Rewriting History 2: The Wider Significance of Mabo v Queenland." *Alternative Law Review* 17, no. 4 (August 1992): 162–165.

Buck, Susan. *The Global Commons, An Introduction.* Washington, DC: Island Press, 1998.

Buckland, William Warwick. *A Textbook of Roman Law from Augustus to Justinian.* Cambridge: Cambridge University Press, 1921.

Business Wire-London. "The RTZ Corporation." March 7, 1996. http://www.encyclopedia.com/doc/1G1-18061968.html (accessed December 1, 2009).

Caratini, Sophie. *Les Rgaybat (1610–1934).* Paris: L'Harmattan, 1989.

——. *Les Enfants des Nuages.* Paris: Seuil, 1993.

——. "Le Rôle de la Femme au Sahara Occidental." *La Pensée* 308 (Oct, Nov, Dec 1996): 115–124.

——. "Les Sahraouis: Entre le temps et l'espace." *Sciences Humaines* 15 (January 1997): 44–45.

Carter, Paul. *The Road to Botany Bay: An Essay in Spatial History.* London/ Boston: Faber and Faber, 1987.

Chatwin, Bruce. *The Songlines.* London: Picador Pan Books, 1988.

Clover, Charles. *Internationale Politik-Global.* German Council on Foreign Relations. Winter 2005. http://www.ip-global.org/archiv/volumes/2005/winter 2005/who-owns-the-sea-.html (accessed December 4, 2009).

Cool, Jenny (Director) *Home Economics: A Documentary of Suburbia.* 1995.

Cooper, John Cobb. "The Problem of a Definition of 'Air Space'." Edited by Andrew G. Haley and Welf Heinrich, Prince of Hanover. *Proceedings of the First Colloquium of the Law of Outer Space.* Vienna: Springer-Verlag, 1959, 38–44.

Coquillette, Daniel R. "Mosses from an Old Manse: Another Look at Some Historic Property Cases About the Environment." *Cornell Law Review* 64 (June 1979): 761–821.

Cordell, Dana. "8 Reasons Why We Need to Rethink the Management of Phosphorus Resources in the Global Food System." *Global Phosphorus Research Initiative.* 2009. www.phosphorusfutures.net (accessed December 1, 2009).

Cornell, Stephan P. and Joseph Kalt. *What Can Tribes Do? Strategies and Institutions in American Indian Economic Development.* Los Angeles: American Indian Studies Center, UCLA, 1992.

Cox, Stan. "'The Basics of Life Belong to Everyone'." *The Land Institute.* March 22, 2002. http://www.landinstitute.org/vnews/display.v?TARGET=printable&article_id=3d10b5ccb7d57 (accessed July 27, 2009).

Cox, Susan Jane Buck. "No Tragedy on the Commons." *Environmental Ethics* 7, Spring (1985): 49–63.

Crang, Michael and N.J. Thrift. *Thinking Space (Critical Geographies).* London: Routledge, 2000.

Cronon, William. *Changes in the Land: Indians, Colonists and the Ecology of New England.* New York: Hill and Wang, 1983.

Cullet, Philippe. "Plant variety protection." *International Environmental Law Research Centre.* 2003. http://www.ielrc.org/content/f0304.htm (accessed December 1, 2009).

Daes, Erica-Irene A. "On the Relations between Indigenous Peoples and States." *Without Prejudice: The EAFORD International Review of Racial Discriminiation* (International Organization For the Elimination of All Forms of Racial Discrimination [EAFORD]), 2, no. 2 (1989): 41–52.

Dear, Michael. *The Postmodern Urban Condition.* Oxford: Blackwell Publishers, 2000.

Deleuze, Gilles. *The Fold: Leibniz and the Baroque.* Translated by Tom Conley. Minneapolis: University of Minnesota Press, 1992.

Deleuze, Gilles and Félix Guattari. *A Thousand Plateaus: Capitalism and Schizophrenia.* Translated by Brian Massumi. Minneapolis: University of Minnesota Press, 1987.

Deloria, Vine and Clifford Lytle. *The Nations Within: The Past and Future of American Indian Sovereignty.* New York: Pantheon Books, 1984.

Derrida, Jacques. *Of Grammatology.* Translated by Gayatri Chakravorty Spivak. Baltimore and London: Johns Hopkins University Press, 1976.

Dickason, Olive. "Old World Laws, New World Peoples and Concepts of Sovereignty." In *Essays on the History of North American Discovery and Exploration*, edited by Stanley Palmer and Dennis Reinhartz, 52–78. College Station, Texas: Texas A&M University Press, 1988.

Disco, Cornelis and Eda Kranakis. "New Industrial Commons in Europe Working Paper Nr. 2009–17." *Tensions of Europe/Inventing Europe.* May 27, 2009. (accessed December 15, 2009).

Doyle, Stephen E. "Comments on the Melbourne Colloquium on the Law of Outer Space." *Journal of Space Law* 26, no. 2 (1998): 213–4.

Eisenzwieg, Uri. "An Imaginary Territory: The Problematic of Space in Zionist Discourse." *Dialectical Anthropology* 5 (1981): 261–85.

Emin, Vahan G. "Spaceflight and the Problem of Vertical Limit of State Sovereignty." In *Fourteenth Colloquium on Law of Outer Space*, edited by Mortimer D. Schwartz, 201–203. New Jersey: Rothman & Co, 1972.

Falk, Richard. *The Status of Law in International Society.* Princeton: Princeton University Press, 1970.

——. "On the Recent Further Decline of International Law." In *Legal Change: Essays in Honour of Juilius Stone*, edited by A.R. Blackshield. Sidney: N.P., 1983.

Farnsworth, Clyde H. "Blaming it all on 'Them'." *New York Times*, May 11, 1997: E4.

Fauchille, Paul. *Traité de droit International public.* Paris: Rousseau et Cie, 1925.

Federal Government of Australia. *Millpirrum and Others vs Nabalco Ltd and the Commonwealth of Australia.* 143. Melbourne: The Law Book Co, 1971.

——. *The National Native Title Tribunal.* December 1, 2009. http://www.nntt.gov.au/What-Is-Native-Title/Pages/default.aspx (accessed December 1, 2009).

Fiore, Pascal. *Nouveau droit international public suivant les besoins de la civilisation moderne.* 2e. Translated by Charles Antoine. 2 vols. Paris: Pedone-Lauriel, 1885.

Flitner, Michael. "Biodiversity: Of Local Commons and Global Commodities." In *Privitizing Nature: Political Struggles for the Global Commons*, edited by Michael Goldman, 144–166. New Brunswick, NJ: Rutgers University Press, 1998.

Fonseca, Eurico. "Dynamic Limitation of the Freedom of Space." Edited by Andrew G. Haley and Welf Heinrich, Prince of Hanover. *Proceedings of the*

Second Colloquium of the Law of Outer Space. Vienna: Springer-Verlag, 1960, 24–6.

Foucault, Michel. *The Order of Things: An Archeology of the Human Sciences.* New York: Vintage, 1973.

Francastel, Pierre. *Medieval Painting.* Edited by Hans L.C. Jaffé. Translated by Robert Erich Wolf. New York: Dell, 1967.

Gagne, Jocelyn. "The Concept of Aboriginal Title at Common Law: A Look at the Nishga Claim." *Saskachtewan Law Review* 47, no. 2 (1983): 309–39.

Gagosian, Robert B. "Abrupt Climate Change: Should we be Worried?" *Woods Hole Oceanographic Institute.* January 27, 2003. http://www.whoi.edu/page.do?pid=12455&tid=282&cid=9986 (accessed December 1, 2009).

Getches, David H. and Charles F. Wilkinson. *Federal Indian Law: Cases and Materials.* 2nd edition. St. Paul: West Publishing Company, 1986.

Getter, Lisa. "Map Maker Fired Over Arctic Chart a Cult Hero." *Los Angeles Times*, May 19, 2001: 1.

Giddens, Anthony. "Preface." In *Now/Here: Space, Time and Modernity*, edited by Deidre Boden and Roger Friedland. Chicago: University of Chicago Press, 1994.

Goldman, Nathan C. *American Space Law: International and Domestic.* 2nd edition. San Diego, CA: Univelt, Inc., 1996.

Goren, David. "Nuclear Accidents in Space and on Earth: An Analysis of International Law Governing the Cosmos-954 and Chernobyl Accidents." *Georgetown International Environmental Law Review* 5 (1993): 855–95.

Gorove, Stephen. "On the Threshold of Space: Toward a Cosmic Law; Problems of the Upward Extent of Sovereignty." Edited by Andrew G. Haley and Welf Heinrich, Prince of Hanover. *First Colloquium on the Law of Outer Space; The Hague 1958.* Vienna: Springer-Verlag, 1959, 69–76.

Green, L.C. and Olive P. Dickason. *The Law of Nations and the New World.* Edmonton: The University of Alberta Press, 1988.

Gregory, Mark. "Rewriting History I: Mabo v Queenland: The Decision." *Alternative Law Review* 17, no. 4 (August 1992): 157–61.

Griache, Janine. *La théorie de l'occupation des territoires sans maître dans l'affaire du Haut-Nil et du Bahr-el-Gazal (1898–1899).* Clermont-Ferrand: Raclot, 1945.

Grossman, Karl. *Master of Space.* January 2000. http://www.thirdworldtraveler.com/Pentagon_military/MasterofSpace.html (accessed December 1, 2009).

Grotius, Hugo. *The Freedom of the Seas, or the Right Which Belongs to the Dutch to Take Part in the East Indian Trade.* Translated by Ralph Van Deman Magoffin. New York: Oxford University Press, 1916.

——. *The Rights of War and Peace.* With Notes by Jean Barbeyrac. Edited by Richard Tuck. 3 vols. Indianapolis: Liberty Fund, 2005.

Grovogui, Siba N'Zatioula. *Sovereigns, Quasi Sovereigns and Africans: Race and Self-Determination in International Law.* Minneapolis: University of Minnesota Press, 1996.

Haley, Andrew. *Space Law and Government.* Appleton-Century-Crofts, 1963.

Haley, Andrew G. and Welf Heinrich, Prince of Hanover (eds), *Proceedings of the First Colloquium of the Law of Outer Space: The Hague 1958.* Vienna: Springer-Verlag, 1959.

——. *Proceedings of the Second Colloquium on the Law of Outer Space: London 1959.* Vienna: Springer-Verlag, 1960.

——. *Proceedings of the Third Colloquium on the Law of Outer Space: Stockholm.* Vienna: Springer-Verlag, 1960.

Hanson, Randel. "From Bads to Goods: Marketing Nuclear Waste to American Indian Tribes." Minneapolis, PhD Dissertation, University of Minnesota, 1998.

Hardin, Garrett. "The Tragedy of the Commons." In *Managing the Commons*, edited by Garret Hardin and J. Baden, 16–30. San Francisco: W.H. Freeman & Co, 1977.

Hardt, Michael and Antonio Negri. *Empire.* Cambridge: Harvard University Press, 2001.

——. *Multitude: War and Democracy in the Age of Empire.* New York: Penguin Press, 2004.

——. *Commonwealth.* Cambridge, MA: Belknap Press of Harvard University Press, 2009.

Harvey, David. *Conference on Globalization.* Santa Barbara, CA, 2003.

Heidegger, Martin. *The Question Concerning Technology and Other Essays.* Trans. William Lovitt. New York: Harper and Row, 1977.

Heim, Barbara Ellen. "Exploring the Last Frontiers for Mineral Resources: A Comparison of International Law Regarding the Deep Seabed, Outer Space and Antarctica." *Vanderbilt Journal of Transnational Law* 23, no. 4 (1990): 819–49.

Heinrich, Welf. "Problems in Establishing a Legal Boundary between Air Space and Space." Edited by Andrew G. Haley and Welf Heinrich, Prince of Hanover. *Proceedings of the First Colloquium on the Law of Outer Space.* Vienna: Springer-Verlag, 1959: 28–30.

Hershey, Amos Shartle. *The Essentials of International Public Law.* New York: The Macmillan Company, 1912.

Herzog, Werner (Director). *Where the Green Ants Dream.* 1984.

High Court of Australia. *Mabo v. Queensland*, (1992). *High Court of Australia.* June 3, 1992. http://www.austlii.edu.au/au/cases/cth/high_ct/175clr1.html (accessed January 1, 2010).

Hirsch, Sharon L. *Symbolism and Modern Urban Society.* Cambridge, MA: University of Cambridge Press, 2004.

Hitchens, Christopher. "The repackaging of Dan Quayle. No mind. No weight. That is to say, very presidential." *Harper's Magazine*, April 1990: 68–78.

Hockney, David. *Secret Knowledge: Rediscovering the Lost Techniques of the Old Masters.* New York: Viking Studio, 2001.

Horvitz, Robert J. "Marconi's Legacy: National Sovereignty Claims in Radio." *Technology and the Public Domain.* Torino: SSRN. http://ssrn.com/abstract=1107832, 2008.

Human Rights Watch. "Human Rights in Western Sahara and in the Tindouf Refugee Camps (Morocco/Western Sahara/Algeria)." *Human Rights Watch.* December 12, 2008. http://www.hrw.org (accessed December 1, 2009).

Hunt, Michael. *Opposition to Mining Projects by Indigenous Peoples and Special Interest Groups.* June 1997. http://www.murdoch.edu.au/elaw/issues/v4n2/hunt42.html (accessed December 1, 2009).

Hunter, David. "Global Environmental Protection in the Twenty-First Century." In *Global Focus: U.S. Foreign Policy at the Turn of the Millennium*, by Martha Honey and Tom Barry. New York: St. Martin's Press, 2000.

Hyman, William. *Magna Carta of Space.* Guest Cottage Incorporated, 1966.

International Court of Justice. *Western Sahara.* Vol. 3 (5 vols). The Hague, 1979.

International Whaling Commission. *International Whaling Commission Homepage.* July 2009. http://www.iwcoffice.org/ (accessed December 21, 2009).

International Working Group for Indigenous Affairs. *Indigenous Peoples – Who are They?* http://www.iwgia.org/sw641.asp (accessed December 15, 2009).

Jameson, Fredric. *The Political Unconscious: Narrative as a Socially Symbolic Act.* Cornell University Press, 1981.

Janos, Brett M. "The Final Frontier: Incorporating Aspects of Culture and History in the Formation of a Workable, Legal Framework for Outerspace." *Selected Works of Brett Janos*, 2009. http://works.bepress.com/brett_janos/1/ (accessed December 4, 2009).

Jooris, Joseph. "De l'occupation des territoires sans maître (terra nullius) sur la côte d'Afrique: L'Affaire d'Angra-Pequeña." *Revue de droit international et de legislation comparee*, 1886: 236–43.

Joyner, Christopher C. *Governing the Frozen Commons: The Antarctic Regime and Environmental Protection.* Columbia, South Carolina: University of South Carolina Press, 1998.

Justinian. *The Institutes of Justinian.* Translated by J.B. Moyle. Oxford: Clarendon Press, 1953.

Kant, Immanuel. *The Critique of Pure Reason.* Translated by Wolfgang Schwarz. Aalen: Scientia, 1982.

——. *The Metaphysical Elements of Justice: Part I of the Metaphysics of Morals (1797).* Translated by John Ladd. Indianapolis, New York: The Liberal Arts Press, Inc., 1965.

Keefe, Heidi. "Making the Final Frontier Feasible: A Critical Look at the Current Body of Outer Space Law." *Santa Clara Computer & High Technology Law Journal* 11 (1995): 345–71.

Keon-Cohen, Brian. "Case Notes: Eddie Mabo and Ors v The State of Queensland." *Aboriginal Law Bulletin* 2, no. 52 (June 1992): 22–3.

Kiss, Alexandre-Charles. *Répetoire de la pratique française en matière de droit international public.* Vol. 2 (7 vols). Paris: CNRS, 1966.

Koppal, Vladimir. "Two Problems of Outer Space Control: The Delimitation of Outer Space and the Legal Ground for Outer Space Flights." Edited by Andrew G. Haley and Welf Heinrich, Prince of Hanover. *Proceedings of the Third Colloquium on the Law of Outer Space: Stockholm.* Vienna: Springer-Verlag, 1960. 108–112.

Korn, Horst, Susanne Friedrich and Ute Feit. *Deep Sea Genetic Resources in the Context of the Convention on Biological Diversity and the United Nations Convention on the Law of the Sea.* Federal Agency for Nature Conservation, Bonn: Bundesamt für Naturschutz, 2003, 1–83.

Kuehls, Thom. *Beyond Sovereign Territory: The Space of Ecopolitics.* Minneapolis: University of Minnesota Press, 1996.

Ladbury, Rick and Jenny Chin. "Legislative Responses to the Mabo Decisions: Implications for the Australian Resources Industry." *JERL*, 1994: 207.

Lalande andré. *Vocabulaire technique et Critque de la Philosophie.* Paris: Presses Universitaire de France, 1983.

Le Doeuff, Michele. *The Philosophical Imaginary.* Translated by Colin Gordon. Palo Alto, CA: Stanford University Press, 1990.

Lefebvre, Henri. *The Production of Space.* Translated by Donald Nicholson-Smith. Oxford: Basil Blackwell Ltd., 1991.

Lefort, Claude. *The Political Forms of Modern Society: Bureaucracy, Democracy, Totalitarianism.* Edited by John B. Thompson. Cambridge: MIT Press, 1986.

Lenskyj, Helen Jefferson. *The Best Olympics Ever? Social Impacts of Sydney 2000.* Albany, NY: State University of New York Press, 2002.

Lessig, Lawrence. "The Architecture of Innovation." *Duke Law Journal* 51 (2002): 177–91.

Liang, Lawrence, Prashant Iyengar and Jiti Nichani. "How Does an Asian Commons Mean?" *Alternative Law Forum.* 2008. http://www.altlawforum.org/intellectual-property/publications/How%20does%20an%20Asian%20Commons%20mean.pdf/view (accessed December 1, 2009).

Lindley, M.F. *The Aquisition and Government of Backward Territory In International Law: Being a Treatise on the Law and Practice Relating to Colonial Expansion.* New York: Longmans, Green and Co. Ltd., 1926.

Linebaugh, Peter. *Magna Carta Manifesto: Liberties and Commons for All.* Berkeley: University of California Press, 2008.

Lipson, Leon. "National Sovereignty of Outer Space." *Harvard Law Review*, April 1961: 1154–67.

Locke, John. *An Essay Concerning Human Understanding.* Edited by Alexander Fraser. New York: Dover Publications, 1959.

——. *Two Treatises of Government.* Edited by Peter Laslett. Cambridge: Cambridge University Press, 1988.

MacKinnon, Rebecca. *What is "Asia" and What is "Commons" Anyway?* January 25, 2008. http://rconversation.blogs.com/rconversation/2008/01/what-is-asia-an.html (accessed January 1, 2010).

MacPhearson, Crawford Brough. *The Political Theory of Possessive Individualism: Hobbes to Locke.* Oxford: Oxford University Press, 1964.

Malbon, Justin. "The Implications of Mabo v Queensland." *Aboriginal Law Bulletin* 2, no. 57 (August 1992): 7–8.

Malcolm, J.R. and L. Pitelka. *Ecosystems and Global Climate Change: A Review of Potential Impacts of U.S. Terrestrial Ecosystems and Biodiversity.* Washington, DC: Pew Center on Global Climate Change, 2000.

Martitz, Ferdinand Von. "Examen de la théorie de la conférence de Berlin de 1885, sur l'occupation des territoires." *Annulaire de l'institut de droit international* (P. Weissenbruch) 9 (1887–1888): 243–55.

McDougal, Myres and W. Michael Reisman. *International Law in Contemporary Perspective: The Public Order of the World Community.* Mineola, NY: The Foundation Press, Inc. 1981.

Mercer, John. *Spanish Sahara.* London: George Allen & Unwin Ltd., 1976.

Milun, Kathryn. *Pathologies of Modern Space: Empty Space, Urban Anxiety and the Recovery of the Public Self.* New York City: Routledge, 2006.

——. "Enforcing the Moratorium Commons: Of Terrorists, Pirates, State-Sponsored Industrial Criminals and Whales." *On the Commons.* February 21, 2007. http://onthecommons.org/node/1095 (accessed December 21, 2009).

——. *The Solar Commons Demonstration Project* at http://solarcommons.org (accessed December 2009).

Monsanto. "Monsanto Ad Sponsoring the Hall of Biodiversity at the American Museum of Natural History Biodiversity Ad." Section D. *New York Times*, June 2, 1998: 3.

Moody, Roger. *The Gulliver File – Mines, People and Land: A Global Battleground.* London: Minewatch, 1992.

Murphy, Colin. "Permanent Resistence in the Western Sahara." *Le Monde Diplomatique*, December 12, 2008. http://mondediplo.com/2008/12/12sahara.

Nabhan, Gary. *Cultures of Habitat: On Nature, Culture and Story.* Washington, DC: Counterpoint Press, 1997.

National Research Council. *Abrupt Climate Change: Inevitable Surprises.* Washington, DC: National Academy Press, 2002, 1.

New York Times. "A New Greenhouse Gas." *New York Times*, July 28, 2000: A1, A17.

"No 2010 Olympics on Stolen Native Land." *Why We Resist: The 2010 Winter Olympics.* January 1, 2010. http://no2010.com/node/18 (accessed January 1, 2010).

Norton, Mark and Stephen Ruth. "Spectrum and Its Influences on 3G and WiFi Architectures." In *Achieving the Triple Play: Technologies and Business Models for Success*, by International Engineering Consortium, 271–82. Chicago: Professional Education International, 2006.

Ostrom, Elinor. *Governing the Commons: The Evolution of Institutions for Collective Action.* Cambridge: Cambridge University Press, 1990.

Peterson, Bruce, et al. "Increasing River Discharge to the Arctic Ocean." *Science*, December 2002: 2171–3.

Polanyi, Karl. *The Great Transformation: The Political and Economic Origins of Our Time*. 2nd Beacon paperback edition. Boston, MA: Beacon Press, 2001.

Popper, Deborah E. and Frank J. Popper. "The Buffalo Commons as Regional Metaphor and Geographic Method." *The Geographical Review* 89, no. 4 (October 1999): 491–510.

Price, David Lynn. *The Western Sahara.* Beverly Hills/London: Sage Publications, 1979.

Rabinow, Paul and Nikolas Rose. "Biopower Today." *Biosocieties* 1, no. 2 (2006): 195–217.

Rawls, John. *Theory of Justice.* Belknap, 1971.

Reuters. "Century zinc mine may not close." *Reuters Online*, November 21, 2008.

——. "Rio Tinto PLC/Ltd – The Merger of CRA & RTZ." http://www.sea-us.org.au/corpfilez/riverofblood.html (accessed December 1, 2009).

Revkin, Andrew. "Eskimos Seek to Recast Global Warming as a Rights Issue." *New York Times*, December 15, 2004: A3.

Revkin, Andrew C. "Inuit Climate Change Petition Rejected." *New York Times.* December 16, 2006. http://www.nytimes.com/2006/12/16/world/americas/16briefs-inuitcomplaint.html (accessed December 1, 2009).

Reynolds, Henry. "Mabo and Pastoral Leases." *Aboriginal Law Bulletin* 2, no. 59 (December 1992): 8–10.

Rifkin, Jeremy. "Biotech Century Treaty to Share Genetic Commons." *The Foundation on Economic Trends.* 2003–2009. http://www.foet.org/past/GeneticCommons.html (accessed January 1, 2010).

Roling, B.V.A. "Are Grotius' Ideas Obsolete in an Expanded World?" In *Hugo Grotius and International Relations*, edited by Hedley Bull, Benedict Kingsbury and Adam Roberts, 297–98. Oxford: Oxford University Press, 1990.

Rose, Carol M. "Romans, Roads and Romantic Creators Traditions of Public Property in the Information Age." *66 Law & Contemporary Problems. 89* Winter/Spring 2003.

Rose, Gillian. *Dialectic of Nihilism: Post-Structuralism and Law.* Oxford, New York: Basil Blackwell, 1984.

Salomon, Charles. *De l'occupation des territoires sans maître: Etude de droit international.* Paris: Giard, 1889.

Sand, Peter H. "Diego Garcia: British-American Legal Black Hole in the Indian Ocean?." *Journal of Environmental Law*, January 2009: 1–25.

Sarat, Austin and Jonathan Simon. "Cultural Analysis, Cultural Studies and the Situation of Legal Scholarship." In *Cultural Analysis, Cultural Studies and the Law: Moving Beyond Legal Realism*, 1–36. Durham: Duke University Press, 2003.

Saxena, Suresh Chandra. *The Liberation War in the Western Sahara.* New Delhi: Vidya Publishers, 1981.

Scargill, D. Ian. "The Decline of Pastoral Nomadism in the Western Sahara." *Geography* 76, no. 2 (April 1991): 331.

Seed, Patricia. "Taking Possession and Reading Texts: Establishing the Authority of Overseas Empires." *William and Mary Quarterly* 49 (1992): 183–209.

Selden, John. *Mare Clausum. Of the Dominion, or, Ownership of the Sea.* Translated by Marchmont Nedham. London: William Du-Gard, 1652.

Sera-Vazquez, Modesto. "The Functional Regulation of the Extra-Atmospheric Space." Edited by Andrew G. Haley and Welf Heinrich, Prince of Hanover. *Proceedings of the Second Colloquium of the Law of Outer Space.* Vienna: Springer-Verlag, 1960: 139–46.

Shiva, Vandana. *Globalization's New Wars: Seed, Water and Life Forms.* New Delhi: Women Unlimited, 2005.

Silk, Leonard S. "Values and Goals of Space Exploration." In *Space and Society* Edited by Howard J. Taubenfeld. New York: Oceana Publications, Inc. 1964.

Smith, Danielle Van Brunt. "Western Sahara Research Guide." *Forced Migration Online.* Refugee Studies Centre/Digital Library. August 2004. http://www.forcedmigration.org/guides/fmo035/title.htm (accessed December 15, 2009).

Smith, Robert J. "Resolving the Tragedy of the Commons by Creating Private Property Rights in Wildlife." *The Cato Journal.* December 2009. http://www.cato.org/pubs/journal/cj1n2-1.html (accessed December 1, 2009).

Speth, James Gustave. *Red Sky at Morning: America and the Crisis of the Global Environment.* New Haven: Yale Unversity Press, 2004.

Steinberg, Philip E. *The Social Construction of the Ocean.* Cambridge: Cambridge University Press, 2001.

Strang, Veronica. *Uncommon Ground: Cultural Landscapes and Environmental Values.* Oxford, New York: Berg, 1997.

Strathern, Marilyn. *After Nature: English Kinship in the Late Twentieth Century.* Cambridge: Cambridge University Press, 1992.

Sutton, Peter. "Dreamings I." In *Dreamings: The Art of Aboriginal Australia*, edited by Peter Sutton. New York: The Asia Society Galleries/G. Braziller Publishers, 1988.

Taylor, C.C. "Archaeology and the Origins of Open-Field Agriculture." In *The Origins of Open-Field Agriculture*, edited by Trever Rowley. London: Groom Helm, 1981.

——. "The Foundation on Economic Trends." *Treaty to Share the Genetic Commons.* 2003–2009. http://www.foet.org/past/GeneticCommons.html (accessed January 1, 2010).

Thompson, V. and Richard Adloff. *The Western Saharans; Background to Conflict.* New Jersey: Barnes & Noble, 1980.

Torres, Gerald and Kathryn Milun. "Translating Yonondio by Precedent and Evidence: The Mashpee Indian Case." *Duke Law Journal*, no. 4 (1990): 625–60.

Tuck, Richard. *Natural Rights Theories; Their Origin and Development.* Cambridge: Cambridge University Press, 1979.

Tyler, Steve. "Post-Modern Ethnography: From Document of the Occult to Occult Document." In *Writing Culture: The Poetics and Politics of Ethnography*, edited by James Clifford and George Marcus, 123–5. Berkeley: University of California Press, 1986.

UKabc. "Porto Alegre Treaty to Share the Genetic Commons." *UK Notice Board.* February 1, 2002. http://www.ukabc.org/genetic_commons_treaty.htm (accessed August 23, 2009).

United Nations. *Outer Space Treaty.* November 30, 1967. http://www.unoosa.org/oosa/SpaceLaw/outerspt.html (accessed December 1, 2009).

——. "Convention on International Liability for Damage Caused by Space Objects." *United Nations Office for Outer Space Affairs.* March 29, 1972. http://www.oosa.unvienna.org/oosa/SpaceLaw/liability.html (accessed December 1, 2009).

——. "Moon Treaty: Agreement Governing the Activities of States on the Moon and Other Celestial Bodies." *United Nations Office for Outer Space Affairs.* 1979. http://www.unoosa.org/oosa/SpaceLaw/moon.html (accessed December 1, 2009).

——. "International Convention on the Elimination of all Forms of Racial Discrimination." *Human and Constitutional Rights Resource Page.* March 26, 2008. http://www.hrcr.org/docs/CERD/cerd2.html (accessed December 15, 2009).

——. *Convention on Biological Diversity.* November 8, 2009. http://www.cbd.int/ (accessed November 8, 2009).

United Nations Commission on Genetic Resources for Food and Agriculture. http://www.fao.org/ag/cgrfa/default.htm.

United Nations Committee on the Peaceful Uses of Outer Space. "Principles Relevant to the Use of Nuclear Power Sources In Outer Space." *United Nations Office for Outer Space Affairs.* 1991. http://www.oosa.unvienna.org/oosa/SpaceLaw/nps.html (accessed December 1, 2009).

United Nations Food and Agriculture Organization. *International Treaty on Plant Genetic Resources for Food and Agriculture.* November 8, 2009. http://www.planttreaty.org/texts_en.htm (accessed November 8, 2009).

United Nations General Assembly. *Resolution 2229 (XXI) of December 20, 1966.* New York: United Nations, 1966.

US Supreme Court. "Cherokee Nation v. Georgia, 1831 (30 U.S. (5 pet.) 1, 8 L. Ed. 25." In *Federal Indian Law*, edited by D. Gutches, 46–51. St. Paul: West Publishing Co., 1986.

Valladao, Haraldo. "The Law of Interplanetary Space." Edited by Andrew G Hanover and Welf Heinrich, Prince of Hanover. *Proceedings of the Second Colloquium of the Law of Outer Space.* Vienna: Springer-Verlag, 1960: 156–68.

Vandana, Shiva and Holla-Bhar Radha. "Piracy by Patent: The Case of the Neem Tree." In *The Case against the Global Economy*, edited by Jerry Mander and Edward Goldsmith, 146–59. San Francisco: Sierra Club, 1996.

Vattel, Emer de. "Le droit des gens, ou Principes de la loi naturelle, 2 vols." *The Online Library of Liberty.* 1758. http://oll.libertyfund.org/?option=com_staticxt&staticfile=show.php%3Ftitle=1858&Itemid=27 (accessed January 2, 2010).

Vergez, Robert. *Early ukiyo-e master: Okumura Masanobu.* Tokyo and New York: Harper & Row, 1983.

Vicuña, Francisco Orrego. "The Regime for the Exploitation of the Seabed Mineral Resources and the Quest for a New International Economic Order of the Oceans: A Latin-American View." *Lawyer of the Americas* 10, no. 3 (Winter 1978): 774–83.

Vogler, John. *The Global Commons: A Regime Analysis.* Second edition. Wiley, 1995.

Watson, Helen and David Wade Chambers. *Singing the Land, Signing the Land.* Geelong, Victoria: Deakin University Press, 1993.

Watson-Verran, Helen. "Renegotiating What's Natural." New Orleans, October 12–15, 1994.

Watt-Cloutier, Sheila. "Testimony of Chair, Inuit Circumpolar Conference." *Inuit Circumpolar Conference.* March 3, 2004. http://inuitcircumpolar.com/index.php?ID=256&Lang=En (accessed December 1, 2009).

Webber, Allen Duane. "Extraterrestial Law on the Final Frontier: A Regime to Govern the Development of Celestial Body Resources." *Georgetown Law Journal* 71, no. 5 (June 1983): 1427–56.

Whorf, Benjamin. 'Languages and Logic'. In *Language, Thought and Reality.* J.B. Carroll. Cambridge, MA, MIT Press, 1956.

Williams Jr, Robert A. "Encounters on the Frontiers of International Human Rights Law: Redefining the Terms of Indigenous Peoples' Survival in the World." *Duke Law Journal*, no. 4 (1990): 660–704.

Wilson, E.O. *The Future of Life.* New York: Knopf, 2002.

Wittgenstein, Ludwig. *Philosophical Investigations.* New York: The Macmillan Company, 1965.

Wong, Ward and Keith Bradsher. "China Joins U.S. in Pledge of Hard Targets on Emissions." *New York Times.* November 26, 2009. http://www.nytimes.com/2009/11/27/science/earth/27climate.html (accessed December 1, 2009).

World Social Forum. *The Treaty Initiative to Share the Genetic Commons.* January 2, 2002. http://www.ukabc.org/genetic_commons_treaty.htm (accessed November 8, 2009).

World Trade Organization. *Agreement on Trade-Related Aspects of Intellectual Property Rights.* August 11, 2009. http://www.wto.org/english/tratop_e/trips_e/t_agm0_e.htm (accessed August 11, 2009).

Worm, Boris, et al. "Impacts of Biodiversity Loss on Ocean Ecosystem Services." *Science* 314 (2006): 787–90.

Young, Orin, ed. *The Effectiveness of International Environmental Regimes.* Cambridge: Cambridge University Press, 1997.

Zoubir, Yahia H. and Daniel Volman. *International Dimensions of the Western Sahara Conflict.* Westport/London: Praeger, 1993.

Index